Kiwis, Wigan
My Life and R

Ces shaking hands with brother Ken before Wigan versus New Zealand
22 October 1947 (Photo: courtesy Robert Gate)

Ces Mountford

By Ces Mountford

LONDON LEAGUE PUBLICATIONS LTD

Kiwis, Wigan and The Wire
My Life and Rugby League

We acknowledge the *Manchester Evening News* archive for permission to reprint material from the *Manchester Evening Chronicle*.

First published in Great Britain in May 2003 by:
London League Publications Ltd, P.O. Box 10441, London E14 0SB

ISBN: 1-903659-10-8

Cover design by: Stephen McCarthy Graphic Design
                              46, Clarence Road, London N15 5BB
Layout: Peter Lush
Printed and bound by: Catford Print Centre, PO Box 563, Catford, London SE6 4PY

Ces Mountford's share of the profits from this book will go to the Institute for Magnetic Resonance Research and the Department of Magnetic Resonance in Medicine at the University of Sydney to facilitate research and education programmes into the improved management for cancer and pain management. His daughter, Carolyn is the Foundation's Chief Executive and Head of Department.

This book is dedicated to Carolyn and Kim, "who endured"; Andrew, Sarah, Ron and the late Charles; all the Mountford family; the fraternity of Rugby League; all sports people (Edna says 'especially the wives!') and cancer researchers everywhere.

Ces Mountford MBE

Ces Mountford was a superb player, particularly during a long and illustrious career in Britain, but he is perhaps better remembered as one of New Zealand's finest coaches and administrators. His contribution to the game was significant and he is fondly remembered still today as a fine ambassador for the game.

His efforts on behalf of Rugby League in New Zealand were recognised in 1987 when he was awarded the MBE in the Queens' Birthday Honours. As patron of the New Zealand Rugby League, I thank Ces for his efforts to develop and foster rugby league in this country and overseas.

Helen Clark

Right Honourable Helen Clark
Prime Minister of New Zealand

WARRINGTON BOROUGH COUNCIL		
H J		28/08/2003
796.3338		£9.95

Wembley triumph: Ces holding the Challenge Cup with his Wigan team mates after the 10-0 victory over Barrow

Foreword: Ces Mountford MBE: "The Rugby League Gentleman"

As a young fellow growing up in Christchurch, then Kumara on the West Coast, I always took a close interest in Rugby League. I followed the representative teams from Canterbury and West Coast and the club sides from both sides of the Alps such as Blackball, Marist, Ngahere and Runanga from the Coast; Hornby, Sydenham, Addington and Linwood from Canterbury. They included many great players: Ces, Bill and Ken Mountford, Chang Newton, Charlie McBride, Nippie Forrest, Micky Ord, Ray and Len Brown, Ray and Gordon Nuttral, Pat Smith, Keith Henry, Ces Davidson, Concrete Smith and my brother Les to name a few.

In those days West Coast was very strong and Canterbury was very hard put to compete with them. I recall Ces Mountford's name and photo along with the match report in the sports papers as a player and captain of the West Coast representative side. He first represented West Coast and South Island as a full-back as a young player and was very unlucky not being selected for the 1939 Kiwi Touring side to England in that position.

I had watched Ces play on many occasions for both Blackball and West Coast and saw him play his last games on the Coast before his departure to England to join Wigan. I believe if Ces had stayed in New Zealand he would have toured England and France with brother Ken in 1947 and I cannot see to this day why Bill Mountford was not selected for that side. He was the best centre three-quarter in New Zealand.

Ces's departing words on leaving for Great Britain were: "I regret leaving the country, but I feel I have acted wisely in accepting the offer to play for the Wigan club. I can assure you that it will always be my endeavour to add prestige to the Rugby League football of the West Coast. On the termination of my contract I intend to return to New Zealand and if not, still a player, I will give to the code my services as a coach." Ces was one of the finest footballers produced on the West Coast.

In England he was known as the "The Blackball Bullet" and the "Little Red Devil" and became the most successful New Zealander of his time to play in the British Rugby League. He added prestige not only to the West Coast, but to New Zealand and the code generally. In his first five years in England with Wigan, he collected 11 winning medals; two of these were from Challenge Cup Final wins at Wembley Stadium, one as captain. In the next years as manager-coach and sometimes player with Warrington, he steered his side to seven trophies including the only double of the Challenge Cup and League Championship in almost 30 years. Ces left New Zealand to make good and did during that period he captained the Rest against Great Britain, played for the British Empire side and captained Other Nationalities against England and France. These internationals were very hard fought.

Ces was always a great help to many Kiwi touring sides to Great Britain and France. The players, management and coaches would seek his advice.

When Ces started to talk about returning to New Zealand, the Warrington club put pressure on him to stay. The players had a special deputation and four members of the training and scouting staff threatened to resign if he left, but Ces was determined to return home just as he promised years before. He turned down another five-year contract with Warrington and a rich offer from Parramatta. What other coach was so highly respected and regarded?

On his return to New Zealand Ces was appointed director of coaching for Rothmans, which included all sports. Later, Ces became secretary-manager of the New Zealand Rugby League (NZRL). Rugby League flourished during this period and by 1971 reached a peak. Ces changed the administration of NZRL from a number of delegates to six directors. The administration then only had two in the office, and far more players and representative football than today.

Administration and officials around the country were sorted out. The provinces outside Auckland such as Taranaki, Wellington, Bay of Plenty and many others showed the benefits of Ces's work and he was producing some great coaches, and international players. There were high standards set on and off the field that lifted the image of our game.

He was one of the very few coaches that not only could teach and give you every opportunity to learn, but carry out individual coaching, one to one, and would teach the basics in movement, and the basics never change.

His coaching booklet was very simple. It was only 12 pages, and thus was easier to learn, not like some: pages and pages - but just hopeless. There were many variations that could be applied by coaches from his manual. Many thought they knew about coaching until they went to Ces's coaching courses, but had to come down to earth, learning there is more to coaching than they expected.

Ces was not given the opportunity to do what he always wanted when he first returned home: to coach the Kiwis. When he did get the opportunity it came late and our international football had been going through a very bad patch. He had to start again and rebuild, which took some time. When the Kiwis were starting to perform and developing promising stars, the New Zealand Rugby League appointed another coach who received the benefit of his years of building. Many of his promising stars went on to professional careers in Great Britain and Australia and reached the top of Rugby League.

After his period with NZRL, the New Zealand Universities Rugby League saw a great opportunity and approached Ces to join them. He accepted the position as national coach. He had two tours to England and France, and one to Australia with the students. Today many of those students are successful professional or business men and credit those tours for the standards that were set and heading them in the right direction in life.

On all his tours, Ces had standards of dress for each meal and dinner in the evening was always formal. He organized the morning 7.00am walk which they all enjoyed as the tour went on. There was great fellowship. Every player and official had a number on tour so we knew if anyone was missing on the buses etc. Only the team and their officials went on the buses to games or trips. The players had their own disciplinary committee and they were able to set standards and fine anyone. Ces always told his player you always go and make yourself known by shaking hands and telling them your name, when at any function. He always said if you have nothing good to say about Rugby League say nothing. When at functions Ces told the players before attending that there was to be no more then two or three in one group and mix with the others. Everywhere he went in England, France and Australia he was highly regarded and respected.

I believe that the NZRL never ever gave Ces a fair go. But they were very fortunate he returned home. His coaching scheme was a success; he put a structure in place for the top administration, and lifted the standards and image of Rugby League. Ces was awarded with Life Membership of NZRL. He was a member of the Legends of Leagues and honoured by the Queen with the MBE.

Ces, Edna and family are very close friends and they were always there to support you in need. We hear from each other weekly and Ces can stand high for what he has achieved in Rugby League throughout the World.

W.O. 'Bud' Lisle is a Member of the New Zealand Order of Merit (MNZM), a Life Member of the NZRL and has been given the NZRL's Distinguished Service Award. He has a lifetime's service to the game in New Zealand. He played until he was 43, wining representative honours at every level except for the Kiwis. He then became involved in coaching, including the Wellington Representative team, and management. Among many posts over the years, he has been a member of the NZRL Council, President and the New Zealand Universities RL for over 20 years; and with John Haynes organised the first Student World Cup in 1986. Now aged 72, he lives in Papakura and still plays an active role in Rugby League.

Note on points and records

During Ces's playing career, a try was worth three points and a goal two points. In part two of the book, we have followed the British custom as counting an international appearance as a match against another country (test or world cup), and not including tour matches against other teams.

Preface: Memories of Wigan and Ces Mountford

When I was growing up there in the 1930s and 1940s, Wigan, with its awesomely deep collieries, massive, gaunt cotton mills, black-faced pitmen and raw-boned pit lassies, was at the very heart of the rough-hewn homeland of Rugby League. The rugged sport symbolized a way of life in the Lancashire town and was a religion for its inhabitants, who attended its services far more regularly than they went to church or chapel. I was born within a piece of coal's throw from Wigan Pier and was one of the faithful, dragged along to Central Park by my father from the age of seven.

The sun shone occasionally on Central Park – more often than not it hid behind battalions of thick clouds that come scudding in over the Irish Sea. At such times rain was not infrequent and at the end of the war fog was much more common than it is now. Inclement weather did not deter the faithful from attending the match, though we preferred dry days when players did not have to squelch through four inches of mud on their way to the try line.

It was on a miserable, damp Saturday afternoon in the autumn of 1946 that I went to Central Park to see Wigan's curtain-raiser for the coming season. It was a foggy day and I had unwisely chosen a place behind the goal posts, so that I could only see play in my half of the field. Wigan's cherry and white shirts were just about visible in the other half, but the opponents' blue ones blended into the autumnal twilight. It was in these less than ideal conditions that I witnessed the début of a new Wigan signing from New Zealand, a certain Cecil Mountford.

I should tell you a little bit about Wigan Rugby League history. Since the historic split between the Northern Union and the southern Rugby Establishment in 1895, Wigan pitmen had carved out not only tunnels in the local coal faces, but also a name for themselves as the toughest, most resilient and most successful rugby players in the British Isles. Year after year in the first half of the century they topped the League with almost monotonous regularity and amassed a glittering array of silver cups in the club boardroom. The greatest source of pride to all us Wiganers was that this success had been achieved almost exclusively by home-grown men and youths. Working down the mine during the week, the stoic pitmen, with limited time for training, had somehow found the fitness and the energy to face tough opposition on Saturdays, triumph time and time again and, incredibly, put Wigan squarely on the world map.

There was one exception concerning this source of talent. Before the First World War Wigan had recruited two New Zealanders: a forward named Charlie Seeling and a centre called Lance Todd. Both were brilliant players, Todd to such an extent that, when he was prematurely killed in a car crash, a Lance Todd Trophy was created to be awarded to the man-of-the -match in the Wembley Challenge Cup Final. In the years that followed, Wigan sporadically talent-spotted in New Zealand, though no recruits ever approached the illustrious standard set by Lance Todd.

The Second World War put an end to bringing players over from down under, but in 1945 the Wigan Rugby League Club decided to re-open the vein of talent in New Zealand. They signed Brian Nordgren, a well-known winger who held the current New Zealand points-scoring record and was a national sprint champion to boot. Nordgren, a tall, blond, handsome 21-year old, looked like a Greek god alongside many of his shorter Wigan colleagues. Though he developed into one of the best wingers in the Rugby League, he took a while to settle and had not yet shown his real form when it was announced that the club had signed on another New Zealander, this time only 5 foot 4 inches. There was some doubt in the minds of the few thousand supporters who assembled to watch Mountford's début on that inauspicious afternoon. Was he good enough to displace promising Wigan youths like Ashcroft, Fleming and Toohey? Wigan had plenty good stand-off halves. Were Wigan directors being a trifle hasty in bringing strangers 12,000 miles to play in unfamiliar conditions?

Central Park debut

One could almost sense a mood of scepticism as the newcomer trotted onto the field surrounded by the usual Wigan heroes. He certainly was diminutive and seemed a bit thin on top at the age of 26. Was there any real force in that short frame? We were soon to find out. After a few minutes' play, scrum-half Bradshaw passed the ball to the New Zealander, who went off like a shot from a gun, heading for the right corner flag. Surely he was holding on to the ball too long – why didn't he pass to the waiting centres? One blue shirt after another went in to finish him off, but somehow they all missed him and his final pass was clearly delivered. A few minutes later he was streaking towards the opposite corner flag, slipping a pass to his countryman Nordgren, who went over to score.

Central Park suddenly brightened up. The sun began to break fitfully through the clouds, lessening the gloom as its rays lit up Mountford's remaining blond hair. The bright spot seemed to zig-zag all over the field for the rest of the half. The new man exuded light and energy, he never seemed to stop running, with or without the ball. He held the ball out in front of him as he ran, challenging the other team to grab it, but they seldom could. He could run to the left and pass to the right and vice versa, often making his opponents run the wrong way. When they hesitated and stopped following him, he promptly ran through the gap and scored himself. He was never far from the ball, monopolising its possession, even backing up for the return pass when he eventually parted with it. In his first game for Wigan he revolutionized stand-off play, imparting to it new elements of speed, lateral running, deceptive acceleration, gap creation and total support.

Wigan half-backs played that way for 30 years afterwards. We witnessed the start of it all. What none of us knew that day was that Mountford had never played stand-off before.

What kind of a man was this diminutive dynamo? What was his breed? What background enabled him to slot in instantly to the well-tried and jealously-guarded patterns of Wigan rugby supremacy? What were the origins of such obvious synergy? These were the thoughts in the minds of the spectators that afternoon as they watched the little Kiwi buzz around continually for 80 minutes with no visible diminishment of his initial bounding momentum. He trotted off quietly at the end, among the pitmen, looking modestly at his feet.

He was 12,000 miles from home, on his first trip abroad, a stranger to our shores, yet already we felt he was one of us. In more senses than one, he was. He was New Zealand born and bred, but his father was an Englishman. Robert Mountford senior joined the merchant navy before the First World War and arrived in New Zealand in 1906. There was gold on the West Coast of the South Island and he signed off to seek his fortune gold prospecting. Like many others he had no luck and, after marrying a local girl, became a coal miner in the small town of Blackball on the West Coast. The miners of Blackball lived a life not dissimilar to that of Wigan pitmen. They spent most of their time underground and hardened their bodies cutting, hacking, hauling and man-handling coal. Like Wiganers, they were hard hit in the glum years of the depression in the 1930s. West Coast miners, like many in Lancashire, are stocky and short in stature. The Mountford family was no exception and Cecil Mountford's frame fitted in well with the other Wigan halfbacks – Bradshaw, Alty and Toohey.

Rugby League was introduced to the West Coast of the South Island in 1915 – 20 years after its establishment in northern England and nine years after Robert Mountford settled in Blackball. This small coal mining village – it had one thousand inhabitants in the 1920s – is situated high up in the hills above the Grey River. The river is well-named for the West Coast of the South Island is often grey, being as rainy and windswept as the Lancashire coast. So when Ces arrived on a watery evening at Wigan railway station in August 1946 at least the menacing skies looked familiar. More than that, he was breathing Rugby League air and the cloth caps and clattering clogs he saw on the streets reminded him that he was again in a mining community.

Ces, born in 1919, lived and breathed Rugby League and pitmen from his earliest memories. His father took him to the matches, as mine did me. By 1936 when I was introduced to Central Park, Ces was already playing for the Blackball senior team. The story of his youth, unfolded in the following chapters, is remarkable by any standards. Only by analysing the career of the young Mountford prodigy can one come to an understanding of how, in his senior sporting life, he became one of the greatest players of all time.

The second of 10 children and encouraged and supported by a sports-mad father and siblings, Ces was an association football star at the age of eleven. Playing for the Blackball Primary School association football team, he was a fast, sharp-shooting centre-forward who actually scored 22 of his side's 25 goals in one season! In spite of his lack of height, at the age of 13 he was playing association football in senior teams and two years later played for the West Coast and was selected for the South Island itself.

Though he played association football on Saturdays, his pitman father made sure he played Rugby League on Sundays for Blackball. He played for the seniors at 15, the West Coast at 16 and the South Island at 18.

In his years at Wigan Ces demonstrated not only a variety of skills, but unbelievable strength, stamina and speed for such a small man. His smallness was, however, deceptive. His stocky frame was carried by legs of great strength, muscularity and suppleness. After leaving school at 14, he and his brother Bob had to lead packhorses, laden with provisions and mining gear, 4,000 feet up the mountainside above Blackball. This gruelling but healthy, strengthening work continued until he was 17, when he went into the coal mines. Like many Wigan youths, physical toil, mining, simple family life and Rugby League were the basic ingredients of Ces's existence.

In these circumstances Ces Mountford was "made" for Wigan and Wigan (and English Rugby League) were made for Ces. His professional achievements, well-documented elsewhere, needed only be summarized in this preface. After his misty debut, Mountford made 74 consecutive appearances for Wigan. The depth of his stamina allowed him to play in 150 out of 160 matches in his first three seasons for the club. No other colleague matched these appearances. He not only ran around to feed others, but he scored regularly, too. In the 1946-7 season he went over the try line 17 times. Remarkable, but actually run of the mill stuff for someone who had scored 31 tries and 67 goals in his last season in Blackball.

The statistics surrounding Mountford's career are impeccable and unrivalled, but they only tell part of his story. At Wigan he won every honour the game had to offer, crowned by two victories in the Challenge Cup at Wembley, captaining the side on the second occasion in 1951. In that match he won the coveted Lance Todd Trophy, but of equal significance was that it was his 217th game for the club – in five seasons. He was the first New Zealander to captain a Challenge Cup-winning side, met the King of England and received an MBE. In later years Ces was elected to the Rugby League Hall of Fame and in 2000 was named as one of the Legends of Rugby League.

So much for Mountford the player. After five years with Wigan he went on to manage Warrington Rugby League Club for 10 years and did it all over again! In 1954 he led Warrington to the elusive Cup and League double. By now one had learnt not to expect anything less from the 'Blackball Bullet'. Beyond Mountford the player and Mountford the manager, there is also Mountford the man. I had the privilege of knowing Ces and his family on an intimate basis for the last three decades of the 20th century, both in New Zealand and Europe. There are many sides to the man which are not immediately evident to one who has seen him only on the playing field. On the pitch his behaviour was the essence of sportsmanship. Few men took such constant buffeting as he took, and none with such serenity. After his fame had spread, Mountford for five years was a "marked man" every time he came onto the field, destined to the close attention and rough handling attendant on such a distinction. All this he bore with a smile to which the years lent grimness, but could never obliterate. There was no malice in his own play and he never retaliated except to ward off unnecessary brutality.

In due course I learnt that the background to his impeccable conduct was his personal, uncompromising sense of morality. His self-discipline was evident, but his smiling, modest manner gave little clue as to his iron will when controlling others. Twice I toured France with him on New Zealand Rugby League tours. His unique coaching skills commanded unbounded admiration and support from his professional players. Even on tour he was constantly honing their skills, always searching for perfection. He praised their efforts, missing no one, but it was clear that he expected, even demanded, excellence from them. His last word as they took the field was that they remember they were playing for New Zealand. Ces was a loyal Wiganer, but he was immensely proud of his rugged West Coast origins and inspired his players to live and breathe the game he loved – and they did.

The French loved Ces for his modesty, his simple, uncomplicated ability to focus on what was effective and right, his professional pursuit of excellence, his invariable fairness, his utter lack of Anglo-Saxon arrogance. We wined and dined with the French after matches – I acted as interpreter – but Ces's demeanour needed little translation. As former opponent of French players in the Other Nationalities XIII and descended from a de Montfort to boot, Mountford commanded French respect like few Anglos could. What impressed them most was, after an evening of great merry-making, he could round up his players, more or less sober, and have them all in bed by midnight. They had to represent New Zealand again in three days.

Ces, happily married to Edna, a wise Wigan girl, was also a kind and inspiring husband and father. Both his children inherited his sporting talent, son Kim being the fastest sprinter in his country at the age of 15 and daughter Carolyn an Olympic hurdles trialist. Both would have made New Zealand's Olympic team had they not unfortunately sustained untimely injuries. Carolyn went on to become a famous cancer specialist, carrying the torch of Mountford excellence into new fields.

Finally, I must mention Ces's try against Leeds at Central Park in 1950, which is described elsewhere in this book. It gave Wigan a famous 13-12 victory over Leeds. It was the only time I saw several thousand Wigan spectators wait outside the ground for a player's exit. There has never been a try like it since. There has never been another player like Mountford, either.

Richard D. Lewis

Richard D. (Don) Lewis was born and raised in Wigan, and is a life-long Wigan Rugby League supporter. He studied languages at University, and now runs an international language school business, and has a world-wide reputation as a language teacher, and expert on cultural diversity. He was knighted by President Ahtisaari of Finland in 1997. He now lives in Hampshire.

Thank You:

Ces and Edna Mountford, and London League Publications Ltd would like to thank the following people for their help and support in producing this book:

Bud Lisle for his work on the book, especially in collecting contributions for the Memories section of the book. His non-stop efforts on this part of the book were invaluable. He gave Ces and Edna constant encouragement over 14 years of intermittent work on the book. *John Haynes* for his work on an early version of the book, especially the first 2 chapters, agreement to use his piece on Ces and Bill Mountford and his help in providing material. *Gerald Ryan* for his work on an early version of the book. *Richard D. Lewis* for co-ordinating the draft that was given to London League Publications Ltd, and his help and support. He has been a long time family friend of the Mountfords, and gave Ces and Edna great support. *Brooke O'Donnell* and *Fiona Sutherland* for their typing and administrative support. *Michael O'Hare* for his patient and careful proof reading. *Robert Gate* for his support, photos, permission to use material from *There were a lot more than that – Odsal 1954*, work on statistics and for writing the introduction. *Peter Kerridge* for his support and information on West Coast Rugby League. *Stan Lewandowski* for his help in contacting past Warrington players. *Andrew Wheelwright* for assistance on Blackpool. *Everyone* who contributed to the book. The *Manchester Evening News* archive for permission to reprint material from the *Manchester Evening Chronicle*. *Stephen McCarthy* for his work on the cover. All the staff at *Catford Print Centre*.

Ces and Edna would like to thank Peter Lush and Dave Farrar from London League Publications Ltd for their work on the book.

However, any mistakes are the responsibility of the authors and London League Publications Ltd.

Introduction: Ces Mountford, Wigan and Warrington

Unfortunately, my father has dementia. He cannot remember what he had for dinner 10 minutes after he has eaten it. I doubt whether he really knows that I am his son. He can, however, remember Ces Mountford: "the fastest stand-off I ever saw. He could boot the ball down the field and be the first to it, even giving the others a start. Little fellow, he was. Blond. Great player. Couldn't half shift. Scored a real try at Thrum Hall once, in a semi-final."

It's funny how the demented can recall things from long ago so clearly. My dad is right. Ces Mountford was a great player and by all accounts he could certainly shift. Maybe he was not the fastest stand-off of all time but there can't have been many who were faster. The fact that he was dubbed "the Blackball Bullet" is an indication of the exceptional speed he possessed. He was indeed a little fellow too, but broad and he had tree trunk legs. At 5ft 4in, or 5ft 5in at a pinch, and depending on which paper you were reading, he was almost the standard height for a half-back in those far-off days of the immediate post-war period. He was a bit heavier than most half-backs though at 11st 5lbs. Those who saw him play remembered him all right.

There were a lot of people to remember him too. Ces was fortunate in that he played in English Rugby League in the days when it was at its most popular, in terms of people paying at the turnstiles, at least. Ces's career at Wigan, from 1946 to 1951, coincided with the peak levels of support for the game. In the 1948-49 season 6,867,189 paying customers attended first class fixtures, with 4,749,223 at league games – four times as many as attend current day professional Rugby League. It was better than that because he played for Wigan, who drew bigger crowds than anyone else, and, in his time at Central Park, won more trophies than anyone else. He was the right man in the right place at the right time.

Some of the present day Super League 'thought police' pooh-pooh the idea that golden ages existed in Rugby League, presumably fearing that the modern game is somehow devalued by comparisons. They are wrong. Ces Mountford played in a golden age, when crowds were huge, when personalities abounded and when competition was strong. Wigan in the half dozen post-war years certainly enjoyed a golden era. Comparisons were drawn with the fantastic Huddersfield 'Team of all the Talents' from around the First World War and with the superb Salford and Swinton combinations of the inter-war period. No one was dogmatic enough to say that Wigan was the greatest, but the team was damn good.

In Ces's days at Central Park, Wigan won the Challenge Cup in 1947-48 and 1950-51 and the Championship in 1946-47 and 1949-50. They took the Lancashire Cup in all five seasons Ces played for them, won the Lancashire

League Championship in 1946-47 and 1949-50, and were runners-up in 1947-48 and 1948-49. Their league position followed this pattern: first, first, second, first, second. Make no mistake, this was a champion team. Its level of success was bettered only by the dominant sides of the 1980s and 1990s, when arguably serious opposition was thinner on the ground.

Team of champions

It was also a team of champions. From number one to number 13 there were men of outstanding talent and, crucially, there was no rapid turn-over of personnel. Many of Ces's colleagues were icons of the game. Full-back was Martin Ryan, a runner rather than a traditional stay-at-the-back kicker and defender. When Ryan, a 1946 and 1950 Lion, was unavailable there was 1950 and 1954 Lion, Jackie Cunliffe, play-anywhere-anytime, Mr Versatile. Jackie had been a Wigan player from 1939 and he was still in the first team in 1960. On the wings there was a choice of four Internationals: Jack Hilton and Gordon Ratcliffe, both Lions in 1950, Johnny Lawrenson, who played in the Ashes-winning Great Britain team of 1948-49, and Ces's compatriot, Brian Nordgren, scorer of 312 tries and 109 goals in 294 games for Wigan. Noggy would have had a wardrobe full of New Zealand caps, if he had not come to England to study law.

In the centres were Ernie Ashcroft, another Lion in 1950 and 1954, and goal-kicking Welshman Ted Ward, who only toured in 1946. Scrum-half, and the perfect partner, to Ces was little Tommy Bradshaw, always ready to run himself silly for Wigan, Lancashire, England and Great Britain.

The forwards were awesome, both in the loose and in the scrummages, which in those days had to be won or there was a good chance of the match being lost. Leader of the pack was hooker Joe Egan, another double Lion, a man who got the ball and ran the game, a master tactician and an inspiring captain. His right-hand man was the gargantuan open-side prop Ken Gee, bedrock of the packs of both Wigan and every type of representative side going. George Banks, Frank Barton, Jack Large, Ted Slevin, Bill Hudson, Jack and Billy Blan, Les White and Nat Silcock were just some of the men whose belligerence, stamina, style and skills created a forward pack which allowed Ces and his back colleagues to enthral hundreds of thousands of spectators year in and year out.

Ces Mountford performed his magic on the great occasions. Many think his finest moments came in 1950, towards the end of the season after Wigan were shorn of eight Great Britain tourists who were on their way to Australia. With Joe Egan among the missing Lions, Ces took the Wigan captaincy for the end of the domestic season. When Halifax went to Central Park and drew 5-5 in the Championship semi-final on 29 April, it looked as if Wigan's hopes of taking the title had departed with their eight Lions. The replay, however, brought an astonishing 18-2 victory at Thrum Hall and Ces scored that dementia-defying try my father recalled over half a century later.

The final, at Maine Road on 13 May, was a no-chance prospect against a full strength Huddersfield team, which had hammered Wigan 27-8 at Fartown just two months earlier. However, Ces led his no-hopers to a 20-2 victory over the flummoxed and embarrassed Fartowners. In the opening minutes Ces's artistry opened up the Huddersfield defence for second-rower-turned-winger Nat Silcock to score a try, giving Wigan a lead they never lost. Thereafter wrote one reporter, "Mountford threw the Huddersfield back division out of gear by his crushing tackling of off-half Russell Pepperell".

A year later Ces led Wigan out at Wembley against his great rival Willie Horne's Barrow. He was the first New Zealander to captain a team in a Challenge Cup final there and, when a rather lack-lustre 80 minutes had elapsed, he was the first Kiwi to receive the Cup after Wigan's 10-0 victory. His own performance, however, had been outstanding and he was awarded the Lance Todd Trophy, another first for a New Zealander. Ironically, the 1951 Cup final proved to be Ces's last appearance in a Wigan jersey.

From being a great player Ces went on to become a successful coach. A 10 year contract with Warrington was itself an extraordinary vote of confidence in his abilities. He was, after all, an untried quantity in that role. Again history shows that he succeeded. Warrington had never enjoyed such riches. The Wire team of the mid-fifties partially rivalled the successes of Mountford's Wigan days. When he left England at the end of his contract it was a great loss to British Rugby League. England's loss was New Zealand's gain, of course. As a coach of coaches and of the national team in his homeland, Ces merely added to his laurels as one of the truly great men of Rugby League in the second half of the twentieth century.

Robert Gate

Robert Gate is a prolific and pioneering Rugby League historian, and has played a major role in developing the history of the game. Among his recent books is *The Great Bev – The rugby league career of Brian Bevan* (London League Publications Ltd 2002).

Ces Mountford: A Legend of League

Ces receiving the MBE from Governor General
Sir Paul Reeves in November 1987

Contents

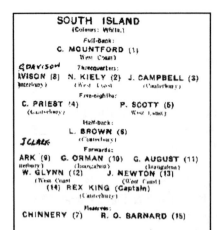

SOUTH ISLAND
(Colours: White.)

Full-Back:
C. MOUNTFORD (1)
West Coast

C DAVISON
Threequarters:
AVISON (8)   N. KIELY (2)   J. CAMPBELL (3)
Canterbury   First Coast   Canterbury

Five-eighths:
C. PRIEST (4)   P. SCOTT (5)
Canterbury   West Coast

Half-back:
L. BROWN (6)
J CLARK   Canterbury

Forwards:
ARK (9)   G. ORMAN (10)   G. AUGUST (11)
Canterbury   Canterbury   Canterbury
W. GLYNN (12)   J. NEWTON (13)
West Coast   West Coast
(14) REX KING (Captain)
Canterbury

Reserves:
CHINNERY (7)   R. O. BARNARD (15)

(Available at Stadium Office Entrance only)
(See Plan on back)

EMPIRE STADIUM, WEMBLEY
No. 45

RUGBY LEAGUE
FINAL
SATURDAY, MAY 1st, 1948
KICK-OFF 3 p.m.

PASS TO
DRESSING
ROOM
A. J. Elvin
MANAGING DIRECTOR
Wembley Stadium Limited

THIS PORTION TO BE RETAINED

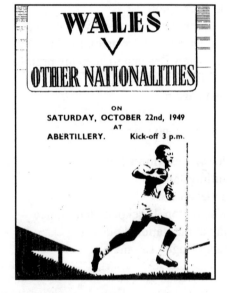

WALES
V
OTHER NATIONALITIES

ON
SATURDAY, OCTOBER 22nd, 1949
AT
ABERTILLERY.   Kick-off 3 p.m.

Memories of great occasions:
Top left: The South Island team sheet for the July 1939 test trial at Carlaw Park. The programme said that Ces was probably the youngest full-back ever to represent South Island – and also the smallest. He was not selected for the tour squad, who arrived in England as war broke out, and were home again eight weeks later, having played two matches. (Courtesy Bud Lisle)
Top right: Dressing room pass for the 1948 Challenge Cup Final.
Bottom: Programme from Ces's international debut for Other Nationalities.

Part 1: My Life and Rugby League

Mountfords playing for Blackball.
Back row: Ces, Ken, father Robert and Bill. Jack seated.

1

Blackball team with four Mountford brothers: Ken and Bill on right in back row, Bob one from right in middle row, Ces in centre on front row, between Johnny Dodds and George Schaeffer.

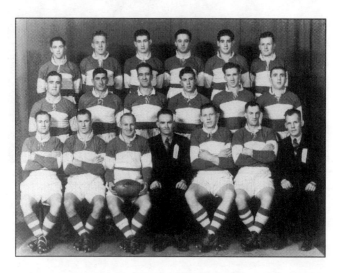

1945 West Coast Representative team. Ces was the team captain and is in the front row holding the ball. Ken Mountford is one from the left in the back row, Bill Mountford is on the right in the back row.

1. My formative years

Along with the other young men of my generation who grew up on the West Coast of New Zealand in such a Rugby League atmosphere, I was enthusiastic about the game and the players who played it. I lived and breathed Rugby League. Doubtless this can in part be attributed to the local interest in the game, which at that time was very high on the West Coast and remains so to this day. The intensity of the enthusiasm for the Rugby League code held by the people who live in the towns and valleys of the West Coast can be likened to the devotion the people of Wales have for Rugby Union. Perhaps it reflects a similar pride and independence of spirit, for which the people of the West Coast is well noted. Great players of the past are still recalled by the Coasters of my generation with admiration and respect, and the deeds of the great West Coast teams of past years are still vividly remembered. Few teams could match West Coast players on their home ground in general toughness and resilience. The Coasters were known to be hard competitors, but always fair.

The West Coast of the South Island of New Zealand is situated between the mighty rollers and surging surf of the Tasman Sea and the snowy mountain chain of the Southern Alps. This means that Coasters live and work in an incredible landscape of spectacular rain forest, which they affectionately call "bush", glacial lakes, snowy mountains and a very rocky coast with many fine ocean beaches. To outsiders, Coasters can appear to be exasperating, cantankerous, unpredictable, rather insular and self-sufficient. This is because they are not understood. They tend to keep their own counsel until they get to know the newcomer. It is said that they are the nicest people in New Zealand, famous throughout the land for their hospitality, their humour, which is a little Gaelic, and their zest for life. Even today people born in the region are members of the most exclusive club in New Zealand – the wild West Coast. The Coasters have retained the characteristics and traditions of fair play, which were the hallmark of the early pioneers. Because they are so isolated geographically, they feel cut off from the mainstream of New Zealand life. Hence they always extend to visitors and visiting teams a warm welcome. They are notorious for their generous pre-match hospitality with touring teams. Doubtless the will to win, to prove themselves once again to the rest of New Zealand and to the world at large, is part of the West Coast psyche. Often, when the final whistle blows, visiting teams are amazed at the results. Another win to the Coast. The whole local community then adjourns to the hotels, pubs or club rooms for the after-match celebrations in which everyone takes part including wives and children.

The town of Blackball, where I was born and grew up played a vital role in developing the Rugby League traditions on the Coast. It was a small coal mining village of some 1,000 people in the 1920s and 1930s, situated high in the hills above the deep menacing swirling waters of the Grey River. The town is surrounded by the steep mountains of the Paparoa Range with its spectacular scenery. Blackball was known in the past to New Zealanders for its coal mine and its Rugby League teams. In the days of my youth its only connection with the rest of the West Coast was by a loose metalled road. I can recall cycling for miles to friends' places. That was the norm in those days. Transport was by Shanks's pony, bicycle, boat or on horseback. You could not grow up in such a community without having some strong feelings, a sense of belonging, being a part of the natural order of things. For some outsiders Blackball was probably the end of the Earth, terribly isolated and lacking in city glamour. Others really enjoy the surroundings. To be alone with nature is an all too rare experience today. It is like that sense of awe and wonder one finds in the outback of Australia or in the Pacific Islands under a wide and starry sky.

My father was born in London on 25 April 1888, within the sound of Bow Bells in the East End. He was one of a family of five, three brothers and two sisters. He passed away on 15 September 1964, three years after I returned to New Zealand. As a youngster growing up in London, he heard much talk of the work to be found in the gold and coal mines of New Zealand. In a sense of spirit and adventure he left school and joined the merchant navy, arriving at Westport in the South Island in 1906. He signed off and went to seek his fortune gold prospecting. Like many others he had no luck, but he struck gold when he met and married my mother Gladys Hodgson, who was a true West Coaster, being born and bred in Rununga. The Hodgson family originated from Yorkshire. The only other source of steady employment on the Coast was the coal mines and thus after his marriage my father became a coal miner.

Family tradition told to me by my English cousins is that we are descended from the de Montforts. Simon de Montfort accompanied William the Conqueror in the Normandy invasion. He is said to be the knight who hacked King Harold to death. Later when playing against a French selection at Carcassonne I was given the keys of the city by the

4

mayor. Carcassonne was the ancient home of the de Montforts. Simon de Montfort was the Grand Master of the ancient order of the Knights Templar. He was tortured and murdered by the French King, Louis.

With the abundance of wonderful native trees on the Coast, the Mountford home was, like most others, built of timber. As our family expanded, we older boys took great pride in helping our father and his brother-in-law, who was a builder, add more rooms until it became a very comfortable home. Coasters are great 'do-it-yourselfers' and that is the reason why they make good soldiers, a characteristic of the pioneer New Zealanders. My father, although short of stature, was an active participant in the coal miners' trade union and took a significant part in the great strike of 1908. Like Paddy Webb, Bill Hickey and many others, he was blacklisted at the Denniston mine near Westport and subsequently accepted employment in Blackball. People who knew my father have said that my short, nuggetty stature and lack of hair make me his double. I was, so to speak, 'a chip off the old block'.

Large families were commonplace at that time. Ours was no exception, consisting of seven boys and three girls. I was the second eldest, being born on 16 June 1919. We were a very happy family, despite the hard economic times of the great depression of the 1930s.

My earliest memories of Rugby League go back to when New Zealand picked its Kiwis to play Great Britain in 1928. During my schooldays at Blackball Primary School, I played Rugby League for the Blackball club. In 1932, I was picked to go to the schoolboys' trial in Greymouth. I remember the year well, because on the icy road we nearly lost our lives when our car spun out of control. Fortunately no one was hurt, and after the trials I was selected to represent the West Coast, this being my first representative football. I was then 13 years old. I also played association football in tandem with Rugby League. Later, the Blackball association football team of which I was a member played against a team called the Millerton All Blacks. In this team were the Ormand brothers who hailed from Newcastle in England. It was a Chatham Cup game, the Challenge Cup of New Zealand association football and we were soundly beaten 5-1. Millerton were a fine side and went on to play in the New Zealand final in Wellington. Association football on the Coast was played on Saturday, as was Rugby Union, while Rugby League was played on Sunday. Thus many of us played both sports. In those days, if a player played Rugby League, he was banned from Rugby Union because he had

5

'professionalised' himself. Many Union players played League on Sunday under a different name. For example, Frank Ryan, the former Mayor of Mount Albert, Auckland, played senior club Rugby Union on Saturday and Rugby League for Auckland University on Sunday under the name of Stanley Baldwin, a former prime minister of England. That was the way it was until recently in New Zealand. As far as the gnomes of the New Zealand Rugby Union were concerned, if you sullied yourself by playing Rugby League, you were banned from playing Union. Instead of Union I played association football.

I was selected to play in the West Coast Schoolboys association football team, which went on to win three provincial games in the South Island Championship in 1933. My father then suggested I should pursue an association football career in England with Chelsea or Arsenal by seeking trials. However, the idea didn't go any further than the thought. It was on Rugby League that my ambitions centred. I liked the cut and thrust of the game and the sense of triumph when I beat a man. I believe association football helped me with speed off the mark, and imbued me with a desire to look for, and to head towards, open spaces on the rugby field. Unlike most New Zealanders, I never played any Rugby Union, the reason being that when a new Headmaster a certain Mr B. Lang, arrived from Auckland, he decided to send a team to the Rugby Union Sevens at Greymouth. I wasn't included because I played Rugby League and it was against his amateur principles. This incident, at that age, had a lasting effect on me and has probably coloured my outlook ever since. Like most Coasters I cannot stand biased and self-opinionated nonentities. They are all really humbugs.

We had a very popular teacher at the school named Jack Crosman, who played Rugby Union for one of the Greymouth Clubs. He was very supportive of me and told me not to worry. It was people like Mr Lang, he told me, who had caused the Rugby League clubs in England to break away in 1895, and the Rugby Union sides in Sydney and the Coast to change to Rugby League. Jack played Rugby Union with the local postmaster, John Dunwoody, and during practice sessions they always found time to help us schoolboys, teaching us how to tackle and many of the other skills common to both codes. Nevertheless, headmaster Lang's attitude was all too common in New Zealand and it is only relatively recently after graduates from the New Zealand Universities Rugby League system have entered the teaching and other professions, that League is

6

able to be in a position to take the sport into the nation's schools. Up to 1950, no university in New Zealand played Rugby League. It was not the done thing. Nor was the game allowed in secondary schools.

Economic depression

I owed a lot to my parents. My mother brought up a family of 10 during the severe years of the great economic depression of the 1930s. The Coast, like all mining communities around the world, was particularly hard hit. Despite this, we were all encouraged by our parents to involve ourselves in sport. As we grew older, my father even became one of the team masseurs. In his early years, my father had been an enthusiastic boxer and it was probably because of this sporting interest that he became involved in fitness programmes and in the treatment of injuries. He had a genuinely amateur approach, not worrying whether matches were won or lost, as long as everyone played well and enjoyed themselves. It was the game that counted, not what we could get out of it for ourselves.

The original Rugby League men of the West Coast had provided a platform for the players of our generation to develop. Several of the pioneer Rugby League players were well known to me. Blackball, as stated earlier, was one of the first three clubs to form on the Coast, the two others being Kohinoor and Hokitika. When I was a senior player, the game had become very firmly entrenched in the families of our town. As players, we felt the keenness of the competition because the standard was very high. We were proud of our club and loved to play for it. That was the secret of the Coast, a kind of *Three Musketeers* brotherhood: "All for one, and one for all".

There was always marvellous support from the participating towns. The number of people living on the Coast at that time was far greater then now. Unfortunately, times have changed and there has been a steady drift to the North Island. When I was playing, it was not unusual to have several thousand people attend a club match despite the fact that these were the years of the great depression. Everyone looked forward eagerly to the weekly game of Rugby League. It diverted them from a life that was otherwise very difficult. Many people were poverty stricken. I know that many families in the north of England, and in the industrial cities of Australia, were similarly affected. The weekly match enabled them, for a short time, to forget the depression and become part of their team.

7

Our family was one of the many affected by the depression; we seemed to live on rice. No wonder it is not my favourite food. To enliven the rice, we dug vegetables from our garden and milk from our cow. I now really wonder how my mother coped. I well remember a moment of sadness at home, when one evening my father returned from relief work, walking into a house with no food in it. This was not frequent, and in the spirit of the times my mother always fed somebody less fortunate than ourselves, as did most of the people on the Coast.

It wasn't all work and sport on the Coast. People were still able to enjoy themselves. There was usually a well-attended dance in one of the towns every weekend and the cinema was open to all on Fridays, Saturdays and Sundays. It also goes without saying that the hotels and clubs were well patronised. Hunting for Captain Cookers (wild pigs), deer, ducks, native pigeons in the dense bush and whitebaiting at the river mouths were part of our everyday lives.

Many a time we would boil the billy, make damper (a pancake-type bread made in the ashes of an open fire) and flapjacks (another type of pancake bread) and sit back and watch the sunset. I can still remember how the setting sun transported the bush to a splendour of rose and gold, while overhead the mountains brooded amethyst in the clear distance. Never in my wanderings around the globe have I seen anything lovelier than a West Coast sunset. For me, the valley at sunset became a bastion of peace which nature had claimed for its own. The Coast has always been a part of me; it is truly the last, loneliest and loveliest place on this globe.

Being part of a large family, as well as bringing joys with the companionship of my brothers and sisters, also brought its obligations. I left Blackball Primary School after sitting the Proficiency examinations and at the age of 13 began work to augment the family income. This was the norm at the time. Behind our family home, the Paparoa Range rose up 6,000 feet and in the depths of the depression the government subsidised the earnings of the gold miners who worked up there. Gold was the one commodity that earned overseas income, so necessary to a bankrupt nation which could not repay its overseas loans.

My eldest brother and I had the job of carting provisions up to the miners, and the heavy work and physical exercise of climbing built up our stamina and physiques. I suppose you could call it natural weight training and with the marvellous panorama of snowy peaks, it was rather more interesting than the gymnasia in which today's footballers often exercise themselves for hours at a time. Our diet was fresh air and I believe the thousands of feet of climbing in those teenage years built up what was later to be much-needed strength in my legs. That strength earned on the mountains seemed to carry me successfully through the hard professional years when we were playing sometimes more than 50 games a season in England. On Monday mornings as a 14-year-old, together with my eldest brother, I was up well before daylight feeding the horses and loading the provisions onto the packhorses for the miners. The winter mornings on the Coast were often crisp and clear and the frost on the ground exuded a cold which we kept at bay with difficulty. The packhorses had to be loaded carefully and the straps pulled hard (sometimes squashing the bread, to the chagrin of the miners), to ensure the load wouldn't slip before the journey began up the famed Croesus track.

Each day of the week we journeyed up to the mining camps with their provisions. We returned sometimes on the same day or on longer journeys we camped out overnight under the stars. On a clear night, we could see the constellations of the Southern Cross in all their glory. With the many thousands of feet we climbed, I am sure we were doing high altitude training well before coaches understood the phenomenon. Certainly, my body's capacity to assimilate oxygen was improved markedly and when I played football at sea level I always seemed to have extra reserves of energy. The going was frequently difficult, as many of the tracks had very steep gorges on either side. Indeed we lost two horses in the three years we carried the provisions and I once sustained a serious leg injury, the scars of which I carry to this day.

The only prospect of steady work in my youth was in the coal mines, so it was into the mines I went, joining my father and elder brother at the age of 16, pushing coal trucks for a living. I was a boy among men during the Rugby League trips to Greymouth's Wingham Park, Runanga and other centres. Returning home, we always called at a hotel in Dobson which was run by a man named Mr Lowe who had only one arm, he lost the other in the First World War. The team had a bob (one shilling - 5p) in the kitty for drinks. (A bob covered three drinks). Being so young, my tipple was lemonade and the men respected the fact that I was still a lad and made sure that I did not indulge.

Modern Rugby League needs both stamina and speed. In my early days there was a great deal of professional sprinting done in New Zealand, from Invercargill in the South, right through to the tip of the North Island.

These games and races were major attractions in a country not then dominated by radio and television. The popularity of these track meets was proved by the large crowds that gathered from all over the country. The West Coast was no exception.

Professional race

My first professional race was at Taylorville, when I was 14 years of age. Alas the township of Taylorville is no more. The sprints were handicap races and the handicapper put me on 10 yards. I won the heat, then the final, and received £10, which was a lot of money in those days. The professionals approached me afterwards to refund their expenses from Christchurch, because they had travelled over the Alps expecting to win. Not being familiar with the procedures pertaining to professional athletics, I asked for advice from the officials. They said the money was mine to keep, but from then on I was off scratch. I still continued to win my share of prizes. I recall one race when my brother Bill raced against me and won; a fact he often reminded me of. Rugby Union frowned on professional track athletics, and if it could be proved that a Rugby Union player took part in such a race he was banned for life from playing Union. Rugby League, the new game, was more accommodating and that could well be another reason why it prospered on the Coast.

The Coast at that time had many fine athletes. Jack Lovelock, the gold medal winner of the mile at the Berlin Olympics in 1936, was born in Greymouth on the Coast. Jack was the son of an Englishman who migrated to New Zealand for health reasons and settled in Greymouth. He was at one time the manager of a gold mine in Crushington, another town which has since vanished. Like Australia and the USA, the Coast has its share of ghost towns. They vanished when the gold disappeared and the goldminers moved on seeking the next El Dorado.

My entry into senior Rugby League, at the early age of 16, was unusual and quite unexpected. I was playing association football at senior club level, and one Sunday in 1935 the Blackball senior Rugby League team found itself short of players. They stopped their bus outside our house before going to a game at Kumara, and picked up both me and a friend of mine called Butch Clark. I was delighted and somewhat nervous to be in my first senior match. The club played me at full-back, which kept me out of the heavy action among the opposing team's forwards. These included one Jim Calder, who went on to represent the Coast and was in the New Zealand representative team against Australia that year.

Examining the major formative years of my career, I followed in the footsteps of the great Johnny Dodds. He was the local Rugby League hero in Blackball and had represented both West Coast and New Zealand. Nicknamed the 'Yank' because he was born in the USA, and playing at first five-eighth, Johnny was one of the second generation of players who played for the West Coast. He began his representative career in 1925. By that time, West Coast had built up a formidable team of top-class players with its representative team's strength emanating from the Blackball, Marist, Inangahua, Runanga and Greymouth clubs. Dodds played in the Combined West Coast-Otago team which defeated Canterbury 12-3 at Monica Park in 1925. Otago was also very strong then with the Christian Brothers' Old Boys club team being the dominant force.

The growing strength of the West Coast was reflected by the result of their game against the visiting Queensland State team that same year, won by Queensland 27-10. Dodds was not only a great Rugby League player but became a prominent selector and administrator of the code. He also found time to train me as a junior player and most of what I did revolved around him and the teams he coached and played in. He taught me the basics of Rugby League, the proper foundation which could be built on later. Johnny Dodds toured Australia with the 1930 Kiwi team, accompanied by two other players from the Coast, Jim Calder and Norm Griffiths. It was from the second generation of Rugby League players that we, the players of the late 1930s, learnt the skills of the game. Dodds also personally guided me in my endeavours as a sprinter. He was certainly a coach for all seasons and well ahead of his time.

Years later when manager at Warrington, I was determined to get more speed out of my players. Harry Lloyd, an Edinburgh Powderhall sprint champion, was employed for that purpose. Lloyd taught me the rudiments of teaching our players style, running action and how to get off the mark quickly, as well as timing correctly with a stopwatch. This all took time, but his assistance was certainly appreciated by both me and the players at Warrington. He was to set a trend. I recall in the late 1950s, we were advised at Warrington that a prominent Rugby Union threequarter who had played for the British Lions in New Zealand in 1959, wished to be considered for a professional career. Harry Lloyd, who acted as a talent scout for the club, was dispatched to watch the pride of the British Lions

11

some 200 miles distant. At half-time, he telephoned me and asked me why he had been sent. The standards we set were so high that he considered the player too slow for the Rugby League game.

During my early years at Blackball, and indeed throughout New Zealand, players would constantly practise goal-kicking. Whether it was in Rugby Union or in Rugby League, it was well recognised then that accurate goal-kicking could be the difference on the scoreboard at the day's end. Finals and test matches always carry the most interest and such matches are often decided by the number of goals kicked. I always liked kicking; it added another dimension to my game and the teams we played against often did not have excellent kickers. For these reasons, I frequently practised goal-kicking at the Blackball Domain. In those days, the 'round the corner instep' kicking style had not been heard of and it was the straight up-and-down toe-end approach that I was acquainted with. In most games I usually took the short kicks and those halfway to the sideline, and if there wasn't a long range goal-kicker available, I took those kicks too. It was said that if you blinked you would miss Mountford's kicks, as I took only one or two paces backwards for distant kicks, none for short kicks.

The late Puig-Aubert of France, I recall, was also a kicker with a short run up, sometimes with a cigarette in his mouth and often wearing a cap. He was a real showman but a superb full-back. His greatest triumph was as a member of the great 1951 French team, which toured and defeated Australia two tests to one. Rugby League supporters will remember the famous Hill at the old Sydney Cricket Ground. The whole Hill rose to sing the *Marseillaise*, so well did the French play in the third test. This spontaneous action confirmed what I already knew, that the Australian fan knows his Rugby League and will always give praise when it is due. It is the same with the Coast. Coasters have no trouble in fraternising with Australians. They tend to speak the same language, direct without any politicking and straight to the point.

Over the years, there had been many fine players on the Coast, but few were recognised by international selection for the 'Kiwis'. There had been since the inception of Rugby League a very substantial increase in the playing strength of the West Coast teams, both in the number of teams playing in the competition and in the quality of play. Yet, during the 1920s the West Coast was consistently overlooked by the predominantly North Island selectors, who tended to think that Rugby League was an all-

Auckland game, and that the rest of New Zealand could have the crumbs. Most of the selectors did not bother to travel to see country players. Many should have been stars, but because they hailed from tiny hamlets in the outback they were unseen and unappreciated. This is perhaps one of the reasons why Rugby League has not succeeded like it should have in New Zealand. On the other hand, our Australian cousins scanned the highways and byways for unseen talent, and continue to do so.

During the First World War, Rugby League ceased to be played in New Zealand except on the Coast where it was actually introduced in 1915. Most of the men joined up to go to the bloody 'playing fields' of Gallipoli and France, many never to return. On resumption of peace in 1918, the returned former players were again available, albeit in reduced numbers due to the ravages of the war. The West Coast's first game against an international side was played in 1920 against Great Britain, with the touring side winning 51-13.

West Coast victory

The code subsequently grew enormously, and in 1946 the tables were turned on the Lions with the West Coast's victory over that fine team, 17-8. I had not long been in England playing for Wigan when the game took place. In conversation with the legendary Jim Sullivan, the Wigan coach, I mentioned to him that I thought the West Coast could defeat Great Britain. This was not something easily accepted by one of Wigan's greatest players and he deemed it an impossibility. When the news of the Coast's 17-8 victory came through, I told him the score. Equal to the occasion as always, he replied quick as a flash, "It must be a bloody misprint." Misprint, however, it was not, for there had been great developments in the code in the inter-war years. New Zealand-wide, Rugby League was threatening Rugby Union as the premier winter sport. With regular inter-provincial games against Canterbury and Auckland, the playing strength and experience on the Coast had increased.

In 1921, Charlie McElwee played for New Zealand against Auckland and the quality of his play was such that he was also selected for the New Zealand team which toured Australia - the first West Coast representative player to do so. The first international West Coaster was Bill Kelly who hailed from Buller. Bill had played for New Zealand in 1912 and for Australia against Harold Wagstaff's touring British side of 1914. Bill

Kelly is the only New Zealander to have represented both countries at Rugby League. He was badly wounded in France in 1915 and never played again. Later though, he was an Australian selector and coached many club sides, his greatest achievements being coaching Balmain with prominent radio announcer Frank Hyde as captain to the 1939 Premiership title. Kelly himself was a player in the 1914 winning Balmain side.

The code's devotees on the Coast in the 1920s were becoming more widely based, with teams in Waiuta and Inangahua. Most importantly, there was also a consistently good administrative approach with J. D. Wingham as President during the 1920s, after whom the West Coast Rugby Central League Ground (not yet then in existence) was to be named. By the mid 1920s, a new group of players had emerged and in 1924 the West Coast defeated Wellington 12-6. The number of senior teams had expanded in the interim with the addition of Nelson Creek and Runanga. There were also further representative honours. The Marist captain, Neil Mouatt, played for the New Zealand team in the first test against Great Britain in 1924 at Auckland. The British side included Jim Sullivan, who was later to be my coach at Wigan. Jim represented Wigan for 25 years, and in nine of them he was also picked for Great Britain. Mouatt was also a member of the New Zealand team which toured Australia in 1925 under the management of J. D. Wingham. In 1926, the popularity of the game had increased so much that a separate league was formed in Buller with its headquarters in Westport. Buller played West Coast in 1926 and 1927, on the first occasion losing 20-17 at Greymouth, but the following year defeating West Coast 12-3 at Victoria Square, Westport. On their way home to Greymouth, the West Coast team defeated Inangahua where a sub-centre to the West Coast League had been formed in 1920.

Thus when I began my Rugby League career in the mid 1930s, there were three strongholds of Rugby League on the West Coast: Buller, Inangahua and West Coast itself. Inangahua was subsequently the centre of a major earthquake and the population has never recovered. Sadly Rugby League in Buller is no more, although I believe there was an attempt to resurrect the game there in 1995.

The growing strength of the game on the Coast was reflected in the results. In 1931 West Coast defeated Canterbury 37-19. The following year West Coast played Canterbury for the Anisy Shield and ran out easy winners 53-26. These were very powerful West Coast teams and from

14

them emerged great Kiwi representatives. The continued growth of the code at club level led to a northern division sub-centre being formed in 1933. There were eight inaugural senior teams, Waitua A, Waitua B, Reefton, Mawheraiti, Grey Valley, Waiuta Rovers and Ahaura. Five of the teams had defected from Rugby Union, similar to what happened so many years ago in England and shortly afterwards in New South Wales. The game was so dominant, it wasn't a question of selecting a West Coast representative team, but rather who to leave out. The local club competition was very fierce and two West Coast teams could have been selected to match any North Island side, so great was the popularity of Rugby League.

So what went wrong? While Rugby League is still the number one winter sport on the Coast, there are fewer teams than there used to be. Rugby Union led a fierce counter campaign to stop the growth of the League code. This was led by the mayor of Westport, Bill Craddock, a well-known pioneer identity. Bill had played Rugby Union football with Bill Kelly at Westport. Kelly had then gone on to represent Wellington at Rugby League before going on to play for New Zealand and later Australia. They remained very firm friends over the years, although Bill Craddock was fierce in his determination to prevent Buller remaining a Rugby League stronghold. I believe Bill Craddock, by his sheer personality and drive, was solely responsible for the demise of Rugby League in Buller. League officialdom had no answer to Craddock's administrative skills and popularity. Rugby Union in Buller owes a lot to Bill Craddock. Lack of good administrators has always been a feature of New Zealand Rugby League officialdom, especially over the last 50 years, and is another reason why Rugby League, instead of becoming the dominant code in New Zealand, as in New South Wales and Queensland, has lost ground over the years. Fortunately, there has now been a resurgence of interest due to the advent of the New Zealand Warriors playing in the Australian NRL and television coverage of that competition.

There was tremendous interest in New Zealand in the touring Great Britain side of 1932. West Coast was well represented in the Kiwi team by Masters at scrum-half. Peter Hart was also selected but had to withdraw because of a knee injury. Coaster Jim Calder was the outstanding player in the test in Auckland. He was named 'player-of-the-day' in recognition and awarded an international cap still very much treasured by his daughter. 1932 stays in my mind because it was the year of my first trip away from

15

the Coast as a schoolboy representative player, travelling across the Alps and through the Otira Tunnel. Upon arrival in Christchurch, I was billeted with the Drury family. Art Drury was the then secretary of the Canterbury Rugby League. His brother Dan looked after me and we remained friends. Rugby League players in those days formed lasting friendships. We might wonder why this is not always the case today.

SOUVENIR
PRICE
SIXPENCE
PROGRAMME
SUNDAY, JUNE 2nd., 1946.

A
U

R
E
V
O
I
R

G
O
O
D

L
U
C
K

The West Coast Rugby League proudly presents this Programme as a Testimonial
—to—
Ces. Mountford
West Coast
and South Island
Rugby League Representative,
on the eve of his departure for England.

The programme that marked Ces's departure for Wigan.

16

2. Blackball Rugby League

To the men and women of the townships of Blackball and Greymouth, I owe the beginnings of my Rugby League career. They have always supported me and I will remain a West Coaster until I die. I have always kept them in my mind wherever I have been. I was proud to be a member of the Blackball club and represent the West Coast. When New Zealand Rugby League followers think of Blackball, they remember the Blackball teams of the 1940 to 1946 era. In that time, Blackball lost only one game in club competition. In four years Blackball scored 2,221 points, with 550 against. Blackball was certainly the Wigan of New Zealand in the 1940s. It came as no surprise to me in England when four Blackball men, Ray Nuttall, McBride, Aynsley and my brother Ken Mountford were selected in the New Zealand side that toured Great Britain and France in 1947-48. What a great side that was.

Between 1939 and 1945 there was great Rugby League activity on the Coast, there were many games in the local competitions. The mines were declared as essential to the war effort with the result that the Coast had a large permanent population. The high grade anthracite coal was required all over the world. This meant more players available for the game.

In the 1942 season, Blackball was undefeated and took the Thacker Shield from Syndenham Rakaia, a Canterbury team, 43-56. We then held this trophy for some time until finally Addington beat us at Blackball. In 1944 our West Coast team beat Canterbury 23-18.

In 1943, Blackball figured in one of the most spectacular inter-club Rugby League games ever played in New Zealand. We went up to Auckland to play the leading side there, Manukau. That all-Maori team had been carrying all before it in New Zealand's strongest Rugby League centre. Blackball's reputation for playing attractive football had become known in Auckland and a record crowd for the club season of more than 17,000 came out in the pouring rain to see us in action.

Most of the Blackball team were engaged in the coal mining industry, an essential industry to the war effort, and as a consequence had only limited time and facilities for training. The long, two-day trip to Auckland did not help us either. Yet it was an eye-opener for the Auckland public to see the way we held the Auckland champions. The heavyweight Manukau pack made sure that Blackball had little chance of obtaining the ball from the scrums, but we made up for this by not relinquishing possession by kicking. We spun the ball, (in those days the six-tackle rule was not part of the game so possession was very important because the number of tackles was not limited) and treated Carlaw Park enthusiasts to a most scintillating display of the same fast and sure handling which we played to full home crowds on the Coast. The Auckland crowd were on their toes cheering our little-fancied Blackball team.

Our display, I am informed, was not equalled at Carlaw Park until the tour of Puig-Aubert's 1951 French team. Halfway through the second half, Blackball led 9-8. I was at five-eighth, and had scored a try. On the outside, my brother, Bill, time and again sliced his way through midfield opposition. It was not just a two-man effort, for the whole Blackball side played well and never wilted under the sustained pressure from Manukau. In the end, the sheer weight of Manukau, combined with the wet conditions, sapped our strength, and carried the day. Seventeen-stone Peter Ririnui burst through our tiring defence to hand on to 15-stone Steve Watene, who gave his winger an easy run to the line. Two more tries in the last minute of the game gave Manukau a 23-9 victory. The Auckland crowd cheered our team to an echo when they left the field. Rugby League, at club level, was the most popular winter game in Auckland at the time. That 1943 Manukau side was studded with international representative players, the best known of whom were the late Steve Watene, who went on to become a Member of Parliament, Peter Ririnui and Jack Hemi. Hemi was one of the finest goal-kickers ever produced in New Zealand, having amazing accuracy and tremendous power. Hemi helped his side to victory with a try and four goals. He was Rugby League's Don Clarke (a famous Rugby Union goal-kicker) at the time.

After this defeat, I went to Huntly and with two friends tried to enlist in the army. My friends were accepted, but I was rejected as I was employed in an industry essential for the war. I was told to return to Blackball immediately. My two friends paid the supreme sacrifice overseas.

Club competition on the West Coast in my time was always very competitive. Probably the most difficult games we had were what one in England would call a local derby. The Gibson and Mulcare families were very prominent in the Ngahere team. The Gibsons worked in the bush, the Mulcares at the timber mills and on their family farm. They were all very hard tacklers and didn't allow much room for attack. We didn't lose many games against Ngahere but never won by a big margin either.

18

Like all young men, my ambition was to play for New Zealand. My attitude to rugby, then as always, was dedication, commitment and to try for perfection. These were also the ideals for most of the Blackball and West Coast players who showed their pride in being Coasters. These attributes, I believe, have at times been missing from New Zealand teams, and are a reason for poor performances. Like the association football teams of England, there are outstanding individuals but they have not always moulded well as a team. Rugby League is a team game, as the little fancied 1995 Queensland State of Origin team proved to the New South Wales star-studded side.

Two outstanding players from the West Coast who, I believe, did not get the recognition they deserved were Micky Ord, a scrum-half, and my brother, Bill Mountford. Bill could play at centre or wing. Only the parochial North Island approach to the game kept them out. I had played full-back for the South Island versus North Island in 1939, but was considered too young for the ill-fated 1939 tour of England. (The tourists arrived just as war broke out, played two games and had to return home). I was only 17 at the time. After the game, I met Herb Cook and George Nepia, who both told me that I was a certainty to be selected for the New Zealand team; but I wasn't. Playing with me in that game for the South Island was Chang Newton, who was also considered to be too young.

Blackball's list of 13 Kiwi representatives has included some legends of New Zealand Rugby League. The 13 are Jim Calder (1928, 1930, 1932, 1935, 1936), Johnny Dodds (1930), Bill Mountford (1946), Ken Mountford (1947-48), Charlie McBride (1946, 1947-48, 1952), Bob Aynsley (1946, 1947-48, 1949), Ray Nuttall (1947-48), Bill McLennan (1951-52, 1952, 1953, 1954, 1955, 1955-56, 1957), Bob O'Donnell (1952), Les McNicol (1955-56), Robin Scholefield (1965), Mick O'Donnell (1977, 1978, 1980, 1981) and Jack Williams (tour manager 1971, 1972). Don Ladner and Gordon Smith both played for the amalgamated club, Blackball and Ngahere, which became Waro-Rakau. These players took part in the game because they loved it. They were proud to represent their club, province, island or country. To them to be selected as a representative player was the pinnacle of success. Monetary advantage did not enter into their considerations. It is significant that the Blackball club ceased to exist in 1969, when it was amalgamated with Ngahere to form a new club, Waro-Rakue (Maori for coal-timber). It had an impressive record in 54 years life as a Rugby League club.

With the demise of the Blackball club went some of the soul of the West Coast Rugby League. Blackball won many national championship titles, held the Thacker Shield, symbol of South Island supremacy in 1943, 1945 and 1946, and was runner-up in the New Zealand club finals three times to Manukau of Auckland in 1943, 1945 and to Addington of Christchurch in 1944. It finally won the National title in 1950 against Mount Albert of Auckland.

In my playing days on the Coast, there were some exciting games played in great spirit. Blackball versus Runanga was always a tough match; the latter always had a good pack of forwards let by the great Billy Glyn. Marist, too, were great competitors led by Billy Mann, my whitebaiting partner in my youth. We played the best we could for our club - winning was what we all wanted. Off the field we were cobbers (friends), the best of mates. The early groundwork of the very talented footballers from the 1930s to the early 1940s certainly showed through. Top players from the past, like Johnny Dodds, Jim Calder, Neil O'Brien, Norm Griffiths, Jonas Masters, Billy Glyn and others, had done their groundwork well with spectacular results. As I have mentioned, it wasn't a question of whom to put into the West Coast team, but who to leave out. Local competition was always very fierce. In addition, we had tremendous input by our administrators, who loved the game and gave their time voluntarily for no material gain. They did it for the Coast. During the 1940s the West Coast teams always had good results in New Zealand provincial games, not losing many matches. The Coast was well represented in the South Island teams and in the New Zealand teams of 1947 and 1948. There were many players in South Island who should have been Kiwis. The South Island had one selector, Auckland or North Island, two. I always believed that Auckland was very parochial. During 1945 and 1946, Johnny Dodds, my old coach, was a New Zealand selector. He was a good mixer, a thinking coach, who liked to socialise and was very popular with the players - a man's man. This was not held in his favour by the powers-that-be and the South Island selector was dropped.

The change was due to the influence of the New Zealand Rugby League Council, all of whom were Aucklanders. This didn't really affect me, as at that time I was already in England playing for Wigan. In retrospect, it was just as well, because it is not in my nature to compromise with mediocre people. It may be thought that these remarks are the utterings of a parochial South Islander, but the facts speak for themselves.

Many South Island players did not get the opportunities they earned, yet the few who were selected could not be ignored and proved to be outstanding Kiwi players, such as McBride, Newton, Aynsley, the Forrest brothers, the O'Donnell brothers, Ray Nuttall, Menzies, Kennedy, Jock Butterfield and my brothers Ken and Bill.

When the Blackball and Ngahere clubs combined in 1969, Gordon Smith was placed in the combined Waro-Rakue Club. Gordon became one of the stars of the 1980 Kiwi team to England and France. We were having a problem with goal-kicking. I had a word with a number of players asking them to come forward if they were capable of kicking goals. A quietly spoken Gordon didn't say anything, so I went over to him and told him I understood that he could kick goals. I asked him what type of boots he had. His were soft toed and low in the heels, not the type needed for kicking. I asked him his size, and found that I had a good pair with square toes. He tried them on, practised kicking and became the most successful goal-kicker on the tour, kicking some vital goals. Gordon still has my boots. He played for Hull Kingston Rovers for several seasons and became a legend in that League stronghold. He returned to New Zealand, coached in Christchurch and coached the New Zealand Universities Rugby League international side. That team was very competitive, as Gordon had all the attributes of a good Rugby League player - discipline, a quick inventive mind, initiative and loyalty to his fellow players.

Another player who spent time in England and Australia playing professional Rugby League and is now living in Christchurch was Mark Broadhurst. Tony Coll has coached the West Coast team and had a very successful year in 1989. All certainly built up reputations that added prestige to the game. I am sure the Australian Kangaroos and the Great Britain Lions, who had to front up to them, would agree with me.

Brian Nordgren

In 1944, West Coast played Auckland at Carlaw Park, the home of Rugby League. We lost in the last minute by a penalty kicked from halfway by Warwick Clark after leading throughout. It was a dubious offside penalty. I returned to Auckland in 1945, playing in a North versus South game, losing 16-8. I gave the last try away by waiting for the ball to bounce, but it bounced in the other direction to Freddy James, who scored near the posts. Playing in that game was Brian Nordgren for the North. Brian was a

21

Coaster, being born in Runanga. He had left as a young lad and joined up in the military forces. It was a strange situation, but in uniform you could play both codes. Thus Brian played for Ponsonby at League as well as for the leading Auckland Rugby Union garrison team. In Rugby Union he was a sensational winger. Brian was the first overseas player signed up by Wigan after the war.

The New Zealand Rugby League protested to their English counterparts about signing a New Zealand player, stating that there was a ban in effect according to an agreement in 1937, which was renewed in 1938 and 1939. However, this agreement lapsed because of the war, and thus New Zealand could not succeed in its appeal. Subsequently, Brian was asked by Wigan if he could assist in helping to get a good first five-eighth. He gave them the names of the captains of the North and South Island teams, one Arthur Kay and me: Ces Mountford. At the time Arthur was 32 and I was 26. So Wigan contacted their agent in New Zealand to approach me. I didn't know this at the time. I had previously been approached in 1939 by Leeds and was entertaining the idea playing for them, but war intervened and that was that.

After the 1945 inter-island match, Bill, my brother and myself were speaking to Scotty McClymont, a New Zealand selector and coach about what the future held in the way of the forthcoming tour. He sharply replied to me: "You don't need to worry, there are five or six better than you in Auckland." Scotty, although knowledgeable in the game, was a self-centred selector, who I believe liked to impose, not consult. He later became very religious which I felt made him even more narrow-minded. I feel that with Scotty and his associates, who were known as the Richmond Mafia, New Zealand League began its decline. The effects are still there to this day. I believe Scotty's main fault was that he was unable to see beyond Auckland. In my opinion, he did understand Rugby League fundamentals but lacked respect from the players.

Shortly after McClymont's reply, I received a letter from the resident Wigan agent, a Mr Griffiths of Ash Street, Avondale, Auckland, offering me an opportunity to go to Wigan. I showed this letter to my brother Bill, who replied: "You have no choice but to take the offer. Scotty made it quite clear that he was not interested in you and the Auckland selectors control the selection." At that time I was studying mining and about to sit for my under-manager's ticket. Mindful of the fact that Wigan had a mining and technical college, said to be the finest in the world, I wrote to the Wigan club asking for more details and informing them that I would like to study full-time at the college in addition to playing Rugby League. The rest is now history. Wigan believed I was the best five-eighth in New Zealand, contrary to the New Zealand selectors.

At the send-off ceremony that the West Coast team put on for me in 1946, I promised the Coast that when my playing contract was fulfilled, I would return to New Zealand and put back into the game all the knowledge I had gained. I felt I owed it to the Coast and to the game. I did my best to keep that promise, but it was not an easy task.

When I finished my studies, a five-year course, I intended to return to New Zealand. The head of the mining department wrote to the minister of mining in New Zealand, asking what he thought my prospects would be in New Zealand. The minister cabled back: "Tell young Mountford to forget about mining, there will be no industry left here in 10 years." This was the main factor in my decision to stay in England after my Wigan contract was finished and accept a 10-year contract to manage and coach the Warrington team. They proved to be 10 good years.

Discipline

On the Coast I was regarded as something of a disciplinarian where Rugby League was concerned, a real killjoy in fact. We once had a visit from a top Wellington club team that was like a holiday for them. The evening before the game, I decided to take a walk to the local cinema. It was usual for some of the players and their girlfriends to meet at the interval and drive to a dance at either Araha or Ngahere. My visit was timely because my brother Bill, Bill Day and Tommy Phillips, together with their girlfriends and Isobel, my future sister-in-law, were about to drive off to attend a dance. Not being a dance fan myself, when told of their destination, I gave them an ultimatum, that if they attended the dance they would be out of the team to play the following day. The girls were not very happy and never forgot or forgave me. Blackball went on to win by a big score. As far as I was concerned the proof of the pudding was in the eating. So it was with captaining or coaching - a lonely position, because you have to keep motivating everyone to continue to be the best.

There was usually a family discussion at the dinner table after our games. In addition to the family, there would always be extra visitors. My father was usually instrumental in inviting all and sundry. In retrospect, my mother and three sisters must have had a hard time with all the cooking and dish washing. I can only thank them for their kindness in putting up with us. But that is the way the Coast was. We shared what we had, a welcome to any strangers. There is a saying, "Once a Coaster, always a Coaster" and to this day I am often filled with nostalgia even though most of the people I knew then have left the area. Life wasn't too complicated in those days; money, transfers and large bonuses were not involved. It was purely the love of the game and life.

On 2 June 1946 I played my last match at Wingham Park, Greymouth, followed by presentations from Bill Meates, the West Coast Rugby League President and a great Marist supporter. Leaving the Coast wasn't easy. Most of my team mates were good enough to play for the English clubs, even if not good enough to play for New Zealand. I had tremendous respect for players from the Coast and South Island, plus the coaches and controlling bodies. They always offered help and advice.

My brother Ken, who toured England and France in 1947 and 1948, was later tragically killed in the Strongman Mine disaster of 1967. I could have been with him, but for the fact that I had accepted an offer to play with Wigan in England. Fate spins its web in strange ways.

Leaving such a close-knit family as mine was traumatic. I was the first to leave home, but the whole family was supportive. I left Blackball on 14 June 1946 by rail car to catch the ferry from Christchurch and then on to Wellington, following by train to Napier where I boarded the Coptic. My uncle and a friend accompanied me to the boat. I received a telegram from Mr Griffiths, the Wigan agent: "Wishing you a safe and happy voyage. Good luck, Griffiths". The Coptic was a cargo ship, and it was a very slow journey to England with five other passengers. I trained in the engine room and helped the cook to make bread. This relieved the tedium a bit. We went via the Panama Canal and the voyage took six weeks. In London I was met by Brian Nordgren and two Wigan directors. Two days after arriving in Wigan I bought a paper, and read that the West Coast had beaten Great Britain 17-8. I was thrilled and spent the day in high spirits.

3. Notes on Ces and Bill Mountford's Blackball Rugby League memories
By John Haynes

Ces thought that Ngahere, situated across the bridge, over the Grey River, was the most difficult team to play against, particularly the tackling of the Gibson brothers and Paddy Mulcare. It was a local derby. There were some former Blackball players there. He said although no-one from Ngahere played for the Kiwis then, they were very solid defensively.

In regard to Marist, Billy Mann first played for Canterbury Rugby Union before playing for Marist Rugby League on the West Coast and created a lot of goodwill. He organised functions between the various clubs. Both Ces and Bill Mountford were mates for many years with Billy Mann and Tony Coll's father Peter Coll. On Micky Ord, who played for Blackball, West Coast and South Island, they said he ran from the base of the scrum expertly and varied his play greatly. He was fast and a good player. Ces felt that if Jimmy Haig and Des Barchard had not been selected in the 1947-48 Kiwis, Mickey Ord would have been a Kiwi but he needed fast finishers outside him.

Rununga was the most difficult club to beat at home. Ces and Bill both spoke of the momentous clash in 1943 at Carlaw Park in Auckland between Blackball and Manakau. They said Peter Ririnui who played for Manukau was a huge man and that Blackball got beaten because the forwards were too small. In the Manukau team was Jack Hemi at full-back, New Zealand full-back, great goal-kicker and line-kicker and came into the backline. Steve Watene was at prop and Blackball seemed to match Manakau in the backs. To go up there the Blackball Club and the players had fundraised selling raffle tickets, but there was very little gate money paid to them although the turnstile showed 19,000 people had gone through the gate. There was a dispute between Jack Redwood of the NZRL, who was from Auckland, and the Blackball team over this as Blackball felt they should be taking some of the gate for their home town.

They said that Ray Nuttall their full-back was very good defensively and came into the backline and was a reasonable kicker. He was a 1947 Kiwi. Jack O'Donnell always played well as was a solid winger. Harry Jamieson a winger was a good finisher and Jock McNaughton at stand-off was a good all round player and served the backs well. Regarding Kirk,

Charlie McBride and Ken Mountford they thought these were the best back three for the South Island for some years. These three were in the New Zealand team which beat Wigan at Central Park in 1947.

Back now to when they played in Auckland, they said that they had to leave Blackball on a Tuesday by rail to get to Auckland by Saturday and there was no pay for them as they were not at work. Blackball had at that time beaten the Rest of the Coast team 27-11. The success of the Blackball team they attributed to being well coached, dedicated and packed full of Kiwis. They always had a good pack of forwards. There was sprint work done with the team running onto the ball and the players were taught to hold the ball out in front and always to attack. They said that they got room to work in off McNaughton at five-eighth. There was also a 60-5 win over Canterbury. When West Coast played Auckland they lost 8-7. Chang Newton stood out in the game, West Coast was awarded a penalty 60 yards out and Ces said if he had let him kick it they would have won the game but he had missed before. Auckland won by a penalty which they said was never a penalty, Jock McNaughton was not off-side in their view and Warwick Clarke for Auckland kicked a goal from halfway. This was the only time West Coast in those days played against Auckland, who never played on the Coast when they were playing.

The Otahuhu Club from Auckland did play in Blackball, and Blackball won 39-10. There was a very good crowd. Blackball took their rugby very seriously, but were not professionals.

Of their brother Ken Mountford, they said he played an extremely brainy game of rugby and that he could read a game. He got very badly and deliberately knocked out by one of the Wigan players when the Kiwis beat Wigan in 1947 in what was a very rugged game. He was always doing something from the back of the scrum with the half-back and played a lot of games on the 1947 tour. Of their brother Bob they said he played on the wing for Blackball. Billy Mountford says of Ces that his attributes were speed, change of pace and good hands. On his own running style, Ces said that he leant over to get a longer stride, would practice sprinting and learnt to hold the ball in both hands. One of his disappointments was that after he went to England Johnny Dodds was replaced as New Zealand selected by Jim Amos. He said that when Johnny Dodds went some people from outside Auckland did not get selected. Ces said that one of the greatest satisfactions he had when playing during this period, which is the early 1940s, was to run Auckland so close at 8-7 because they were

26

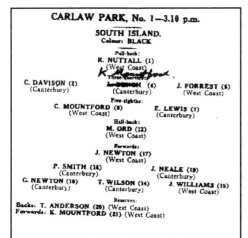

CARLAW PARK, No. 1—3.10 p.m.

SOUTH ISLAND.
Colour: BLACK

Full-back:
R. NUTTALL (1)

Three-quarters:
C. DAVISON (2)   L. DINNICH (4)   J. FORREST (5)
(Canterbury)   (Canterbury)   (West Coast)

Five-eighth:
C. MOUNTFORD (6)   E. LEWIS (7)
(West Coast)   (Canterbury)

Half-back:
M. ORD (12)
(West Coast)

Forwards:
J. NEWTON (17)
(West Coast)
P. SMITH (16)   J. NEALE (19)
(Canterbury)   (Canterbury)
G. NEWTON (10)   T. WILSON (14)   J. WILLIAMS (15)
(Canterbury)   (Canterbury)   (West Coast)

Reserves:
Backs: T. ANDERSON (20) (West Coast)
Forwards: K. MOUNTFORD (21) (West Coast)

South Island team 16 September 1944 against North Island at Carlaw Park. Ces is at five-eighth. Ken Mountford is listed as a reserve, but played at threequarter.

playing very good rugby; so was Blackball and to be accepted to go to Auckland to play Manakau. This was the great achievement of the boys from Blackball.

It was their considered view that the Blackball team in 1946 when it was playing at its best could have beaten a number of English sides. They say that that was proved when West Coast beat Great Britain in 1946 when Great Britain toured in New Zealand. They recalled miners like Chang Newton and his mates filling 72 boxes of coal before training on training days. Charlie McBride was a great low tackler and was one of their amazing lightweights.

On playing in Blackball, they said that any team that came down there they just had to win to get recognition. They said that there were six Mountfords playing at Blackball and that they were pretty instrumental in getting the others out to train. Ces said of Johnny Dodds that he always regarded him as the best coach ever and a good friend never getting rewarded for his efforts.

Of the tour to England, and Ces deciding to go and play professional in England before it went, Ces said that with Pat Smith being back as captain, it was obvious he wasn't going to be captain and that there was no chance for him. He believed that they were unlucky in that there was no proper administration in the West Coast capable of influencing the New Zealand selectors. Ces and Bill said that they trained and played together and knew each others play really well. In the Blackball team, Micky Ord got them going really well and once Jock McNaughton had got the ball

27

away quickly it gave Ces room to move and Bill had the speed to catch up with Ces. They said that they planned moves and often Ces would go around or call Bill through on the inside. The best move they had was for Ces to go on an angle and to call Bill in off close. They said they always got good service from the inside-backs and they got the ball quick enough to be able to do things. Peter and Billy Kirk were always covering. The latter was a great player, who had the same style as Peter Mountford.

One of Bill Mountford's great disappointments as it turned out was that in 1950 he received an offer to play for Manly in Sydney but he was not permitted by the New Zealand Rugby League to play in Australia there being a ban by NZ on NZ players going overseas. Typically Billy said he wouldn't have worried but the next year the New Zealand Rugby League let others go.

Ces also mentioned about when he arrived in England it was a very wet day. One of the first things that happened was a very nice card that he received from the great George Smith who had toured with the first New Zealand Rugby League team the All Golds in 1907-1908, but he didn't have a chance to contact him. He also said that when he first got to Wigan he started to make some breaks, but that the opposition started to be able to anticipate this. He then had to take himself out on the park and teach himself how to sidestep properly. Once he had learnt this and mastered it he was able to get through more often.

During one of my conversations with Bill and Ces Mountford we visited the ground at Blackball where they played all their rugby. This brought back terrific memories and they said that the crowds were quite huge by comparison with the numbers in the area with between 4,000 and 5,000 people watching the games. They got changed in the local hotel, and went there afterwards as well. Bill at one point also pointed to the hedge which was next to us on the ground and he said with a smile that this is where some of the locals used to play "two up" when the game was on. This Ces obviously didn't agree with and he said that it never happened. I think Bill was having a bit of fun with Ces, but that it was nevertheless true. The thing which amazed me about Ces was just how much he thought about rugby. He made sure that other players got to training on time and thought about the matches they played. Bill seemed to me to be slightly more relaxed. I feel it was this intensity of purpose which actually took Ces through his rugby, to England and later into coaching and administration. He was quite literally totally committed to the game.

28

4. My days as a professional at Wigan

I arrived at Wigan on a dismal, dreary, rainy day and felt homesick for the green fields of the far away West Coast. I wanted to return home. I missed the high country of the Southern Alps, the rainforest, the surging surf, the spectacular sunsets and most of all my wonderful family and close friends.

When the Wigan directors met me in London they gave me a contract to sign. Brian Nordgren advised me not to sign this until I had perused and understood it thoroughly. For that advice I am perpetually grateful to him. The directors were upset with Brian because there were rumours that other clubs were after me and I might not sign. Brian and I became good friends and the best of team mates. In addition, on my second day in Wigan, Brian introduced me to Edna, a young lady who was later to become my wife.

My first day at Wigan was spent with Jim Sullivan, who was one of Great Britain's greats. Jim had represented Great Britain as a full-back on numerous occasions and had become a successful coach. Firstly, a photograph was taken with Jim and two directors as a form of welcome. We then stripped ready for the running track. Jim asked many penetrating questions about which position I played. My answer was second five-eighth. He was confused by the terminology used in New Zealand that he said was wrong, and replied: "You mean, you play centre". According to British Rugby League, you are either a right or a left centre. To make this quite clear to me, Jim outlined the numbering and terminology used: No. 1: full-back, No. 2: right wing, No. 3: right centre, No. 4: left centre, No. 5: left wing, No. 6: stand-off half, No. 7: scrum-half, No. 8: open side prop, No. 9: hooker, No. 10: blind side prop, No. 11: open side second-row, No. 12: blind side second-row, No 13: loose-forward.

This was my first lesson in the English way, yet it took from 1946 to 1988 for the International Board to agree to these numberings. Australia was the main objector and New Zealand was not very keen either. I often hear people in the media, radio and television, say inside and outside centre. There are no such positions in Rugby League. If the scrum is on the left-hand side of the field or the 10 yard mark, the left winger is near the left hand sideline, then the scrum-half will be at the scrum and a pass length away the stand-off half, then the left centre, right centre and right wing. Having sorted all that out, Jim said to me: "You are too bloody small to be a centre. You are only big enough to be a stand-off half and we have plenty of those." Shades of the New Zealand selectors.

29

He was right, of course, but it wasn't a very good introduction. Wigan *was* well blessed with a number of stand-off halves and I doubt whether Jim really wanted another. At that time, the club had Jackie Fleming and Ted Toohey, very nice fellows and good footballers, so the competition for a place in the first team was on. My first game was a charity game, the week after my arrival, for the Wardonia Cup. It was up to me to produce the form if I wanted to be included in the first team. My selection wasn't popular with Jim Sullivan because he had spent much time with the local players who knew about the moves and how to work them properly. Jim was acknowledged as one of the greatest tacticians the game has ever produced. Unfortunately, his coaching ability and personality were at odds with me because I was used to Johnny Dodds and the New Zealand way of doing things - open and inquisitive rather than adversarial.

I must have made a favourable impression on the selectors during the charity game against Warrington, for I went on to play 74 consecutive games for Wigan until an injury forced me out. This was a poisoned arm sustained during the Kiwi visit in 1947. Jackie Fleming and Ted Toohey went to other clubs, Toohey to Barrow and Fleming to Warrington. Toohey later played for Great Britain. Rugby League football was rich in England after the war, and a very high standard was set. Now and then I would inform the British players that there was much talent in New Zealand also. However an overseas ban was being enforced on New Zealand players by the New Zealand Rugby Football League, who sought to protect what they considered to be their assets. The players were given no say in this. Thus no more players were allowed to go to England or Australia. My brother Bill, a very good centre with plenty of speed, had trials with the Manly Sea Eagles in Australia. He was offered terms by Manly, but was not allowed to accept the contract by the New Zealand administration. I cannot understand, to this day, why amateurs in New Zealand had to get a clearance to change countries. I agree that players who are receiving money on contracts should be controlled by transfer terms, but amateurs should be in charge of their own destiny.

New Zealand Rugby League should have had a similar organisation to that in the United Kingdom where one can sign either as an amateur or as a professional. New Zealand at that time, I believe, was beset by little people with mediocre minds, who administered the game. They retarded the game by their lack of understanding. Rugby League was on the slippery slope of decline, and it has never fully recovered. The administrators of the late 1940s have a lot to answer for.

In New Zealand, the system then was that a player had to play six test matches before being free to turn professional overseas. There were many players who were accomplished enough for some English clubs but who wouldn't get selected for the Kiwi team. There had to be a way where amateurs are free to join overseas clubs during their career. Placing a transfer fee on an amateur was hard to understand, unless it is to bolster finances for the administration which is incapable of paying its way.

I played from 1946 to 1953 and I found Rugby League at the top in the United Kingdom very competitive. The training was similar to that I brought through in the coaching scheme in New Zealand in the 1960s, instructing coaches how to teach. This is the way of the future, but many of the little people do not comprehend this. They want success now, even though there is no groundwork set up to achieve this.

Upon arrival at the dressing rooms at Central Park for training one found all the players' gear hanging up on their respective hooks: jersey, shorts, socks, boots and spikes. The spikes were used first; after stretching exercises, a few warm ups and half a dozen runs through, it was straight to the cinder tracks and on your mark, get set, go - the players always being timed for 40 yards. After about six timed sprints, it was then run up to 20 yards, then accelerated running through to 60. It was then a matter of taking the field and doing PT work, two fast laps.

One lap was taken at 75 per cent full out and then one was walked, then another lap 75 per cent full out. After that it was a return to the dressing room, off with the spikes and on with the boots. This was where I proved to be a novice, but I was soon knocked into shape by the players who knew all the moves.

Master scrum-half

Bradshaw was a master scrum-half who knew all the short cuts and variations. We had Ernie Ashcroft right centre and Ted Ward left. Ernie was 13½ stones, Ted 15 stones. The variety of play from these players was tremendous. Also the ability of these three to talk variations in play was amazing; they read the game as it progressed. Bradshaw would say: "I'll come around you or go blind", or Ted would say: "Have a go and beat your opposite number", or I would tell Bradshaw to go on his own. The

31

more the scrum-halves ran, the more variety of play was introduced in the backs, and of course we had masterly full-backs, Martin Ryan and Jackie Cunliffe, coming into the backline. We also had extremely talented wing three-quarters in Brian Nordgren, Jack Hilton, Gordon Ratcliffe and Johnny Lawrenson. They were either scoring tries or making them. In making tries, they would often come in from the blind side, then take a pass from the scrum half or an inside pass from the stand-off breaking the opposite backline, the ball going along our backline for the wing to score in the opposite corner. The man behind all these moves was the master tactician, Jim Sullivan.

These days I often wonder where all the variety of the moves has gone. We tried so hard to teach players how to read the game; where the opposition was standing and from that a decision could be made about what to do. If there are more players on one side than another, one goes in the direction where there are the least number of players and one should run to the outside of players, not barge up the middle. One could continue to discuss tactics and their variations for some time. Today, it is paid coaches who have the limelight not tactical players, like the American gridiron game.

In my five years at Wigan, we won the Challenge Cup twice, the Championship twice and the Lancashire Cup five times. The last was a knockout competition for Lancashire clubs. Successful coaches plan a game and require players to stick to it. A good coach will always add to the natural talent of a player and brings out the best by not suffocating such talent, but encouraging it. Such coaches, like top-class administrators in the league, are far too rare. Winning, no matter how, is the main task, not spectacular play utilising natural ability. Teams exist to boost the ego of paid coaches, paid administrators and directors. Players are now a commodity, an asset to be disposed of, traded or dropped. Instead of being participants, our young people are now watchers, like those in the USA.

Joe Egan was captain of Wigan when I went there and a regular selection as hooker for Great Britain. The forwards in our team had a wonderful understanding, taking the ball up, turning in the tackle and sending each other through the gap with the backs following on to complete the moves. The quick service from play the ball by the forwards to the backs was spectacular. It was Rugby League at its best, and it brought in the crowds.

After my third year at Wigan, Joe Egan was appointed coach at Leigh and I was made captain of Wigan, which was a great honour. I was privileged to receive the Lancashire Cup from the Earl of Derby. The Earl was a prominent supporter of Rugby League, a very fine person, a gentleman. The code in England was fortunate to have him as a patron.

At this time there was tremendous competition in Rugby League in England. The standard of club football was very high. The rivalry between the leading Lancashire clubs, Warrington, Wigan, St Helens, Leigh, Oldham, Swinton and Salford was always very keen, with large crowds attending matches. The Easter weekend derby, between Wigan and St Helens on Good Friday at Wigan, was attended by a sell out crowd of 42,000, with thousands turned away. I recall that the main street, Standishgate, leading to Central Park, was a veritable sea of people so thick that one could have walked on their heads. On Easter Monday we played Warrington and on the Saturday in between Widnes. We were grateful when the Monday was over. Fixtures at Christmas time were similar with games played on Christmas Day and Boxing Day, including the return derby at St Helens.

While Wigan rarely lost games in my time at the club, if we did lose, we usually took it well, giving full credit to the opposition and always sharing a drink with them afterwards. We never liked losing, but we had to admire any team that was good enough to beat us. One thing that always upset me on such occasions was the look on the Wigan directors' faces, which were sour and they persistently questioned us about who was responsible for the loss. Some clubs were good losers, some were not. It is a good sportsman who can smile when his team loses; that's the way it should be for directors and administrators as well. The trouble is that many of them never played League at senior level, if they played at all. They did not allow for the human element, but expected players to perform like machines.

After the Lancashire Cup matches, club competition games continued, with Saturday matches, until Christmas. There were few holidays in those days for players during the season. We even had games on New Year's Day, so that by January players were beginning to fade a little and felt very pleased to resume normal fixtures: one match a week. From the end of January it was a case of looking forward to the Rugby League Challenge Cup, which ran on a knockout basis until the final took place in April or early May.

Clubs, by this time, were also starting to assess their chances in the top four play-offs for the championship - which games they could afford to win or lose. It was like the modern day Super League in Australia or Great Britain. Generally at this stage one could see whether one's team had a chance of winning the Lancashire or Yorkshire Championships. The play-off among the top four for the overall Championship Trophy was played after the Wembley Challenge Cup Final.

There were far more games played during the seasons following the Second World War than today. At Wigan we played up to 54 games in one season, including the pre-season Wardonia Cup charity game between Wigan and Warrington.

Each club had its distinctive playing style. Widnes was one of the most difficult clubs to play against; they were very strong in defence, unlike many of the other clubs, who played more open rugby.

Changes in personnel from time to time brought new faces to the team and with them new tactics were devised. The loss of Joe Egan was keenly felt; in some respects it was a body blow for Wigan. He was everything to the team, always capable of pulling a game out of the fire when we were losing. One day, when playing against Leeds, defending on our line and behind 11-10, Joe said to me: "Follow me, I'll see you through". This he did and I ran off Joe and went on to score at the other end of the field. That was Joe Egan, a real Rugby League legend, a League immortal. Will we ever see his like again? They must be out there, in the playing fields of England, Wales, Australia, France, the Pacific Islands, New Zealand and new emerging nations. All we have to do is find them.

Joe Egan's replacement as a hooker turned out to be George Curran, another Wiganer, who played at Wembley in the 1951 Challenge Cup Final and previously toured with Great Britain and played for Salford. Wigan had two other hookers, Ron Mather and Harold McIntyre. Sometimes George Curran played blind side prop while Ron Mather hooked. Tommy Bradshaw at scrum-half had contracted fibrositis and was out of action for a year. Fortunately for Wigan, Johnny Alty was available and signed up the club. He came from the Leigh area and was an instant success, always prepared to run on his own if the tactics warranted it. A running scrum-half creates gaps and takes the pressure off the back line. Jack soon built up a combination with Billy Blan, our loose-forward and me. Wigan was certainly very fortunate at that time in having two great scrum-halves in Bradshaw and Alty.

34

My five years on the playing fields for Wigan included some momentous and some very endearing moments for me. A highlight for me at Wigan was going to the Wembley Final in 1948, my first 'Royal' Wembley, meeting His Majesty, King George VI and receiving a medal from Her Majesty, Queen Elizabeth, who became the Queen Mother. Winning the Championship was another highlight, for a very special reason. Wigan had eight players who missed the match as they were on tour to Australia and New Zealand in 1950. We had already won the Lancashire Championship and earlier in the year the Lancashire Cup, but we were knocked out of the Rugby League Challenge Cup. Warrington went to Wembley that year and won the cup. The great Australia forward, Harry Bath, was a member of that side and was the first Australian to captain a Wembley Challenge Cup winning side.

The Championship

When Wigan played Halifax at the Championship semi-final play-off in 1950 the result was a draw at Wigan, 5-5. The club only paid £3 for a draw at home and there was almost a riot amongst the players. The contract with players was £7 to win, £3 to lose, a draw away from home was calculated as a win, a draw at home was a loss. It was my job to represent the players and to meet the board of directors to discuss the matter. I was soon informed in no uncertain terms that we were all aware of the terms of our agreements. The directors said there would be 'plenty on' for the replay the following Tuesday.

After the drawn match with Halifax, team selection for the replay was very important. It was suggested that the big problem for Wigan in the Halifax game was Kia Rika, who was playing on the wing for Halifax. The answer was to play Silcock, a forward, on the wing for Wigan to mark Rika out of the game. Silcock had plenty of natural speed, and the change worked; we won by 18-2. We went on to Halifax and won easily, receiving £25 for the win, so the directors were true to their word. We met Huddersfield in the Final at Maine Road, the Manchester City football ground. The crowd was over 65,000.

Because of his semi-final performance, Silcock was then left in the team on the wing to mark Lionel Cooper in the Championship Final. Jim Sullivan wasn't very happy with Silcock's selection and made his views known. However he was proved wrong. Huddersfield had a very good team for the final, with famous players such as Russell Pepperell, Pat Devery and John Hunter, to name a few. Wigan was not expected to win, because we were without eight regular players, who were touring. In the first five minutes of the game we won a scrum. I beat my opposite number, passed to Silcock, who went on to score under the posts. This initial shock proved too much for Huddersfield, though they never gave up and there was even a counter attack by Australian Pat Devery, late in the game. He beat me and looked like getting away, but I managed to turn around and catch him from behind. Pat was an excellent footballer, one of Australia's post-war Rugby League heroes. But we won that final 20-2.

Another highlight was Wigan's Wembley Challenge Cup final in 1951. Unknown to me at that time, it was to be my last appearance wearing the famous cherry and white colours. In that year we were in the running for both the Wembley Rugby League Challenge Cup and the Rugby League Championship. In the Challenge Cup semi-final, Wigan played a very strong Warrington team. Harry Bath kicked a penalty goal early in the first half for Warrington and Jackie Cunliffe scored a try for Wigan in the second half to win the game 3-2.

Our final league Championship game was against Gus Risman's Workington team, who had already beaten us in the League at Borough Park. At Central Park they won again, 14-9. We scored three tries, but could not convert any of them. This put Workington into the semi-final, when they had to play us yet again. During the Central Park match before that semi-final of the Championship, I received a serious hip injury and was down to a walk. As a result I failed a fitness test and couldn't recover to play in the semi-final. Workington won the match 8-5, so the double was gone. Workington Town, led by Gus Risman, played very well.

All that was left for Wigan in 1951 was the Wembley final; we had already won the Lancashire Cup and the Lancashire Championship. I was a doubtful starter for the match right up to the Saturday. I travelled with the team to Brighton on the Thursday before the final with a possibility of playing, which I did, although only 85 per cent fit. We went on to win the Cup at Wembley. I captained the side and was awarded the Lance Todd Trophy for the man-of-the-match. The team was given a great welcome home in Wigan. More than 70,000 fans turned out and lined the streets when we arrived by train and bus from London. A reception at the town hall given by the mayor was followed by another at Central Park.

The day after arriving home, I visited our club doctor and was given instructions on how to treat my injured hip. Jim Sullivan's response to these instructions meant that I never played for Wigan again. The captaincy of Wigan had already made it the most difficult season of my whole career. Jim Sullivan and I just couldn't get on, although I gave him all the support and praise possible. His initial resentment at my signing for Wigan in 1946 never really seemed to dissipate. Despite this, my stay in Wigan was a great and wonderful experience, as I generally had the support of the directors and fans and made many good and lasting friends. It was also where I met my wife, Edna. I have never regretted my decision to sign for Wigan.

Players

One of my greatest opponents was Barrow's stand-off half Willie Horne, not the fastest player but his variation in play was a challenge, I always had to be on the alert. Dickie Williams, stand off for Leeds was also in this category. I had many 'battles' with those two, battles of wits, they were, they didn't need to resort to biff tactics. Albert Johnson, the Warrington winger was a class played I admired, he could easily beat an opponent.

Joe Egan, hooker, Tommy Bradshaw, scrum-half and me were a unit in the Wigan team. Joe was the best, a great forward and excellent hooker, getting more than his share of the ball. Tommy Bradshaw was also in this category, retrieving the ball, he was a fast distributor or playmaker in modern terms, which gave me a good start. Joe and Ken Gee were always protective of us 'little folk'. Ernie Ashcroft and Ted Ward left and right centres would carry on where I left off. Ted was a vigorous player and could often call the tune. Brian Nordgren, Gordon Ratclilffe and Jack Hilton, wingers had good finishing speed.

The artistry and kicking of Martin Ryan and Jackie Cunliffe, fullbacks, was pleasing. In fact every player in the Wigan team of that era was an artist in their own right. I would add that they were fitter than players today without having the high tech equipment available today. They didn't have the luxury of interchange; it was hard slog, usually in harsh winter weather once a week, sometimes more than once, for 80 minutes. Many players worked on Saturday mornings going straight to the ground from work, travelling to away games every other week. They didn't have today's money either.

During my term at Wigan we played an Italian team in 1950 winning 49–28, two days later we beat a Welsh club team 72–29.

One memory is the humour of the Wigan team. North country humour is very funny and clever, you would think they had scriptwriters. I was often the victim of this when first arriving at Wigan, due to my different ways and accent, I suppose, but I coped and was soon integrated. The same humour can be heard on the terraces.

At Warrington I admired Brian Bevan and Harry Bath, two stalwarts of the team. I was fortunate in always having good team mates at Wigan and good teams at Warrington. It was the same in New Zealand when I was also involved with university Rugby League.

My future

It was in 1951 that I discussed my future with the head of the mining and technical college, Mr Chalmers, who as already mentioned, contacted the minister of mines in New Zealand. The telegraphed advice from the minister was to forget about mining in New Zealand. I should have known that politicians should not be taken for granted and made my own enquiries from other sources. I next contacted my very good friend and mentor, Les Owen, who suggested I get legal advice about my position at Wigan, as my second three year contract still had a year to run and the situation between Sullivan and myself had not improved.

I discussed the matter with a local solicitor who referred me to a Queen's Counsel. The silk advised me to pay back to Wigan a third of the money for my three year contract, and if they accepted that I would be free to do what I wanted. I really wished to return to New Zealand as I missed my family. After receiving the telegram from the Minister I decided to stay in England. As well as graduating from mining, I had qualified as a Grade One Coach, one of the first five to gain that top rating after attending Lowther College in Wales. This was a very pleasant and rewarding experience, which gave me the opportunity to meet with some of the most talented sports people in the United Kingdom. Our tutors in the teaching methods were lecturers from Oxford and Cambridge. Most sports were represented on this course. Possibly it was because of this background that years later I accepted the offer of the President of the New Zealand Universities Rugby League, Bud Lisle, to coach the New Zealand University team.

5. Playing for Wigan

This chapter is excerpts from a series that Ces wrote in the early 1950s for the *Manchester Evening Chronicle*, headed *What the Crowd Doesn't Know* about his time at Wigan. It has been edited to avoid duplication of material that appears elsewhere in the book. We are grateful for permission from the *Manchester Evening News* archive to use this material.

On the Monday before the start of the 1946-47 season I watched a seven-a-aside Rugby League tournament at Central Park and was impressed by the play of Tommy Harrison, the Salford scrum-half. I said so to Tommy Bradshaw, who was to partner me so brilliantly at scrum-half for Wigan.

The irrepressible Tommy, guessing I was thinking Harrison might pip him for international honours in the season ahead, said: Reet. He IS good, but a'll show him – and thee." Braddy WAS reet too. He did get the honours.

Braddy, I shall never forget. No stand-off could want a harder –working or more co-operative scrum-half. With his brilliance went a bouncy confidence that was infectious.

You hear it said that a good pack makes a scrum-half. Equally, a good scrum-half can help to make a pack. Time and again I heard Braddy – a basket maker by trade – geeing up the big fellows like a featherweight second briefing a heavyweight boxer.

As they gathered for the scrum, Braddy would stage-whisper to Joe Egan: Make sure tha gets it this time, Joe." Then turning to Billy Blan: "Thee come up alongside o' me, Billy, and I'll send thi thro.'"

A great-hearted jack-in-the-box was Braddy, whose career might have been even more spectacular had fibrositis left him alone. In the early weeks of the season Braddy, that great club loyalist Ernie Ashcroft and I talked moves and practised them for hours on end, and later Ted Ward, back from the tour, joined in.

They did me a great deal of good, for in New Zealand the whole concentration had always been on fast, open play but always on orthodox lines, whereas, as I soon learned, the emphasis over here was on tactics and planned moves.

As the two pre-season practice games approached, snatches of conversation made me painfully conscious of the fact that if I got into the Wigan team somebody would have to go out. The thought had never occurred to me before, despite the obvious inevitability of it, and it was worrying as I was anxious not to make enemies. Furthermore, I had the idea that the man I would displace, Jack Fleming - who later left for Warrington, then moved to

Widnes and back to Wigan - was well liked by Jim Sullivan. In fact, I felt and still feel that Jim would have preferred me to go from Central Park rather than Jack. The fact that few words passed between Jack and myself in the time before he left for Warrington suggested that he had not taken my appearance on the scene cordially, but he and I remain good friends and it is always a pleasure to meet him.

Blow to Ted

At least Jack was spared the humiliation Ted Toohey suffered only a few minutes before the start of our Wardonia Cup game at Warrington the week before the League season opened. Ted was stripped in the dressing room when word reached Jim Sullivan that Johnny Lawrenson, just back from the services, was to play instead. Ted didn't say much, but his face showed how deeply he resented such a late change, and I must say I felt extremely sorry for him. Not surprisingly he left Wigan shortly afterwards for Barrow where he gained international honours. Later he went to Leigh and is now at Workington.

Straight talk

The two practice games had been trying ordeals for me, though the moral and playing support of Tommy Bradshaw and Ernie Ashcroft gave me confidence, and an early break through in the first practice made me feel more sure of myself. Actually, Toohey had slipped as I cut past him, and it made the break appear the more spectacular.

The games showed me I had still something to learn of English methods of play. For instance, I have never been accused of shirking a tackle, and, in fact, it was tackling a big forward which smashed my knee and ended my playing days. But after the first practice game the other players asked me forcefully why I didn't take my man when the other side got possession from the scrums. I explained that in New Zealand the practice was to drive the opponent towards the scrum-half and breaking forwards to make the tackle doubly sure, not to take him on the open side and risk his getting away in the wide open spaces.

Hesketh helps

Well, I was never too young or too old to learn, and I was grateful when a Wigan director, Mr George Hesketh - an older generation will remember him as a great half-back with Wigan and Oldham - took me on to the pitch and showed me how I ought to take my man. There was at least one comforting word after the first practice game. As I left the field the veteran Wigan supporter, the late Jim Worthington, told me: "You'll do, lad, when you settle down"

I'm afraid it was only in the late stages of the Wardonia Cup game at Wilderspool that I did anything. I scored a try and Wigan won by 30 points to seven.

With Ted Ward, Martin Ryan, Joe Egan and Ken Gee still away with the tourists, we went into our first game of the season at Belle Vue. Belle Vue included Mel Tierney (later with Rochdale), playing his first game at full-back, Stan McCormick and at half-back Kenny and Watkins, who gave Tommy Bradshaw and myself a tough afternoon. We won 12-11.

Comparatively easy victories in the first, second, and semi-final rounds of the Lancashire Cup (against Rochdale, Salford and Oldham respectively) gave me no indication of what cup-ties are really like, but the final was to teach me. By that time I had settled down and was having a good spell, and Tommy Bradshaw and I had developed a grand understanding. In addition, our Tourists back, though Ted Ward had gone home to Wales because of his mother's illness. So we went into the final at Swinton against Belle Vue, whom we had trounced in a game at Central Park the previous Saturday 68-0. I don't think they tried an inch that Swinton. . !

It felt as if they threw everything at us bar the kitchen stove and they gave me the hiding of my life. Kenny was round my neck most of the game like a long lost brother and, when I slipped him, Stan Powell (later Warrington), playing at centre, would streak in our centres so that I couldn't get my pass in.

Blunders

I remember breaking through on three occasions towards Brian Nordgren, but without success. Blan scored a try for Wigan and Manning a try for Belle Vue. Three goals by Johnny Lawrenson gave us the Cup.

11 Medals

That Lancashire Cup final victory over Belle Vue was a happy augury for me. It was, in fact, the first of six successive Lancashire Cup final victories for Wigan, and gave me the first of the 11 winning medals I gained with the club - two Challenge Cup medals, two League championship medals, two Lancashire League championship medals, and five Lancashire Challenge Cup medals. When Wigan won the sixth I had joined Warrington. Twice we lost in the championship play-off semi-final - once to Bradford Northern and later to

41

Workington. BUT I WAS NEVER ON THE LOSING SIDE IN A FINAL IN THIS COUNTRY. [The only losing medal Ces received was his last match as manager at Warrington, the 1961 Championship Final.] But, for all its happy omens, that Belle Vue game ranks in my mind as one of the two outstanding examples of the worst type of game, especially for the big occasion.

The second was Wigan's Rugby League championship final victory by 13 points to four over Dewsbury at Maine Road the same season

Poor Braddy

Never in my life have I seen such close spotting and heavy tackling dominate a team's tactics as they did Dewsbury's that day.

While I took a drubbing, Braddy had a nightmare of a game. The opposing scrumhalf, Royal, and the forwards never let up on him, and I have never seen a player hurled down and picked up so often in one afternoon.

How he lived through it I don't know. Nor, I bet, does Braddy. At half-time we were two points down, the result of a goal by full-back Jimmy Ledgard, now with Leigh, but we managed to get on top in the second half.

Wigan's Lancashire Cup victory over Belle Vue followed by a short French tour which enabled me to achieve my second ambition - to play in France - and which I thoroughly enjoyed. Everything seemed to be going swimmingly, but the stern reality of professional football was driven home deeply the first time I captained Wigan - against Warrington at Central Park.

With six players on county duty, we lost 3-4, and I had the additional mortification of seeing my opposite number, Mel de Lloyd, drop the two goals that topped our try by Atkinson.

As Tommy Bradshaw and I walked from the ground after the match we couldn't help over-hearing the acid comments of the knots of spectators. They left no doubts to our burning ears, that our supporters were severe critics, despite the long unbeaten run that had preceded that game.

Soon afterwards my first game in Yorkshire, against Bradford Northern at Odsal, was equally unfortunate.

We were leading 5-4 in a game in shocking conditions when, in the 25th minute of the second half, in my eagerness to gain possession I fielded a kick in an offside position. Ernest Ward's penalty shot went over after hitting an upright, and Bradford won 6-5.

McCue tribute

What Ken Gee said to me at the time and after the match merited colour. His flow was superb, but the content highly censorable.

42

Poor Ken. I couldn't blame him. He had played one of the greatest games of his career -and that is saying something - for the lion hearted player whose football brain equalled his great brawn. I don't propose to go through all the games in my first season, but one or two stand out as highlights – for instance the league game we won at Widnes 2-0.

The game had a joyful yet sombre note. Tommy Bradshaw so out-played opposing scrum-half Tommy McCue that one writer said the red light had shone for McCue as far as international honours were concerned, even though McCue was one of the great tacticians of our game.

Whatever Tommy McCue himself may have thought, he was great sportsman enough to come over at the end of the game, shake Braddy by the hand and congratulate him on a wonderful game.

My biggest disappointment in that first season with Wigan was our defeat at Central Park by Leeds in the third round of the Rugby League Challenge Cup competition.

They beat us 5-0, and I had a feeling from the early play that our number was up when, in the first-half Bert Cook, Leeds' New Zealand full-back, kicked a goal from half-way despite the torrential rain.

If I ever saw greatness in defeat it was in our captain, Joe Egan, that day. He took the rap for a mistake that was never his. But not a murmur from him after the game.

But we had our revenge against Leeds when we beat them 21-11 in the League Championship semi-final at Central Park.

Best since 'Waggy'

The Sporting Chronicle said of us after that game: "No one who has watched Wigan's sustained progress this season has ever doubted their right to a place in the final.

Week after week, in all sorts of conditions, they have played Rugby of the highest class, highest speed; daring football of wonderful entertainment value, with individual brilliance allied most intelligently to remarkable effective team work in the best combination I have seen since Harold Wagstaffe led Huddersfield, best of all four-cup winners."

And, believe it or not, the writer was a Yorkshireman!

Switch move

So, in my first season in English Rugby I won a League championship medal, a Lancashire League championship medal and a Lancashire Challenge Culp medal. True, Wembley was still a dream, but with such a grand team it

43

couldn't be too far away.

I had played in France, and the critics here had been more than kind. One even said that by attacking in one direction and switching my pass in the other I would revolutionise the game, though I think I was no pioneer in that.

What is equally important, I had found grand team-mates, real friends and welcoming homes that made me feel that that friendly town, Wigan, was home.

In 1950, Wigan won a famous victory over Huddersfield in the Championship Final, with eight senior players absent, on the way to Australia with the British Lions. Ces wrote the following about what happened after the final:

[Our plan of playing Silcock on the wing to mark Lionel Cooper] worked beautifully, and the "haven't a chance" Wigan won 20-2. The team had a day out, with a bowling competition, in celebration, and in the hope of fostering good relations in the club I organised the presentation of a fountain pen for Jim Sullivan.

Jim was obviously moved when we sprang the surprise on him, and in act, was in tears as he told us that it was the first time a presentation of that kind had ever been made to him.

For a considerable time it had been apparent, to me that, at least under the surface and some times above, Jim was not exactly an admirer of mine, and I had always had the feeling that he could well do without me, but I was intent on striving for a happier understanding. He had his job to do – and I make no reflection upon his ability to do it – and I had no intention of trespassing on it. My concern was to be part of a happy and contented team, most of all while I was captain.

As Wigan started the 1950-51 season with the tourists not yet back, I was again acting captain. It had all the promise of a wonderful term. The team was good and did well in the opening games.

The day my daughter Carolyn was born the crowd, informed of the news over the loudspeakers, roared its congratulations as I led the team out for the game against Huddersfield. And the boys helped the celebrations with a grand 45-13 victory. Who could ask for more?

I was well satisfied, but I had trodden on corns and given some wrong impressions by taking during the close season a course in coaching and had organised a successful coaching school for boys at Central Park, an essential piece of work to qualify for my Grade 1 certificate.

Because of what the whispering gallery said – and how they spring up in football clubs and among some sections of supporters - I must emphasise that I was not after anybody's job. I was intent on playing and my contract had still two seasons to run.

What I told Joe

Shortly after his return from the tour Joe Egan was placed on transfer at his own request, the fee being £5,000. Joe had his eye on a player-coach job and soon went to Leigh.

I am anxious to make it clear that I had no desire to retain the captaincy Joe had so meritoriously carried. In fact, when he asked what I thought of his transfer request I told him frankly: "If I had my way you wouldn't go. You're a fine hooker and there is a place at Wigan for you and the others for a long time to come."

He replied quietly: I had to look after my future. You've done very well while we've been away. I could only repeat what I told him before, that well as we had played there was always room for men of tour standard. That wasn't flattery. It was obvious fact.

Irritating

When Joe left I took the captaincy for the rest of the season. We were doing well, but the whispering gallery was still at work. This time, about Christmas, the old referee, the late Ben Ennion, told me for my own good that it was going round the town that Wigan were intent on signing Len Constance, the stand-off half, and that one Wigan director, Mr. Joe Taylor, was making no secret of it. In fact, they did sign Constance after I had left.

Now I hold that a club can sign any player it likes, and no player should resent being dropped if he is replaced by a better player, but it comes a bit hard on a player to hear of an impending signing as a piece of public property, and that at a time when he is captaining a side doing so well.

In the last League game of the season, against Workington at Central Park, I was badly injured in the thigh and ribs in a tackle by Bill Ivison. I finished the game a passenger, and the defeat cost us the Lancashire League championship.

The Saturday after the defeat by Workington we had to meet them again at Central Park in the semi-final of the League championship play-off, and the prospects of my playing were extremely dim. I could do no training and when on the Wednesday I tried training with the players on our day out at Southport it was just hopeless.

George Hesketh immediately told Jim Sullivan to return with me to Central Park and give me more treatment. With the chance of pulling off the double, all I wanted was for us to get through that semi-final.

Despite all the careful attention from Sully and at home during the week I was not fit enough to turn out against Workington in the Championship semi-final. Instead I watched the game from the side-lines, a disconsolate spectator as Workington got on top and stayed there.

In the dressing room after the match Jim Sullivan, alone after the players had left, was in tears. I must confess I myself was pretty close to crying. That may sound sentimental for Rugby League men, but defeat at that stage of a long league programme has its own poignancy. To the public, it may lack the almost glamorous despair of defeat in the Wembley Final, it brings to the mind weeks and weeks of arduous games in fair weather and foul, of courageous striving and great comradeship amongst team-mates - and then in 80 minutes it is all over without any tangible token of honours.

You can well imagine how both Jim Sullivan and I, and indeed, the whole Wigan team felt. Yet within minutes that awful whispering gallery was spreading the story that I was pleased that Wigan had lost without me in the side - and people who ought to have known better believed it, and spread it.

By what twist of logic they arrived at the view that I could derive satisfaction from a defeat which had cost me the chance of another championship medal is beyond me. But there it was.

Trophy trouble

As we left the Wembley pitch for me to receive the Cup from the Duke of Gloucester, [after beating Barrow 10-0 in the 1951 Challenge Cup final] I said to Billy Blan: "I'll take the Cup, but you will get the Lance Todd Trophy."

You will recall, of course, that that trophy, in memory of a grand New Zealand player who later managed the brilliant Salford team of Red Devils, is awarded by the votes of experienced Rugby League journalists covering the Wembley final to the player who they consider has given the finest performance in the game.

As I said at the time, and have repeated several times since - as far as I could see in the hurly-burly, of the game I thought Billy Blan had played a "blinder" which would have carried off the trophy. I was surprised yet, I must admit, proud, when the journalists' majority vote awarded it to me.

Billy was obviously disappointed and could not be blamed for that, but some of my detractors took a very early opportunity to fasten on the decision to whisper trouble and Blan and I found ourselves unwittingly and unwillingly involved in an atmosphere which was deplorable.

Conscious though I was of the honour, I soon realized it was something of an embarrassment. But what could I do? It had been awarded to me by men whose judgment of the Rugby League game was reflected in their responsibility of reporting the final for their newspapers. If I had made the gesture of handing the trophy to Billy it would have looked like an ungrateful kick in the teeth to critics.

Efforts in vain

Moreover, I could well imagine those who didn't like me making capital out of such an action with a sneer at "Mountford's magnanimity."

I was beginning to feel that all my efforts both as captain and I hope, to foster happy relations, not only in the club as a whole, were all in vain. Yet I had no intention of leaving Wigan even then, and it was heart-warming to see how those loyal supporters, realistic critics of the game though they are, turned out in their thousands to welcome us home that Monday night.

At the civic reception when I expressed the team's thanks I explained that I was happy to have under my contract another season with the Wigan club and that at the end of that time I would be returning to New Zealand.

Thinking back over that time, I still feel that I meant what I said – that despite the frictions which were occurring in one or two places, I wanted to go on giving what was left of the football in me to the club which had given me the chance to play Rugby in Europe and in whose company I had shared in so many glorious and hard fought triumphs.

[My injury] had recurred during the Wembley final [now] reasserted itself in full force, and on the advice of the club doctor I went to Central park with his instruction that the treatment I had been receiving should be continued.

I found Mr Hesketh, the chairman, the secretary Wilf Ward, and Jim Sullivan in a coffee bar not far from the ground. As we walked from the coffee bar Mr Hesketh and I behind Jim and secretary Ward, I told the chairman I did not like the atmosphere which had developed in the club.

It was obvious that he, too, was well aware of it, was watchful against its developing further and was intent on preventing its development if he, personally, could help it.

Victory over Barrow in the 1951 Wembley final didn't make me feel any happier about the atmosphere which had developed in the Wigan club.

I had already told chairman George Hesketh that I didn't like it and as I was on my way to Central Park to receive treatment for a thigh injury I met director Joe Taylor. He asked me how the injury was getting along and I told him, "Not too good, I'm afraid." He answered: "Well, it doesn't matter now we've won the Cup." That was the end.

He may have meant well. Maybe with the pain nagging at me I was oversensitive, but I don't think so. The fact that was eating into me was that for years in New Zealand I had played football because I loved every minute of it and at Wigan it had been exactly the same - as far as the football was concerned. Football may be your career - a New Zealand expert had once written that it was my religion - but you have got to love it or get out of the atmosphere which is detracting from game. And how I had loved Wigan, especially with triumphs those games had brought for so many of us. Grand fellows, football fanatics who of their own volition would spend hour after hour perfecting their technique and fitting it into what had become a smoothly running football machine.

Sad farewell

I was a sad man as I walked into Central Park and chatted for a short time with Bert Barnes the club's baggage man. In quiet, deserted surroundings of an historic enclosure so used to the clamour of excited thousands it was almost as if I was taking a sad farewell. Slowly I walked home to Lessingham Avenue hoping that the gentle exercise would ease the pain in my injured thigh. Back home I told my wife that I would never go back to Central Park to put on a jersey again, and that we would go back to New Zealand.

I was prepared in accordance with my contract to repay Wigan with the proportion of the signing on fee for the period not served. [As outlined elsewhere, the rest of this article explains how Ces applied for the manager post at Warrington.]

Before I accepted the Warrington offer, however, there came an unofficial or semi-official approach to keep me at the Wigan club. One Sunday morning a Wigan director called at my home and, saying that he was speaking for three or four other members of the board as well as himself, asked me if I would stay if I were given the job of player-coach, with the coach's wage added to those or player.

He'd belt me

I told him that I would not consider taking another man's job, and added: "Old as I am, if I did and my father were here he would not hesitate to belt me for it." He held strong principles on action like that.

How much the director may have been influenced by what might have been happening elsewhere I do not know, but shortly after came the news that Jim Sullivan had met Huddersfield officials to discuss their offer for him to become their trainer-coach.

I knew nothing of Jim Sullivan's offer from Huddersfield until I read that report, and, as I say, I don't know whether the Wigan board did. Jim, of course, went later to St Helens, where he is carrying on the good work.

It is an interesting coincidence that Jim met the Huddersfield officials a few hours before Warrington announced my appointment as manager and

Wigan board were discussing my letter ending my contract with them which had enclosed a cheque.

Cheque returned

They later announced that they were returning the cheque and asked that I should "loyally and faithfully fulfil my part of the agreement.

I had always tried to give the club loyal and faithful service, and my departure was in strict accordance with the terms of my agreement. So, having offered the Wigan club £500, I joined Warrington as manager in the summer of 1951.

Wigan had taken the matter to the Rugby League Management Committee on the ground that Warrington had committed a breach of the by-laws by "inducing" me as a registered player to leave the club for which I had been registered. As I have made clear there was certainly no inducement by Warrington. .

[After outlining the settling of the dispute over his registration as a player with Warrington, which had included the notable feat of being named in both team line ups in the match programme for the 1951 Wardonia Cup season-opening match, and playing for neither because of the dispute; Ces reflected on leaving Central Park] I am happy to say that there are no ill-feelings left. Just as the scars we suffer in the rough and tumble of the game heal and are forgotten, so it is with personal differences behind the scenes. The main point is that the good of the game must always come first.

Wigan welcome

It is a tribute to the warm-heartedness of Wigan that I am still a welcome visitor to Central Park and Wigan homes. I am truly grateful for it and for the letters which I treasure, which came from Wigan supporters in the midst of the controversy when I left, saying many nice things about me, not least one from "two popular side patrons," Vera and Glyn Keegan, of Lamberhead Green.

Managership has brought its achievements and disappointments, just as playing did, but there is a great joy in still being in the game and in being able to devote time to an aspect I have always enjoyed – the encouragement and development of the youngsters

I have tried in this series to show through my own experiences that players and officials are, after all, human beings with hopes and worries, good days and off days. The players who swap heavy tackles on the field may be the best of pals off the field.

Both did our best

You may have guessed that Jim Sullivan, as coach, and I, as player, weren't always unanimous in our days at Wigan, but that didn't alter the fact that we were both intent on doing our best for the team and club.

So with club boards and committees. They have many problems to contend with - financial, administrative, and, not least, personal. While the supporter can pick and choose the games he wants to see club representatives are often watching strange teams in the hope of spotting new talent, watching the "A" team, or undertaking long journeys with the first team for games which might be anything but attractive.

It all adds up to the fact that any game may have behind it a complexity of problems which the public cannot know. Still, this Rugby League game of ours is the greatest in the world. Let's keep it that way.

Wigan RLFC 1946-47: League Champions, Lancashire Cup winners,
Lancashire League winners, Wardonia Cup winners.
The back row is the club's directors, with coach Jim Sullivan on the right.
Players: Standing: E. J. Ashcroft, E. Ward, B.C. Nordgren, M. Ryan, H.
Atkinson, G. W. Ratcliffe, J. Lawrenson, J. Hilton, F. Barton, G. W. Banks.
Sitting: W. Blan, K. Gee, T. Bradshaw, J. Egan (capt), C.R. Mountford, J.
Blan, F. Tracey, J.Cunliffe.

50

6. Great Occasions at Wigan
By Peter Lush and Dave Farrar

Wembley Challenge Cup Finals

1948 Bradford Northern 3 Wigan 8
Wembley Stadium. 1 May 1948. Attendance: 91,465

The 1948 final was very important for the Colliers, as it was nearly 20 years since they had won the Challenge Cup, in the first Wembley final in 1929. They had been back to the twin towers in the first final after the Second World War in 1946, but lost narrowly to Ernest Ward's Bradford Northern 13-12. This was a repeat of the two-legged Challenge Cup final of 1944, which again had seen the Odsal men victorious.

Wigan had had a strong cup run in 1948. In the first round, Castleford were beaten over two legs by an aggregate score of 46-7. In the second round they brushed Leeds aside by 17-3 at Central Park. In the third round they had some work to do to beat Warrington at Wilderspool by 13-10. In the semi-final at Station Road, Swinton, Wigan beat Rochdale Hornets by 11-0 before 26,000 spectators. On their way to Wembley Wigan had only conceded 20 points and were confident of a second Wembley success.

In the sports post-war boom it was no surprise that the attendance was a world record 91,465 and Wigan were keen to make it a Lancashire double as Manchester United had already won the FA Cup. It was a right royal occasion as both teams were presented to the King. George VI.

It was the half-back partnership of Bradshaw and Mountford that laid the foundation for the ultimate victory. It was a fumble by Batten that brought Wigan their first try, as winger Hilton quickly hacked the ball past Bradford fullback Leake and touched down, Edward Ward converting. An almost identical error by Wigan's Gordon Ratcliffe gave Alan Edwards a gift try, Ernest Ward missed the kick.

In a terse and tense final there was no further score until the last minute when another Leake error led to a Bradford drop-out, a poor kick put Wigan in position for prop Barton to score, Ward missed the kick but Wigan were triumphant by 8 points to 3. It was the success of Bradshaw and Mountford in subduing the Bradford halfback pair of Davies and Ward that throttled any attacking play of the Bradford backs and the Wigan forwards kept the Bradford six, which included the eighteen stone Frank Whitcombe, Ken Traill and Trevor Foster, in check.

Wigan: Ryan; Ratcliffe, Edward Ward, Ashcroft, Hilton; Mountford, Bradshaw; Gee, Egan, Barton, White, Blan and Hudson.
Scorers: Tries: Hilton, Barton. Goal: Edward Ward.
Bradford Northern: Leake; Batten, Case, Ernest Ward, Edwards; Davies, D. Ward; Whitcombe, Darlison, Smith, Foster, Tyler and Traill.
Scorer: Try: Edwards.

1951 Barrow 0 Wigan 10
Wembley Stadium. 5 May 1951. Attendance: 94,262

In 1951, Wigan was looking to repeat their success of 1948 against a free scoring Barrow side. Again it was tight defence that had seen Wigan get to Wembley. In the first round they had easily brushed aside Rochdale Hornets over two legs by 50-5. They saw off Batley by 16-8 in the second round at Central Park. In the third round Huddersfield was beaten 2-0 at Central Park.

The semi-final was a close affair. Warrington was despatched 3 points to 2 at a packed Station Road in front of 44,621 fans. A Harry Bath penalty had given Warrington the lead, and with five minutes left the cup holders looked set for a Wembley return. Then Ces Mountford's midfield run drew the Wire's defence, he passed to full-back Jackie Cunliffe, who made for the corner, passing to Brian Nordgren to touch down. Ken Gee missed the kick, as he had with three previous penalty attempts, but Wigan held out for last few minutes to claim a cup final place against Barrow.

At Wembley, it was again to be Wigan captain Ces Mountford's match, and he became the first non-British player to win the Lance Todd Trophy awarded to the 'man-of-the-match'. One reporter noted "His persistency exemplified by personal effort to keep his side constantly in the attack, threw a tremendous burden on Barrow's defence, which in spite of heroic effort, twice was compelled to capitulate during the last quarter of a surprisingly one-sided contest." The headlines included "Mountford has double Wembley triumph" and "Mountford made myth of Wigan fears".

Mountford also had the distinction of being the first New Zealander to captain a winning side at Wembley. The game itself was exciting and was described at the best of all the Wembley finals played at the great stadium. It was the battle at half-back between Mountford and Barrow's Willie Horne that was decisive and Horne was never completely able to overshadow the Wigan captain.

The only score in a tight first half was a Gee penalty goal after Blan had been floored. It was 20 minutes into the second half when Mountford combined with Broome to put Hilton in at the corner. It was prop Gee who sealed the game after barging over with two Barrow players failing to prevent him. To cap a great day Ces Mountford kicked the conversion to send the Wigan contingent in the 94,262 crowd home happy. Wigan had won the cup and had only conceded 15 points in the whole competition in doing so. It was a fitting end to Ces Mountford's Wigan career.

Wigan: Cunliffe; Hilton, Broome, Roughley, Nordgren; Mountford, Bradshaw; Gee, Curran, Barton, Silcock, Slevin and Blan.
Scorers: Tries: Hilton, Gee. Goal: Mountford.
Barrow: Stretch; Lewthwaite, Jackson, Goodwin, Castle; Horne, Toohey; Longman, McKinnell, Hartley, Grundy, Atkinson and McGregor.

Rugby League Championship Finals
At this time the top four teams contested the Rugby League Championship at the end of the season. First played fourth and the second and third teams met in the semi-finals, with the Final on a neutral ground to decide the title.

1947 Wigan 13 Dewsbury 4
At Maine Road, (Manchester City FC). 21 June 1947. Attendance: 40,599

Wigan had finished the season top of the Rugby League table, and beat Leeds 21-11 in the semi-final to reach the Championship final against league runners-up Dewsbury. Their Yorkshire opponents had beaten Widnes 5-2 to reach the final. The whole winter had seen dreadful weather. With midweek matches difficult to arrange due to the economic situation, the final was played on 21 June at Manchester City FC's Maine Road ground. A crowd of 40,599 came to see the climax of the season.

Tries from Nordgren, Lawrenson and Bradshaw gave Ces Mountford a second medal to join the Lancashire Cup one he had won earlier in the season, and meant that Wigan retained the Championship. But it was never easy. After four minutes Ledgard dropped a goal for Dewsbury, and they kept their 2-0 lead until half-time. But early in the second half, Ledgard failed to gather a loose ball, and Ernest Ward sent in Brian Nordgren for a try. Ward kicked the goal to put Wigan 5-2 ahead.

In a tough match, Dewsbury loose-forward Street was injured. While he was receiving treatment, Lawrenson scored, after Mountford had made space to pass to Ernest Ward. Bradshaw add a further try, with a conversion by Ward sealing the match for Wigan.

According to one report, Dewsbury tried to "counteract the brilliancy of Mountford" by moving Clark to stand-off, "but the move was of no avail". Alfred Beecroft's report said that "at half-back Bradshaw and Mountford gave

[Wigan] superiority which they turned to account." One of the newspapers pointed out that in his first season for the club, Mountford had played 53 consecutive games.

Wigan: Cunliffe, Nordgren, Ward, Ashcroft, Lawrenson, Mountford, Bradshaw, Gee, Egan, Banks, Barton, W. Blan, J. Blan.
Scorers: Tries: Nordgren, Lawrenson, Bradshaw. Goals: Ward (2).
Dewsbury: Ledgard, Armitage, Clark, Sacker, Withington, Gilbertson, Royal, Hammond, McKeating, Pearson, Cox, Holt, Street.
Scorers: Goals: Ledgard, Holt.

1950 Huddersfield 2 Wigan 20
At Maine Road (Manchester City FC). 13 May 1950. Attendance: 65,065.

As outlined elsewhere in this book, this was one of the most remarkable victories in Wigan's history. Without eight first-team regulars who had gone on the Lions' tour to Australia, Wigan, captained by Ces Mountford, beat a strong Huddersfield side 20-2 at Maine Road to win the Rugby League Championship. Wigan had finished top of the league table; Huddersfield had been runners-up. In the semi-final, Wigan had drawn 5-5 with Halifax at Central Park before winning 18-2 at the Shay. Huddersfield had beaten Swinton 9-0 at Fartown. A massive crowd of 65,065 saw Wigan's triumph.

Ces Mountford was involved in Wigan's first try. His run and pass set up Silcock to score in the corner. Ward kicked the goal from the touchline, and eleven minutes later Nordgren scored Wigan's second try. The half time score was 10-0. Further tries from Broome and Blan, and another Ward goal made the final score 20-2, Bawden scoring Huddersfield's solitary goal.

One report said that Ces Mountford "now stands supreme as the game's best halfback. Mountford, indeed, could seriously advance claims to be the game's greatest player this season." Another said "Biggest honours went to one of the smallest players on the field, Wigan's New Zealand outside-half Cecil Mountford. His inspired play time and again split wide the opposition."

Wigan coach Jim Sullivan claimed it was the 'Greatest Victory in Rugby League history'. He said: "Our boys played grandly. There was never any doubt from the first that we would win. We achieved success against what seemed impossible odds, all by first-class teamwork and superior fitness and finish. I am very proud of them."

Wigan: Ward, Silcock, Broome, Roughley, Nordgren, Mountford, Alty, Slevin, McIntyre, Barton, Hudson, Large, W. Blan.
Scorers: Tries: Silcock, Broome, Nordgren, Blan. Goals: Ward (4)

54

Huddersfield: Hunter, Cracknell, Bawden, Devery, Cooper, Pepperell, Banks, Daly, Mundy, Wilmot, Morrison, Nicholson, Owens.
Scorer: Goal: Bawden.

Lancashire Cup

The Lancashire Cup is no longer part of the Rugby League calendar. But for many years it, and the Yorkshire cup the other side of the Pennines, were seen as a prestigious trophies, strongly competed for in the first half of each season. Wigan won the trophy for an unprecedented five consecutive seasons during Ces Mountford's time at the club. He did not play in the 1947 final due to injury, but had played in all the previous rounds, so was given a medal. That year Wigan beat Belle Vue Rangers 10-7 at Warrington.

1946 Wigan 9 Belle Vue Rangers 3

At Station Road, Swinton. 26 October 1946. Attendance: 21,648

Wigan beat Rochdale Hornets 81-9 (over two legs) in the first round of the Cup, and then Salford 50-0 (over two legs) in the second round to reach the semi-final. A 21-7 win at Oldham took Wigan to the final at Swinton on 26 October. A crowd of 21,648 saw the Colliers win the Cup for the eighth time.

Wigan had beaten their Manchester-based opponents 68-0 a few weeks earlier at Central Park. This match was much tighter, with only two tries, one to each team. Belle Vue had learnt from their earlier defeat, and tough tackling posed problems for Wigan.

Wigan took the lead after two minutes. J. Blan gathered a loose ball from a scrum near the Belle Vue line to score. Lawrenson missed the conversion, and five minutes later, Manning scored for Belle Vue to level the scores, Powell missing the conversion. Two penalties from Lawrenson gave Wigan a 7-3 half-time lead. The first, for offside, had gone in off the post. The second half was scoreless until near the end when Lawrenson converted a further penalty, given for obstruction. So Wigan retained the Cup in a hard fought match with 42 scrums.

Wigan: Ryan, Nordgren, Lawrenson, Ashcroft, Ratcliffe, Mountford, Bradshaw, Gee, Egan, Banks, W. Blan, Atkinson, J. Blan.
Scorers: Try: J. Blan. Goals: Lawrenson (3)
Belle Vue: Harris, Tolan, Waring, Powell, Barr, Kenny, Watkins, Thomas, Jones, Glendenning, Gwyther, Brown, Manning.
Scorer: Try: Manning.

55

1948: Wigan 14 Warrington 8

At Station Road, Swinton. 13 November 1948. Attendance: 39,015

Wigan faced local rivals St Helens in the first round, again over two legs. A 24-9 win at Knowsley Road in the first leg was followed by a narrow 8-7 win at Central Park. In the second round, Wigan won 18-5 at Salford, and in the semi-final beat Belle Vue Rangers 22-9.

The final was held at Swinton on 13 November, with 39,015 supporters present for a hard-fought clash with Warrington. The Wire was unbeaten, and the crowd was 3,000 higher than for the Great Britain versus Australia test match three weeks earlier. Warrington was favourites, but first-half tries from Gordon Ratcliffe and Ted Ward, with three goals from Ward, put Wigan in a strong position. Palin had replied for Warrington with a penalty, and just before half-time Johnson scored a try. So Wigan led at half-time 12-5. Bevan scored for Warrington in the second half, but Wigan hung on to win 14-8, frustrating the Wire again.

Wigan: Ryan, Ratcliffe, Ward, Ashcroft, Lawrence, Mountford, Alty, Gee, Egan, Barton, Silcock, W. Blan, Hudson.
Scorers: Tries: Ratcliffe, Ward. Goals: Ward (4).
Warrington: Jones, Bevan, Pimblett, Peake, Johnson, Fleming, Helme, Derbyshire, Cotton, Riley, Bath, Featherstone, Palin.
Scorers: Tries: Bevan, Johnson. Goal: Palin.

1949: Wigan 20 Leigh 7

At Wilderspool Stadium, Warrington. 29 October 1949. Attendance: 35,000.

Wigan won the Cup for the fourth consecutive year with a comfortable win over local rivals Leigh. The final was at Wilderspool on 29 October, with 35,000 present. To reach the final, Wigan beat Oldham 54-33 over two legs in the first round, despite losing the second leg 19-9 at Watersheddings. Swinton were dispatched 33-13 at Central Park in the second round, and Cumbrians Workington Town 30-17 in the semi-final.

The match was described as "rough and vigorous as rugby is entitled to be", but most of the "delightful football" came from Wigan. It was Brian Nordgren's day, with four tries; Billy Blan and Jack Hilton also scored tries. Ken Gee only converted one goal; otherwise the score could have been embarrassing. Wigan led 8-2 at half-time. Cleworth scored a second-half try for Leigh, and Ledgard scored two goals. One report said that "Ledgard was constantly extended" although "his defence was superb", while Martin Ryan, the Wigan full-back "had an afternoon's defensive holiday".

Wigan was so strong that one reporter felt that the whole team, apart from Kiwis Mountford and Nordgren, should be picked for Great Britain.

Wigan: M. Ryan, Hilton, Cunliffe, Ashcroft, Nordgren, Mountford, Bradshaw, Gee, Egan, Slevin, Barton, Hudson, W. Blan.
Scorers: Tries: Nordgren (4), Hilton, Blan. Goal: Gee
Leigh: Ledgard, Wood, Kerwick, Harris, Cleworth, Rowe, Riley, Edge, Stephens, Wheatley, C. Ryan, Pawsey, Burke.
Scorers: Try: Cleworth. Goals: Ledgard (2).

1950: Wigan 28 Warrington 5
At Station Road, Swinton. 4 November 1950. Attendance: 42,541.

A record crowd of 42,451 gathered on 4 November, and saw Wigan win the Cup for a fifth consecutive time at Swinton's Station Road ground. Wigan had beaten Cumbrians Whitehaven 54-4 over two legs in the first round, and then got a bye in the second round. The semi-final saw local rivals St Helens beaten 9-7. On the day of the final, Warrington was top of the league with 20 points from 11 games; Wigan was second with an identical record. But once again the Central Park side beat the Wire in a cup final, this time by 23 points, a far greater margin than in 1948.

Reports said that Wigan were at "their brilliant best". Warrington could not make their superiority in the scrums pay, and Wigan's defence was sound. Cunliffe scored Wigan's first try, converted by Gee. Warrington replied with a penalty from Palin, but further tries from Nordgren and Slevin, both converted by Gee, gave Wigan a 15-2 half-time lead.

Roughley scored for Wigan after the restart. Warrington's hopes were then hit when they lost Gerry Helme through injury. Nordgren and Alty added further tries, and Gee scored another goal, before Naughton scored Warrington's only try. Warrington's day was summed up near the end when Bevan kicked through from his own half, but lost the ball under Wigan's posts. But even a Bevan try would not have made any difference to the final result.

This was Ces Mountford's first Lancashire Cup final as captain. One report said that he "led Wigan in brilliant style from the out-half position." Another said he was the 'director-general' of the Wigan attack.

Wigan: Cunliffe, Ratcliffe, Broome, Roughley, Nordgren, Mountford, Alty, Gee, Mather, Barton, Slevin, Silcock, W. Blan.
Scorers: Tries: Nordgren (2), Cunliffe, Roughley, Alty, Slevin. Goals: Gee (5)

Warrington: Frodsham, Bevan, Ryder, Naughton, Johnson, Knowelden, Helme, Derbyshire, Fishwick, Featherstone, Bath, Ryan, Palin.
Scorers: Try: Naughton. Goal: Palin.

Matches against the tourists

In these days of winter Rugby League, a regular highlight was tours from Australia and New Zealand. The tourists would play a full programme of matches against club sides as well as the test matches. These contests were taken very seriously.

Wigan 8 New Zealand 10

At Central Park. 22 October 1947. Attendance: 24,089

The Kiwi tourists played 27 matches on this tour, winning 16, drawing one and losing 10. In the test matches against Great Britain, the Kiwis lost the first test by one point, won the second 10-7, and then were well beaten 25-9 at Odsal, in front of a 42,685 crowd, in the third.

Ces will have played against many of the Kiwis. Perhaps the highlight was a rare game against his brother Ken. Ces was invited to the civic reception given for the tourists before the game by the mayor of Wigan.

This was no exhibition match. A newspaper report said that "no keener fought match has been seen at Central Park, certainly no better defence has been shown against Wigan. New Zealand's tackling in the last half hour was beyond all praise; it was magnificent. How the players stood up to the hammering in that period was remarkable." The report also said that Ces "was the live-wire of [Wigan's] attack, and showed excellent judgment with his touch-kicking, particularly when pressed."

Ces was involved in an early passing move that put Ratcliffe in at the corner to give Wigan the lead. Ward missed the conversion. After 23 minutes, Forrest scored under the posts for the Kiwis, and Clarke converted, giving the Kiwis a 5-3 lead, which they held until half-time.

After 51 minutes, a fine passing move resulted in a Mountford try. But sadly for Wigan fans, it was Ken who scored, following a passing move involving Clarke, Anderson and McBride. Clarke added the goal, so the Kiwis were 10-3 ahead. Wigan now pressured the Kiwi line, with Ratcliffe, Nordgren and Egan all going close to scoring. Egan then set up Blan to score near the posts, and Ward converted.

Wigan continued to press for the winning try, but the Kiwi defence could not be broken. A newspaper report said that "a draw would have been a fitting result was the general view." It did say that Ces had "played heroically", but Ken's team won on the day.

Wigan: Ryan, Nordgren, Ashcroft, Ratcliffe, C. R. Mountford, Bradshaw, Gee, Egan, Banks, Barton, W. Blan, Bowen.
Scorers: Tries: Ratcliffe, Blan. Goal: Ward.
New Zealand: Clarke, Forrest, Robertson, Anderson, McInnarny, Clark, K. Mountford, Pye, Smith, Johnson, McBride, Newton, Hardwick.
Scorers: Tries: Forrest, K. Mountford. Goals: W. Clarke (2).

Wigan 16 Australia 11
At Central Park. 20 October 1948. Attendance: 28,554.

A year on from their narrow defeat against the Kiwis, Wigan went one better and beat the tourists. The club's last success against an Australian side had been 37 years before. The Australians were struggling; it was their sixth defeat of the 13 matches they had played so far on tour. Their final record was 15 wins and 12 defeats from 27 matches. They lost the test series against Great Britain 3-0. At the pre-match civic reception, the Australian manager, William Buckley, said that they regarded the fixture as the "fourth test match".

Bob Pemberton's report was headlined: "Wigan took sting out of Australians. Mountford and Alty had them guessing." His report said that the Australians were well beaten, and that Joe Egan won the scrums 41-20. At half back, "Mountford and Alty were in brilliant form and the Australians could never subdue this lively pair."

After eight minutes, Lawrenson scored in the corner to give Wigan a 3-0 lead. Three minutes later, Ratcliffe scored to put Wigan 6-0 up. Graves, who apparently was the tourists' most dangerous threequarter, replied for the tourists. However, he then missed a simple conversion. However, Australia then took the lead. Gibbs got the ball from Wigan full-back Martin Ryan, who put Schubert in to score. Graves converted, so Australia was 8-6 up, a lead they kept until half-time. Six minutes after the break, Ashcroft scored a try to restore Wigan's lead, Ward converting to make the score 11-8. Ratcliffe then ran through from the half-way line to score. Ward added the goal to put Wigan 16-8 up. McMahon replied for Australia, but Graves' conversion hit the post, and Wigan held on to win 16-11. Ces was injured near the end, and the crowd booed the incident. But generally the match had been played in a good spirit.

Wigan: Ryan, Ratcliffe, Ward, Ashcroft, Lawrenson, Mountford, Alty, Gee, Egan, Barton, Silcock, Atkinson, Blan.
Scorers: Tries: Ratcliffe (2), Lawrenson, Ashcroft. Goals: Ward (2).
Australia: Churchill, McMahon, Dimond, Pegg, Graves, O'Connell, Thompson, Hand, Schubert, Gibbs, Rayner, Hall, Tyquin.
Scorers: Graves, Schubert, McMahon. Goal: Graves.

"That Try": Wigan 13 Leeds 12. Northern Rugby League.
At Central Park. 7 September 1949. Attendance: 25,000.

Wigan were on top in the first half, taking a 6-2 lead. Ces scored a "superb solo try" to give Wigan the lead after 20 minutes. Cook replied for Leeds with a penalty, but then Nordgren scored a try to make the half-time score 6-2. Ces injured his knee soon after the interval, and was reduced to limping on the wing – there were no substitutes in those days. Gee scored a penalty for Wigan, 8-2, but then Ratcliffe lost the ball, Clarkson scored, Cook converted and Wigan's lead was 8-7. Ces's kick was charged down, and Arthur Clues scored, Cook converting to give Leeds the lead. Gee scored another penalty to reduce Wigan's arrears to a single point. Then with six minutes left, Clues and Gee were sent off.

With seconds left, and Wigan still 12-10 down, Ces got the ball from the last scrum of the game. Overcoming his injury, he darted through the Leeds defence. Using fellow Kiwi Brian Nordgren as a foil, he kept running for the corner, and scored after a superb run of sixty yards. There was great excitement, and hundreds of people waited for Ces outside the ground after the game to give him "a wonderful ovation". Reporter Tom Reynolds said that it was "the most spectacular try that Mountford ever scored."

Ces told a reporter after the game: "If any Leeds player had touched me, I would have fallen over, and my main thought was to keep away from them. I daren't have drawn them to me. When Proctor looked the other way I knew it was my chance as I felt I could beat Dickie Williams for speed. I also knew there was only time left for one solo break through and it was fortunate that some of the Leeds backs anticipated a pass to Brian Nordgren and moved in that direction. I forgot the pain of my injury, but it was the first thing that I remembered after touching down." The report said that his wife Edna was 'mobbed' by overjoyed spectators in the stand. One supporter was so excited that he said that Ces "can have my bacon ration for next week."

Richard Lewis was at that game. He recalls: "As the referee prepared to blow his whistle, Mountford came inside, took the ball from Bradshaw and ran for the left hand corner flag. With more than half the field to go, Leeds players converged on him. He swerved and beat one or two. Shrugging off the effects of his injury he twisted past one or two more blue shirts and prepared to pass to Nordgren. The Leeds defence took the dummy and Ces ran through the gap only he could see and, buried under Leeds defenders, plonked the ball over the line to win the match 13-12."

Wigan: Ryan, Ratcliffe, Broome, Ashcroft, Nordgren, Mountford, Bradshaw, Gee, Egan, Barton, Silcock, Slevin, Hudson.

60

Scorers: Tries: Mountford (2), Nordgren. Goals: Gee (2).

Leeds: Cook, Wright, Bartlett, Proctor, Verrenkamp, Williams, Feather, McMaster, Kearney, Kendrick, Clues, Murphy, Clarkson.

Scorers: Tries: Clarkson, Clues. Goals: Cook (2).

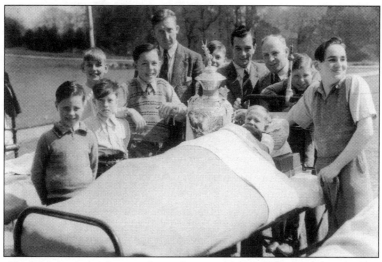

Cheering up the patients: Wigan players with the Challenge Cup visiting a local hospital. Players: Jack Hilton, Tommy Bradshaw and Ces.

1948 Challenge Cup Final: Ces presented to King George VI.

61

Ces being presented with his Other Nationalities cap by Mr Conroy, vice-chairman of Wigan RLFC

A 1950 cartoon of Ces

"That try" – Ces scoring in the last minute against Leeds
at Central Park, 7 September 1949,winning the game 13-12.

7. A Rugby League Wedding
by Edna Mountford

When Ces and I first met, I had never attended a Rugby League game, though I was, like most Wiganers, interested in a distant sort of way. I wasn't actually a Wiganer by birth. Brian Nordgren introduced us first and then Jim Sullivan, whom I knew very well because he played golf with my boss, invited me to accompany the team as well as their wives and girlfriends, for a Sunday day out to Buxton. It was a very pleasant day and subsequently these meetings became something of a habit. From the start I was informed, just in case I had other ideas; that Ces didn't intend staying in England after his contract with Wigan expired. There was a veiled insinuation that a permanent relationship wasn't on the cards either.

By this time Ces had moved from Mrs Critchley's digs to Pemberton with the Websters, who were a childless couple having lost their only son as a baby during an air raid on Sheffield. Mother and baby were trapped under the house for two days until being rescued. Perhaps, because of this, Ces was treated like a son - no player could have been better looked after.

Somewhere along the line, there was a change of mind or heart. The marriage proposal came as quite a surprise. The announcement was made on Christmas Eve when a small party was arranged at my home. We had previously bought the engagement ring in Southport. The announcement duly made, I settled down to the engagement with the nuptials to be held sometime in the future, at a time when it didn't interfere with rugby. To my amazement a suggestion was made that we marry very soon, in January, the reason being that Ces's brother Ken was coming over as a member of the 1947-48 touring Kiwi side, would attend the wedding and be best man. So there we were, four weeks after becoming engaged, at a marriage ceremony. It was 18 months since Ces had arrived in England.

Four weeks to prepare for a wedding from scratch was, in a post-war utility climate, simplified. With clothing rationed and on coupons, an elaborate wedding was out of the question. One had to buy an outfit, which had to last many a long day, and, as it was mid-winter, it had to be something warm. One didn't however need coupons for the hats so I went to town on this item, which was made by a young male milliner.

The wedding cake was made by my mother, one tier, for which she had to collect pickled eggs in a jam jar offered by various relatives. The wedding breakfast was at home presided over by a Mrs Frost, who attended to the catering at Central Park. There were relatives and a few close friends in attendance, because we had told very few people. The only ones at Central Park to know were two of the directors, Tom and George Hesketh, Jim and Eve Sullivan and Brian Nordgren, who all attended the ceremony. We didn't want a big fuss. Permission had to be granted by the club for Ces's absence from Tuesday to Friday. We were married at 9.30 am and on a train to London at 1.00 pm. We were just boarding the train when the first of the press posse raced into the station.

All didn't go as planned, however, because Ken - the main reason for the rushed wedding - wasn't able to make it after all. The touring party were stranded in France due to bad weather. However, we went ahead with the ceremony and took some of the wedding cake with us to London. The New Zealand team arrived in London that night, Ken bringing French champagne with him, which we drank with the wedding cake in a quiet moment at our hotel. We stayed the first night in London at the Euston Hotel, in Euston. The second night we stayed at the Royal Hotel, Russell Square, where the Kiwis were staying. It was the last night of their tour, so of course they had a night out on the town. At some unearthly hour, there was a 'choir' outside our bedroom door. The renderings were quite tuneful, but we feigned sleep and didn't open the door.

While we were in London we had tracked down some lost relatives of the Mountford family. Ces's father had left London at a very early age and lost touch with three brothers and one sister. We decided to place an ad in the *News of the World's* 'Missing' column, listing the names and all relevant information. To our astonishment, we received a letter from one of Ces's uncles a few days before going to London (a neighbour of his had seen the advert while peeling potatoes) so we were able to arrange a gathering of the clan for dinner at the Royal Hotel. It was a very emotional meeting, the brothers with the distinctive Mountford look, their wives and offspring. The eldest son of Cecil in London was named Robert after Ces's father and vice versa. One sister was missing, Aunt Sylvia, who lived in Melbourne, Australia, but we visited her later on our way to New Zealand by ship. Ken also attended the reunion dinner. Afterwards, while we were all sitting in the lounge reminiscing, Ken handed round a bag of sweets and lollies, said good-bye and rushed off. When Ces remonstrated, Ken replied: "We can only spare an hour for entertaining". He was quite a character and no doubt was one of the 'choristers' that same night.

We were able to say farewell to the Kiwi team when they left for home the following day. After the wedding we received a beautifully decorated wedding cake from Ces's mother and family. It arrived in perfect condition, so we had another celebration and also a longer honeymoon in the off-season when we flew to New Zealand for eight weeks. We received many parcels containing honey, cakes, butter, tinned meats and fruit from the family - they certainly helped the rationing situation.

New Zealand: first impressions

What were my first impressions of New Zealand? For months I had been regaled with stories of eternal blue skies and sunshine. As it turned out we arrived early on a cold May morning while it was still dark. The first thing to attract my attention was a cobweb of wires on the horizon: power and telephone lines and anything which could be was slung into the air. This rather detracted from the beautiful scenery, which I had been told to expect. After toying with a huge meal of steak and two eggs at an Auckland eatery - a gourmet delight we had promised ourselves while enduring rationing in England, my next impression was of noisy plumbing. Toilets and baths are still noisy to this day and while living in a two-storey house, letting out the bath water was a gurgling experience. I can't understand why this should be so in New Zealand and Australia and not in other countries I have visited.

I chose to travel to the West Coast by train and boat mistakenly thinking that this would give me an opportunity to view the scenery. This was not so, as our journey was overnight and the only scenery I saw was people rushing for pies and tea at each stop. We had a sleeper, but sleep was not possible. After wondering if we were running on corrugated iron I was told that the shuddering was due to the narrow gauge railway track.

Also, I was surprised to find that there is trouble with the sound 'th' in the New Zealand language, I have some knowledge of teaching English as a foreign language and found this a major problem in European countries, to hear 'fift' and 'sixt' said in New Zealand even by radio and television announcers rather surprised me.

Left: Ces, Edna and Brian Nordgren on Ces & Edna's wedding day – 27 January 1948.
Right: Ces relaxing by riding a horse. The Wigan directors were always worried about one of their top stars going riding!

1950: Wigan versus Huddersfield Championship Final. Lionel Cooper (on right) faces a Wigan challenge from (left to right) Silcock, Ces and Broome.

7. Other Nationalities
By Peter Lush

The Other Nationalities team had played three games before the First World War, and then had been revived in the 1920s and 1930s. It then included Welsh and Scottish players. After the Second World War, it joined the European Championship for the 1949-50 season, and mainly consisted of Australian and New Zealand players, with some Scottish players, notably Huddersfield's Dave Valentine. Wales had their own team in this period. Australia and New Zealand did not select players based in Great Britain for their international squads, so some of the sport's great players, including Ces and Brian Bevan, never played for their countries. The Other Nationalities team, despite the bland name, was in fact a high quality side and a force on the international scene at the time.

Wales 5 Other Nationalities 6
At Abertillery. 22 October 1949. Attendance: 2,000

Ces made his international debut in Other Nationalities' second match of the season. The first had been a 13-7 win at Workington over England. This match took place in dreadful conditions: driving, freezing rain and lightening. The conditions got so bad that both captains asked the referee to abandon the match, but he refused. Despite the conditions, reports of the match say that the quality of handling was good. Bevan opened the scoring after six minutes. His try in the corner was not converted, and at half-time Other Nationalities (ON) led 3-0. With eight minutes left, the Welsh full-back Sid Williams failed to clear and Lionel Cooper scored to put ON 6-0 up. A late try by Welsh stand-off Jack Davies, which he converted, made the score 6-5, but ON hung on to their lead to win.

Wales: S. Williams, A. H. Daniels, J. B. Mahoney, N. Harris, L. Williams, J. Davies, W.M. Banks, T. Danter, F. Osmond, E. Hawkins, T. J. F. Foster, W. J. D. Howes, B. V. Goldswain.
Scorers: Try: Davies. Goal: Davies.
ON: J.C.H. Hunter, B.Bevan, A.H. Paskins, P.C. Devery, L.W. Cooper, C.R. Mountford, D. Jackson, R. E. McMaster, K.H. Kearney, A.H. Bath, A. Clues, J. Payne, D.D. Valentine.
Scorers: Tries: Bevan, Cooper.

67

France 8 Other Nationalities 3
At Marseille. 15 January 1950. Attendance: 22,580

Bevan and Cooper missed this narrow defeat against a strong French team, with Puig-Aubert at full-back. *Le Meridional* said: "Mountford was a constant danger to the French team, it often taking three men to stop this little red devil. The best player on the field, Mountford beat his opponents with astonishing ease: fully a rugby genius, the little new Zealander gave us an exhibition that will long be remembered, and he fully deserved the applause of the crowd."

The French team dominated the scrums in the first half, but despite this the half-time score was 3-3, Leeds winger Bartlett scoring for ON, and Contrastin scoring for France. But despite ON's scrum work improving in the second half, France scored a further try and Dejean kicked a goal to win 8-3. This was France's only win in the European Championship that season, and England won the title on the basis of a better points difference than the ON side.

France: A Puig-Aubert, V. Cantoni, G. Comes, P. Dejean, R. Contrastin, C. Galoup, R. Duffort, A. Ulma, G. Genoud, A. Beraud, H. Berthomieu, E. Brousse, R. Perez.
Scorers: Tries: Contrastin (2). Goal: Dejean.
ON: J. C. H. Hunter, R. Bartlett, A.H. Paskins, P.C. Devery, B. C. Nordgren, C. R. Mountford, D. Jackson, R. E. McMaster, K. H. Kearney, J. Daly, A. Clues, R. S. Robson, D. D. Valentine.
Scorer: Try: Bartlett.

France 16 Other Nationalities 3
At Bordeaux. 10 December 1950. Attendance: 28,000.

Another large crowd saw France win conclusively against ON, captained by Ces for the first time. This was a golden period for France, who under Puig-Aubert's leadership would win a famous test series victory in Australia the next year. Puig-Aubert put France ahead after five minutes with a penalty. Crespo added a try on 20 minutes, which Puig-Aubert converted, to give France a 7-0 half-time lead. Three minutes into the second half, Ces passed to Brian Bevan who ran fifty yards to score. But another try for France by Mazon, and three more goals from Puig-Aubert left France as clear winners. A report of the match said that they "were on the offensive practically throughout and were sound in defence."

However, the game was marred by a clash between Arthur Clues and French second-rower Edouard Ponsinet. Clues went to tackle Ponsinet high; the French player ducked and received a blow that Clues later said moved his scalp up one-and-a-half inches. The injury was so horrific that one ON player vomited at the sight of it. Ponsinet was very badly injured, and this feud would return to future matches between the teams.

France: A Puig-Aubert, V. Cantoni, J. Crespo, Y. Treilhes, R. Contrastin, C. Galoup, R. Duffort, L. Mazon, M. Martin, A. Beraud, E. Ponsinet, E. Brousse, G. Calixte.
Scorers: Tries: Crespo, Mazon. Goals: Puig-Aubert (5).
ON: H. E. Cook, B. Bevan, R. Bartlett, I. W. Clark, L. W. Cooper, C. R. Mountford, D. Jackson, R. E. McMaster, A. H. Bath, J. C. Daly, A. R. Clues, J. R. Mudge, D. D. Valentine.
Scorer: Try: Bevan.

England 10 Other Nationalities 35
At Wigan. 11 April 1951. Attendance: 16,860.

Mistakes by England contributed to this easy win for ON. Ces was facing seven of his Wigan team mates on their home ground. Ces captained the ON side again. A further attraction for the crowd was the appearance for ON of former Australian Rugby Union captain Trevor Allan, who had joined Leigh for a £5,000 signing-on fee a few months earlier.

Early on, Ratcliffe dropped a pass, which Cooper seized on to put Devery in at the corner. A penalty by Devery put ON further ahead, and then Bevan intercepted a pass by Gibson to score between the posts. Harry Bath converted. Mudge added another try, Bath again converting. Dean scored a penalty for England, but another Bevan try, this time converted by Devery, made the half-time score 20-2 to ON. Ashcroft set up Cunliffe for England's first try after half-time, with Dean converting. But Bevan completed his hat-trick, scoring under the posts from a passing moved started by Ces, and Devery converted. Valentine scored again for ON, Devery converting. England fought back for Ratcliffe to score near the corner. ON finished the scoring with a try from Daly, Devery converting to seal a clear victory.

Despite this great win, ON again finished as runners-up on points difference in the final table. France, ON and England all had 4 points from 3 matches, but France's points dfference of +23 beat ON's +18. Despite two victories, England's points difference was -2.

England: J. Cunliffe, G. W. Ratcliffe, E. J. Ashcroft, E. Gibson, G. Clark, K. Dean, T. Bradshaw, K. Gee, A. Wood, F. Barton, G. Palmer, N. Silcock, W. Ivison.
Scorers: Tries: Cunliffe, Ratcliffe. Goals: Dean (2).

ON: J. C. H. Hunter, B. Bevan, T. Allan, P. C. Devery, L. W. Cooper, C. R. Mountford, D. Jackson, J. C. Daly, T. McKinney, J. R. Mudge, H. Bath, R. S. Robson, D. D. Valentine.
Scorers: Tries: Bevan (3), Daly, Mudge, Valentine.
Goals: Devery (5), Bath (2).

Wales 18 Other Nationalities 16
At Warrington. 15 April 1953. Attendance: 8,449.

The Rugby League had decided at the end of the previous season to play Wales' 'home' matches in the north of England, hoping to attract better attendances. This was the first time Warrington staged an international match, and marked Ces's return to the international stage, following his controversial move from Wigan.

Despite 'playing away', Wales had had a successful season, and the destiny of the title rested on this match. A win or narrow defeat for ON would secure the title for them, a big win for Wales would given them the title. Ces had his Warrington team mates Brian Bevan and Harry Bath with him in a strong ON side.

As so often on major Rugby League international occasions, it rained. This reduced the attendance, and resulted in a treacherous pitch. ON dominated the first-half to take an interval lead of 13-7. A further ON try after the break saw them 16-7 ahead, and surely the title was safe. But the Welsh team fought back, and a late try from Harris, converted by Evans gave them a narrow 18-16 victory. But ON won the title on points difference. Theirs was +24, both Wales and England, despite both having four points from three matches, were -3 and -6 respectively. So Ces and his team mates, led by captain Lionel Cooper, collected the Jean Galia trophy and winners' medals from Jean Galia's widow.

Wales: J. Evans, D. R. Bevan, L. Williams, N. Harris, T. Cook, R. Williams, W. M. Banks, M. Condon, P. T. Harris, E. Gwyther, G. Parsons, C. Winslade, G. James.
Scorers: Tries: Williams, N. Harris, P. T. Harris, Parsons. Goals: Evans (3).
ON: J. Phillips, B. Bevan, T. Allan, P. C. Devery, L. W. Cooper, C. R. Mountford, N. Black, J. C. Daly, W. Ellean, J. R. Mudge, A. H. Bath, A. C. Clues, D. D. Valentine.
Scorers: Tries: Cooper, Black, Clues, Valentine. Goals: Bath (2).

Representative Match: Lord Derby Memorial Game

Great Britain Tourists 23 The Rest 16
At Wigan. 4 October 1950. Attendance 25,000

Ces captained The Rest in this representative match. He faced five of his Wigan team mates, but had Central Park colleagues Jack Broome and Ted Slevin in his team. The occasion raised over £1,500 for the Lord Derby Memorial Fund, but a newspaper report said that: "there was no real bite in the play, and as often happens when footballers of any code are not under any pressure the standard of play suffered badly and the game generally was untidy." The reporter said that it might have been a better game if Wigan had worn the cherry and white jerseys used by The Rest.

Street gave the Tourists the lead, and they were on top for the first 20 minutes. However, Broome cut through some poor defence to equalise for The Rest, Cook converting to give them the lead. Ward made the score 5-5 with a penalty, and then scored in the corner from an opening created by Cunliffe. Bevan put the rest ahead with a try in the corner, Cook adding the touchline conversion. Ward brought the scores level again at 10-10 with a penalty.

In the second half, Martin Ryan won the game for the Tourists. He set up Danby to score, then scored himself after an interchange of passes with Ward. Ward converted both tries. Bevan and Cooper replied for The Rest with tries before Danby scored again to secure the game for the Tourists.

Great Britain Tourists: M. Ryan, A.H. Daniels, E. Ward, E. J. Ashcroft, T. Danby, J. Cunliffe, T. Bradshaw, K. Gee, J. Egan, E. Gwyther, R. Ryan, F. Higgins, H. Street.
Scorers: Tries: Danby (2), Ward, Ryan, Street. Goals: Ward (4).
The Rest: H. E. Cook, B. Bevan, J. Broome, L. Williams, L. W. Cooper, C. R. Mountford, G. J. Helme, R. E. McMaster, L. Marson, A. G. Prescott, A. C. Clues, E. Slevin, D. D. Valentine.
Scorers: Tries: Bevan (2), Broome, Cooper. Goals: Cook (2).

71

Rugby League Coaching School at Lowther College, 1950.
Ces is on the right in the front row; RFL General Secretary
Bill Fallowfield is standing behind him.

Ces presenting the Wigan players to the Duke of Gloucester,
Wembley Challenge Cup Final 1951.

9. Managing Warrington

In 1951 my wife saw an advertisement in the *Sporting Chronicle*, seeking a coach for the Warrington Rugby League club. While I wasn't enthusiastic, my wife (who was always very supportive) typed an application that I signed and posted without high hopes. To my surprise, the following day I received a telegram from Peter Ward, chairman of the Warrington club, asking me to telephone him right away. I made arrangements to meet him and discuss the matter further. Initially I asked why the previous coach, Chris Brockbank, decided to leave. The reply was that he was buying a business in Blackpool. I knew Chris was a very successful coach and would be difficult to replace. I informed Mr Ward that I was only interested in a long-term contract as manager-coach and explained that this was necessary due to the change in my future plans, as I had intended to return to New Zealand. Mr Ward said they were very interested in me and we had a full and frank discussion. We agreed on a 10-year contract. I returned to Wigan, and discussed the offer with my legal adviser, who agreed that it was a good one. My solicitor then applied to Wigan for my clearance as a player, copies of the request going to the Rugby League. Wigan objected to my transfer as a player, but they had weakened their case by having accepted my money in repayment for the third year of my second contract.

I then moved house to Warrington with my family and commenced my job as team manager-coach. It was like going into a new world. Before the year was over, the Rugby League cleared me to play for Warrington. I was then player-manager and coaching, ably assisted by Les Hockenhull, a very talented young secretary with a good knowledge of the game. We worked well together for 10 years - a very productive partnership. He was a very helpful, obliging individual who was not interested either in himself or position, a rare talent - a true Rugby League man. He attended to everything; no job was too small for him. Coaches with such a secretarial support are indeed very fortunate.

A number of the older players who served Warrington well in the past were retiring and it was a case of rebuilding the team and filling key positions with new players. This was a challenge I accepted gladly. My first two years were not easy and saw little result. I even returned to the playing field myself, but after 18 months I was injured while playing, with the result that I did not don my boots again. This was in October 1953.

73

At that time we were well positioned on the Championship ladder and well into contention for both the Championship and the Challenge Cup. We went on to win both trophies, but for the Challenge Cup, but we had to have a replay in Bradford. We drew with Halifax at Wembley 4-4.

Odsal replay

The replay was at Odsal Stadium, where we won 8-4. There was a record crowd of officially 102,569 (unofficially probably nearer 120,000) to see us win the double. The crowd was quite unexpected by police and Rugby League officials, and stories of gates being broken down. There was tremendous traffic chaos. The team arrived at the stadium on time, but Edna remembers the coach with the wives and girlfriends being held up, and missing their pre-match meal. Fortunately, the players had been on time for theirs. Until recently, it was the largest crowd ever to attend a rugby match of either code in the world. Traffic was still returning to Warrington at 5am the following day.

Our preparation for big games was fairly simple compared with today. Usually for important games we would spend a few days at Blackpool's North Shore, but for the Odsal replay we went to Ilkley. One episode in the game I will never forget, that was when Gerry Helme scored the winning try. At half-time I spoke to him, telling him to run when the opportunity arose. He scored the winning try doing that. Gerry was a brilliant half-back when he ran with the ball. If he wasn't running, the tempo slowed down.

We then beat Halifax in the Championship Final three days later. It was the first time the double had been won for some 20 years. In all, Warrington won three trophies that year. We had a wonderful group of players with tremendous team spirit. With all the games we played against them in the Challenge Cup and the Championship, and an end-of-season visit to Ireland, where we played them twice, we developed a friendly relationship with the Halifax players.

1955 Championship

We retained the championship the next year. We played Oldham in the Championship Final at Maine Road, Manchester. We spent a few days before the game at the Royal Hotel, Bispham, on the North Shore at

Blackpool. These visits were made very comfortable by the staff. Our requirements for the players were always met. The bracing wind from the North Sea meant that our early 7.00am walk along the promenade was brisk. The walk was rather a shock initially, but together with the oranges eaten en route, became a regular occurrence, and an opportunity to meet informally with their fellow team members. Also, the players could talk to me if they had any problems. It also meant, somewhat sneakily, that I ensured that they weren't out of bed too late the previous night.

As for the game, which we won 7-3, my main memory is of Harry Bath kicking the winning goal, and that Warrington and Oldham played very well in atrocious conditions: wet, cold and windy. We received the trophy from the Earl of Derby, who I knew very well by then, having received many trophies from him.

Brian Bevan

In every Rugby League era there exist shining stars who, through inimitable talent, magnetise the crowds and bring them eagerly through the turnstiles in their thousands. In the last part of the 20th century and after the Millennium, Shaun Edwards, Ellery Hanley, Martin Offiah, Va'aiga Tuigamala, Iestyn Harris, Kevin Cunningham, Kris Radlinski, Jason Robinson and Henry and Robbie Paul have been such luminaries. In the post-war era of 1946-56 there were an equal number of brilliant individuals who dominated their club scene. Star-studded Wigan, with Joe Egan, Martin Ryan, Tommy Bradshaw, Brian Nordgren, Ken Gee and Billy Blan, was the most fortunately-endowed team, but Pat Devery and Lionel Cooper of Huddersfield, Ernie Ward and Eric Batten of Bradford Northern, Albert Johnson and Harry Bath of Warrington and Willie Horne of Barrow were all intriguing talents and great crowd-pullers.

It is questionable if any players of that era, sensational though they were, could outshine Brian Bevan. Playing right wing for Warrington he was a household name for devastating speed, uncanny elusiveness and sheer, cussed originality. A weird-looking, emaciated Australian, he looked nobody until he got the ball. After that he was a law unto himself. How could you catch him? If he had a yard start, it was impossible. If you left a couple of yards between you and the touchline, he simply ran round you. If you hugged the touchline to stop this, he took off on a sickening diagonal sprint towards the left-hand corner flag, leaving opposing wingers and centres completely nonplussed over who was supposed to mark him. When they half-heartedly tried to intervene, he ran across the face of them. There is nothing in the book about defence against this tactic. He scored almost as many tries way out left as he did on the right. After banging the ball down, he would walk modestly back, bandy-legged, huffing and puffing like a cardiac case. In all the years I played against him and with him, I can only recall half a dozen times when he was well and truly grabbed. He was a phenomenal will-o'-the-wisp rarely touched by normal players. You could say he didn't like being tackled!

Brian Bevan was an enigma, his skeletal body a contrast in so many ways. I first met him as an opponent when I played for Wigan and played with him in several Other Nationalities teams. When I became manager-coach for Warrington I had the task of managing this talent. My first encounter with him was in the dressing room when I began my 10-year contract with that club.

I was intrigued to see rows of dressing strips in various sizes stuck to the walls and being applied to Brian's toes, fingers, ankles, wrists and elbows while the other players waited for attention in various other ways. I didn't wish to be a 'new broom' on the first day so waited a while before approaching Brian and suggesting he arrive at the ground earlier for this procedure so that other players didn't have to wait. He agreed to this.

A unique sportsman

Brian Bevan was unique as a sportsman, quietly spoken, mostly in monosyllables. I never had any problem with his training and coaching though I think some of the other players found him difficult to understand. More often than not he would answer questions with a nod and his greeting in passing anyone would be a nod.

On the field, Bev was a star, a shining light. Covered in plasters, with a bald head and minus teeth, he looked anything but awesome and one wondered at his extraordinary talent when playing Rugby League. He had incredible speed off the mark as well as a baffling change of pace which left opponents grabbing at empty air.

Whizzing along in top gear he would suddenly come to a screeching halt, mesmerising his pursuers, and then take off in a completely different direction. It was almost impossible to lay a finger on him when he employed this tactic. I was one of those mesmerised during my playing days with Wigan. His reading of the game and the strength in that frail body was remarkable. Some players and fans thought that his defence was suspect but he usually made up for any slips and was a certainty to be selected if fit and sometimes when not fit, in important games.

Socially and personally, he was shy. He would dissolve into the background at gatherings, many people would find it difficult to hold a conversation with him though I never had that problem. He would listen intently, head bowed. I always spoke to him privately - not with the rest of the team. He had his own wavelength.

Brian totally concentrated on his game as a winger believing that he was one of the best in the world. There is no doubt about it - he was. As mentioned, I played with Brian in the Other Nationalities team. He was a good team mate, never any trouble and focussed on the game.

Brian married a Warrington girl, Doreen, and had two lovely daughters. The last I heard of Bev before he died, he was working as a barber in a prison. There sure wouldn't be any loose talk. There will never be another Bev.

Development

My management at Warrington was very innovative, assisting the local amateur League and developing schoolboy football in co-operation with the many schools in the area. Twice a year I would organise coaching schools for teachers, teaching them the skills of the game. There would be 30 teachers in attendance at each course, which were very friendly, relaxed occasions. After attending lectures and demonstrations, teachers had the opportunity to coach on the playing fields. We always finished with a short game. You cannot beat practical experience. By the end of my 10 years with Warrington, we were signing young men who had been coached by teachers who had been through our coaching courses. On the completion of my 10-year contract, despite another offer from Warrington, I decided to return home to New Zealand, my native land. It must have been hard for my family, especially Edna, but I felt the time was ripe.

In the 1955-56 season, the Warrington board of directors decided that no further money would be available for signing high class players; we had to develop junior players throughout the local area. Only rarely did we break this rule. There weren't many, if any, 'cheque book Charlie' coaches in those days. Coaches had to produce their own players or go under. I firmly believe the Warrington board of directors were absolutely right in their decision to invest in the future of local talent. We had proved this at Blackball on the Coast. You cannot buy loyalty, discipline, good fellowship and love of the game. You have to build for the future, have a five-year plan and be committed to carrying it out. Then there will always be players waiting in the wings who want a chance to show their skills. If senior players know there is enthusiastic young talent breathing down their necks, it tends to keep them on their toes.

Touring teams

I was often in contact with touring teams from 'down under' during my time at Warrington. The 1959-60 Australian tourists arrived in England during a very hot 'Indian summer'. In a change from past arrangements, they spent some of the tour staying in Lancashire, and the team and supporters were at the Victoria Hotel in Stockton Heath, near our home in Appleton.

There was great excitement that the tourists were coming – the hotel was refurbished and looked a picture. I attended the team's first training run, and arranged for some injured players to receive treatment. Edna sat in the car watching the training, and Ern Keefer, who was from Queensland and was one of the team's managers, asked to sit in the car out of the heat. She could hardly believe that a Queenslander found England too hot. That was the start of a friendship between us that lasted until he died last year.

I kept in touch with the team, and Edna and I would invite the managers home for supper and a chat round the fire. Older members of touring teams usually appreciate a taste of home. Touring can be very lonely.

When the party left, Edna was presented with a bone china tea service in yellow and gold, almost the Australian colours. A very young Johnny Raper, Reg Gasnier and Harry Wells were among the players on that tour.

The first game of the tour was against Warrington. There was a huge crowd. After a few minutes, Brian Hambley came off with a badly injured nose. I came down from the stand, accompanied by our club doctor, Dr McClelland, and Jack Argent, the Australian manager.

I suggested that a replacement be allowed, so that the opening game of the tour wouldn't be spoiled by one side being a player short. The others were dubious, but eventually agreed. A player was sent on, and jack Argent put him in Hambley's jersey, ruffled his hair and put a plaster on his nose. This subterfuge may have been accepted by the Warrington crowd, but not by Tiger Black, whose commentary was being broadcast to Australia. No announcement had been made, he knew it wasn't Hambley, and hoped the new player didn't get the ball so he didn't have to mention his name.

Of course, substitutes were not allowed then. The truth came out, and there were pressmen on our doorstep for days. Warrington lost in the last few minutes, and the players blamed me for getting losing money. A sporting gesture turned slightly sour.

One player on that tour, Brian Clay, was injured, and in Warrington General Hospital. He wanted to go to a match at Wilderspool, and the ward sister, Vivienne, who we knew as other tourists had been in the hospital. She agreed as long as I returned him straight back to hospital after the game.

Unfortunately, I had to take two other players to hospital, and asked Jim Challinor to take Brian back. Edna phoned the ward sister the next morning to say that Brian had enjoyed the game. There was an ominous silence on the phone – it turned out Brian had been caught trying to climb in through a window at 2.00am. Jim had taken him home for dinner. Fortunately, Vivienne didn't lose her job, but later did leave nursing to marry Jack Argent, who came from Australia for the ceremony.

I was put in a difficult position by the managers of a different Australian tour party. They asked if I could coach their team one Sunday, while they took their coach on a trip to Blackpool. I was horrified at this idea, thinking of how I would feel if I was in the same position as their coach. But the Australian managers were worried about how their team was performing; they said it was for the good of the tour and Rugby League. I reluctantly agreed, so for a couple of Sundays their coach was taken on unexpected outings to the coast.

A similar incident happened with a Kiwi team. I was asked to travel to Ilkley to coach and speak to the Kiwi team. I did it as a favour. Two players later told Edna that after I had left, Scotty McClymont told the team he hoped they had enjoyed the talk, coaching and advice from me, but now to forget it all and get down to work with me – I'm the coach. It was probably an understandable reaction.

1961 Championship Final defeat

The 1961 defeat by Leeds was an anti-climax at the end of my career in England. The weeks before the game had been very traumatic for me and the family, and the team who had become so involved in my departure.

I was offered another five year contract, but that didn't really suit me, as it would have interfered with an important part of our children's education and would have been more difficult for them to adjust to an eventual return to New Zealand. Also in the back of my mind was my promise to return to New Zealand.

There were deputations to the Board by the players and staff to try to keep me, and then many farewell functions. There were threats of resignation by players and training staff. All this was happening while we were preparing for the big game, packing, selling the house and organising travel. This was not the usual atmosphere for preparation for a final, but it couldn't be avoided as we had to be ready to leave by the time my contract finished. It was the end of 10 years at the club.

The players were so determined to win the game as a parting present for me that I think they tried too hard and mistakes crept into their play. This is the only losing medal I have for tests and finals. Jack Arkwright threw his away as he was leaving the field, a gesture seen by a lot of people. It was very sad to see his despair.

The scene in the dressing room afterwards displayed more than the loss of a game. It was the end of my career in England as I then thought – my time at Blackpool came later out of the blue.

My parting gift to Warrington had been signing Parry Gordon, who turned out to be a great player and clubman for the Wire.

8. Great occasions at Warrington
By Peter Lush

The 1953-54 season was the greatest in Warrington's history, winning the Championship, the Challenge Cup and the Lancashire League. Yet all this was achieved without Ces's services as a player, the knee injury that finished his playing career had happened in October 1953.

The road to Wembley.

The first round of the Challenge Cup saw lowly Bramley beaten 47-5 over two legs. A mere 2,048 supporters saw Brian Bevan score six tries in the Wire's 30-5 victory in the second match at McLaren Field.

The second round draw produced a much tougher fixture. Warrington had to travel to Watersheddings to face Oldham, who had one of the best teams in their history at this time. A 21,000 all-ticket crowd saw the Wire win through 7-4, on a pitch of snow and heavy mud. But early in the second half, Oldham was 4-2 ahead through two penalty goals from Bernard Ganley. As so often, it was Brian Bevan who rescued the game for Warrington. A magnificent run in those conditions saw the Australian winger score under the posts to win the game for his team. Even the Oldham supporters, disappointed as they were, applauded his run.

Two weeks later, Warrington travelled to York in the third round, and won 26-5 to secure a semi-final spot. Leeds was the final obstacle on the road to Wembley. A crowd of 36,993 saw the Wire win through 8-4 at Swinton's Station Road ground. Leeds was a strong side, with Lewis Jones and Arthur Clues among their stars. But a try from Jim Challinor gave the Wire the lead, Harry Bath made it 5-0 with a penalty, and Brian Bevan – again, inevitably – scored a try five minutes before half-time. Warrington's 8-4 win took the club to Wembley for the fourth time.

Challenge Cup Final: Halifax 4 Warrington 4
At Wembley Stadium. 24 April 1954. Attendance: 81,841.

Warrington faced Yorkshire opposition again in the Final. Halifax had one of the strongest defences in the league, and would be tough opponents.

In the history of Rugby League, this is one of the 'forgotten' matches, overshadowed by the replay at Odsal 11 days later. Reports of the match say that it was a poor game. Griffiths scored two penalties for Halifax, who led 4-0 at half-time. Harry Bath scored two in the second half. Between them the pair missed 11 kicks (Bath seven, Griffiths four). Bevan had one good run in the second half, but generally the play was forward dominated. In the second half there was even slow handclapping as Halifax tried to slow play down to defend a 4-2 lead. With the scores level, Halifax narrowly missed a penalty that would have won the game, and changed Rugby League history. But it was not to be, and the Wembley final petered out into anti-climax.

Halifax: T. Griffiths, A. H. Daniels, T. W. Lynch, P. Todd, D. R. Bevan, K. Dean, S. Kielty, G. M. J. Thorley, A. Ackerley, J. Wilkinson, A. Fearnley, D. Schofield, D. Clarkson.
Scorer: Goals: Griffiths (2).
Warrington: E. Frodsham, B. Bevan, J. Challinor, A. Stevens, S. McCormick, H. R. Price, G. J. Helme, D. Naughton, F. Wright, G. Lowe, H. Bath, A. Heathwood, R. Ryan.
Scorer: Goals: Bath (2).

Challenge Cup Final Replay: Halifax 4 Warrington 8
At Odsal. 5 May 1954. Attendance: 102,569.

Despite the dull draw at Wembley, the return of the Cup Final to the north for the first time in many years in peace time clearly caught the public imagination. The official attendance was a world record for decades until recently beaten at the massive Stadium Australia. The real attendance, as crowd control collapsed and many entered the ground without passing through the turnstiles, was probably around 120,000. Miraculously, there was not a major disaster, which would have seen the occasion remembered for the wrong reasons.

Whatever Bradford Bulls go on to achieve at this ground, the name Odsal will always be associated with this match. Ces Mountford took his players to relax in Ilkley for a few days before the game. Their coach battled through the traffic, and the game kicked off on time. In those days, the teams walked down from the dressing rooms through the crowd to get to the pitch. The players were used to big crowds in those days, but this was unprecedented. The previous highest crowd at Odsal was 69,898 for Warrington's Championship semi-final against Leeds in 1950.

Warrington scored first; Jim Challinor touching down after eight minutes to put the Wire 3-0 up. For Halifax, Griffiths scored a penalty for offside just before half-time. Warrington's 3-2 lead did not reflect their superiority in the first half. Harry Bath had again been having an off day with the boot, and had missed four penalties. However, he scored one in the second half to make the lead 5-2. Griffiths replied five minutes later: 5-4 to Warrington. Then 13 minutes from time, Wire scrum-half Gerry Helme scored in the corner to make the score 8-4, and the cup was heading for Wilderspool. And everyone got home eventually, with traffic heading away from the game for hours afterwards.

Halifax: T. Griffiths, A. H. Daniels, T. W. Lynch, W. Mather, D. R. Bevan, K. Dean, S. Kielty, G. M. J. Thorley, A. Ackerley, J. Wilkinson, A. Fearnley, D. Schofield, D. Clarkson.
Scorer: Goals: Griffiths (2).
Warrington: E. Frodsham, B. Bevan, J. Challinor, R. Ryder, S. McCormick, H. R. Price, G. J. Helme, D. Naughton, F. Wright, G. Lowe, H. Bath, A. Heathwood, R. Ryan.
Scorers: Tries: Challinor, Helme. Goal: Bath.

The Championship Final: Halifax 7 Warrington 8
At Maine Road (Manchester City FC). 8 May 1954. Attendance: 36,519.

Between the Challenge Cup Final and the Odsal replay, Warrington had beaten St Helens 11-0 at Wilderspool in the Championship semi-final to reach the Final. Halifax, who had finished top of the final league table, a point clear of Warrington, beat Workington Town 18-7 in their semi-final, so the teams would meet again in the Championship Final.

The match took place three days after the Odsal replay. The match 'only' attracted 36,519 supporters to see another hard-fought contest. The whole game was shown live on television, which maybe meant some fans stayed at home. And maybe the cost of a trip to London and the Cup Final replay had caught up with other supporters.

Warrington was bidding to win three trophies in a season for the first time ever, and to do the Cup and Championship double for the first time since Swinton achieved this in 1927-28. The Wire's cause was not helped by falling behind after only three minutes. Stan Kielty stole the ball from Eric Frodsham, and put John Thorley in to score, Griffiths adding the goal. Bath narrowed the lead with penalties in the 10th and 24th minutes, but after 27 minutes, a penalty from Griffiths gave Halifax a 7-4 lead which they held until half-time.

Another Bath penalty on 51 minutes reduced Halifax's lead to 7-6. Clarkson hit the post for Halifax with a penalty, but then Bath won the game for the Wire with a 64th minute penalty. Warrington kept this lead for the final 16 minutes to take the Championship. Bevan had a try disallowed for offside near the end, but it made no difference to the final result.

Halifax: T. Griffiths, A. H. Daniels, T. W. Lynch, P. Todd, D. R. Bevan, K. Dean, S. Kielty, G. M. J. Thorley, A. Ackerley, J. Wilkinson, A. Fearnley, D. Schofield, D. Clarkson.
Scorers: Try: Thorley. Goals: Griffiths (2).
Warrington: E. Frodsham, B. Bevan, J. Challinor, R. Ryder, S. McCormick, H. R. Price, G. J. Helme, D. Naughton, F. Wright, G. Lowe, H. Bath, A. Heathwood, R. Ryan.
Scorer: Goals: Bath (4).

1954-55: The Championship retained

Warrington made little impact on the cup competitions in the 1954-55 season, losing at Widnes in the first round of the Lancashire Cup, and 9-4 to Bradford Northern on an ant-climactic return to Odsal in the first round of the Challenge Cup. But the end of the season Championship play-off produced some glory.

Warrington had finished top of the League. In the play-off semi-final, old foes Halifax was the visitors to Wilderspool. A crowd of 22,311 saw the Wire win 17-9 to reach the final at Maine Road.

The Championship Final: Oldham 3 Warrington 7
At Maine Road (Manchester City FC).14 May 1955. Attendance: 49,434.

There had been heavy rain before the match, and the first half was hit by a further storm and hailstones. Parts of the pitch were flooded, and the match resembled one in January or February rather than mid May. Warrington survived an early attack by Oldham which resulted in Barrow touching down in the corner, only for the touch judge to rule that he had touched the corner flag. Soon afterwards, Bevan came close to scoring. Then after 24 minutes, Bath passed to Challinor, who put Bevan in to score. Warrington held their lead for little more than 10 minutes, Frank Pitchford scoring for Oldham five minutes before half-time. At the break the scores were tied at 3-3.

The teams put new kit on at half-time, but soon were as muddy and wet as in the first half. Five minutes into the second half, Harry Bath scored a penalty from wide out to give Warrington the lead. He secured victory for his team with a further penalty, from 40 yards out, five minutes from time. Thus, Warrington retained the Championship, and Oldham finished as runners up in three competitions: the Championship, the Lancashire League and the Lancashire Cup. They had also finished second in the Rugby League final table. Despite the conditions, reports say that it was a tremendous match. The Earl of Derby presented the trophy and winners' medals to Warrington.

Oldham: F. Stirrup, R. Barrow, R. Cracknell, A. Davies, T. O'Grady, F. Daley, F. Pitchford, H. Ogden, J. Keith, K. Jackson, C. Winslade, S. Little, B. Goldswain.
Scorer: Try: Pitchford.
Warrington: E. Frodsham, B. Bevan, J. Challinor, A. Naughton, L. Horton, J. Honey, G. Helme, D. Naughton, T. McKinney, G. Lowe, S. Phillips, H. Bath, R. Ryan.
Scorers: Try: Bevan. Goals: Bath (2).

The following season, Warrington won the Lancashire League, but lost in the semi-final of the Lancashire Cup to Widnes and at home to Hull in the Championship semi-final. One trophy that was won was the ITV Trophy. This involved the game in a rare outing to London, as all the matches were played at Queen's Park Rangers FC's Loftus Road ground in west London, and were on television. Warrington beat Wakefield 33-9, and then Leigh in the final 43-18 to secure the trophy. Brian Bevan scored two tries in the final, which was played before a crowd of 3,173. The competition was not repeated.

1959-60: The Lancashire Cup returns to Wilderspool

The Lancashire Cup was always a hard fought for trophy. Warrington's last victory had been before the Second World War, in the 1937-38 season, so this triumph was well overdue. For the first time, after eight years at the club, Ces was given sole responsibility for team selection. Previously, the side had been chosen on a majority vote of the directors and manager.

Warrington had to travel to Cumbria for the first round, as the draw took them to Workington Town. The Cumbrians were not the force they had been in the early 1950s, and were heading for 19th place in the league. Warrington won 33-12, and in the second round had a shorter journey to Leigh. This time, the Wire won 29-2, in front of 13,952 fans. Ally Naughton scored a hat-trick of tries.

Six days later, Warrington travelled to Central Park to face Wigan in the semi-final. There was great interest in the match, and 30,637 crammed into the ground. The match was Brian Bevan's 527th game for Warrington, a new club record.

The match lived up to expectations. Wigan took an early 10-0 lead, with tries from Cunliffe and Ashton, both converted by Ashton. Warrington fought back with a try by Terry O'Grady, converted by Fraser, to make the half-time score 10-5 to Wigan. After 52 minutes, Warrington levelled the scores, Edwards touching down and Fraser converting. Bevan then set up Denis Karalius to score, 13-10 to Warrington. Holden then scored out wide for

Wigan, but Ashton missed the conversion. 13-13, but with seconds remaining, Jim Challinor won the game for Warrington with a drop-goal from 25 yards out. So Warrington won 15-13, and reached their first Lancashire Cup Final since 1950.

Lancashire Cup Final: St Helens 4 Warrington 5
At Central Park. 31 October 1959. Attendance: 39,237.

Warrington returned to Central Park for the final, to face St Helens. Tough opposition – St Helens had won their first 12 league games of the season and were the Champions. The Karalius brothers were due to be on opposing sides, but Vince (St Helens) and Denis (Warrington) were both injured.

St Helens took the lead with an unusual score. Rhodes hit the bar with a penalty from far out, but Warrington managed to play the ball forward in an offside position, and thus Rhodes scored an easy penalty. Then Warrington scored a controversial try. Greenhough kicked ahead, Bevan touched down as van Vollenhoven kicked the ball. Despite St Helens protests, the try was given, and Fraser converted from near the touch line. Rhodes kicked a further penalty, so at half-time Warrington led 5-4.

The second half was scoreless, despite constant St Helens pressure. The Warrington forwards were magnificent, and they held out to take the cup back to Wilderspool.

St Helens: A. Rhodes, K. T. van Vollenhoven, D. Greenall, J. B. McGinn, J. Prinsloo, A. J. Murphy, W. Smith, A. E. Terry, T. McKinney, A. G. Prescott, B. Briggs, R. Huddart, F. Terry.
Scorer: Goals: Rhodes (2)
Warrington: E. G. Fraser, B. Bevan, J. Challinor, L. Gilfedder, T. O'Grady, R. J. Greenhough, J. Edwards, N. Silcock, P. Lannon, A. Brindle, J. Arkwright, H. Major, A. Naughton.
Scorers: Try: Bevan. Goal: Fraser.

The following season was to be Ces's final one at Warrington. In the cups, the Wire went out in both competitions in narrow defeats at Wilderspool. In the Lancashire Cup, Leigh won 9-8 in the second round in September. In the Challenge Cup, Warrington won 39-0 at Doncaster, with 4 tries from Bevan, before Featherstone won 13-10 at Wilderspool in the next round. Featherstone finished ninth in the league that year, but it was disappointing.

Warrington finished runners-up in the league table, five points behind table topping Leeds. In the Championship semi-final, Swinton came to Wilderspool. A crowd of 24,237 saw two tries from Bevan and one from O'Grady took the

86

Wire through, Fraser and Gilfedder adding goals. It was 5-5 at half-time, and Bevan won the game for Warrington in the second half. Thus Warrington reached their first Championship Final since the 1955 victory over Oldham. ￭

1961 Championship Final: Leeds 25 Warrington 10
At Odsal. 20 May 1961. Attendance: 52,177.

As Ces outlines elsewhere, by the time the final came, it was clear that he was leaving Wilderspool, despite the efforts of the players to persuade him to stay on. He took the team to Ilkley before the game, as he had before the 1954 Odsal replay. The players were desperate to win. But so was Leeds, who, despite the high status of the club in the game, had never won the Championship. The 1961 Final was their sixth, and their captain, Lewis Jones, was coming to the end of his career. It was Warrington's 12 post-war final, including the Odsal replay, and Bevan had played in all of them. It was to be his last appearance in a major final. All these factors attracted a crowd of 52,177 to Odsal, the scene of Ces's greatest triumph as a manager.

Leeds' pack turned out to be the decisive factor in the game. Hooker Simms won the scrums 29-10, and at half-time, Leeds led 10-0, having dominated the game. Fairbank and Evans had scored the tries. The Yorkshire side increased their lead to 18-0 before the Wire could score. Jim Challinor touched down, and added a second try five minutes from time. Laurie Gilfedder converted both tries, but Leeds scored again before the end to make the final score 25-10. Ken Dalby's *The Headingley Story* says that Leeds "brilliantly led by Lewis Jones, [rose] to the occasion in glorious style and reduced Warrington to bewildered also-rans."

Ces told Jack Bentley from the *Daily Express*: "We got the flutters. They started four hours before the kick-off. You should have seen 'em. The occasion was too big for us." So Warrington ended as runners-up, disappointing for Ces and his players, but second place in the league table and a Final outing was still an acceptable end to his Warrington career, and an improvement on seventh place in the table the year before.

Leeds: K. W. Thornett, W. Rosenberg, D. Hallas, V. N. Hattee, E. Ratcliffe, B.L. Jones, C. Evans, D. Robinson, B. Simms, T. Whitehead, J. Fairbank, D. Goodwin, B. Shaw.
Scorers: Tries: Hallas (2), Jones, Evans, Fairbank. Goals: Jones (5).
Warrington: E. G. Fraser, B. Bevan, J. Challinor, J. Pickavance, T. O'Grady, R. J. Greenhough, J. Edwards, D. A. Brindle, W. Harper, J. Arkwright, L. Gilfedder, H. Major, A. Naughton.
Scorers: Tries: Challinor (2). Goals: Gilfedder (2).

As has been outlined elsewhere in this book, Ces's departure from Wigan to Warrington was controversial. In the 1951 pre-season Wardonia Cup, he was named in both team line ups, but played for neither. This cartoon was published at the time of the match.

Below: Happy times at Warrington: Gerry Helme on the run to his match-winning try against Halifax at Odsal 1954.
(Photo: Courtesy Robert Gate)

11. A wife in Wigan and Warrington
By Edna Mountford

Gone are the days when Wigan was looked upon as a town of mines, cotton mills, clogs, lamplights and the pier and the butt of music hall jokes. These were instigated by the late George Formby Senior, who was born in Wigan. I suppose that Wiganers can really thank him and George Junior for putting Wigan on the map, one way or the other.

George Formby Junior was, of course, born in Wigan and was a regular follower of the club's fortunes, as also was the comedian Tom Moss who had a touring show. Whenever they came to the Wigan Hippodrome or Warrington Theatre the team would be invited, they were always acknowledged and drawn into the programme. The last time we heard from Tom, he was living in a cottage near Blackpool.

Another follower of Wigan was the England footballer Sir Stanley Matthews, who lived in Blackpool and often attended the Good Friday derby between Wigan and St Helens, if not playing football.

As wives and girlfriends of the players we did have our moments. As a break from training for the men and also the general tedium for us, we were sometimes taken to Manchester for dinner and a show. One I particularly recall was a Tex Ritter show preceded by a Chinese meal.

One of the players with Warrington at that time was Tony Storey, brother of David, the author of the book and film *This Sporting Life*. Tony was a psychologist and at that time worked in a boy's remand home near Warrington. We sometimes went there for dinner and our two youngsters were most interested in the boys who had been 'naughty'. These boys had built a very impressive swimming pool. David was also a painter, many of his paintings were stacked against the wall at Tony's because David was between residences at the time. The paintings fascinated me - apart from thickly applied paint, there were screws, springs, anything and everything that would stick to paint.

Another Warrington supporter was Colin Welland, also a writer and television personality, probably best remembered for his part as a copper in *Z Cars*. Colin wrote several pieces about Ces. I first met Colin at the Fulham Football Club, which then had dual codes of association football and Rugby League. Colin was a director on the Rugby League side. The New Zealand Rugby League team played a game there one evening during the 1980 tour. When I went into the clubroom at half-time I heard Colin asking for Ces. At full-time we did have an enjoyable chat with him. Colin lived within sight of the ground.

In Wigan, we became friends with the Owen family. Les Owen had become Ces's mentor and friend from the time he arrived in Wigan and was a very much-valued friend. Les kept horses at his Wigan home and was a keen rider, as was Ces, having had the experience of keeping horses himself and riding them up the mountains in Blackball.

Most Sunday mornings, Les and Ces were to be seen heading for the estate of the Earl of Crawford and Balcarres who resided at Haigh Hall, Wigan. Most of the Earl's estate was open to the public.

Ces eagerly looked forward to the riding on Sunday mornings. He found it relaxing, especially after a game on Saturday. There was no Sunday football then. The Wigan directors weren't very enthusiastic, though, at the thought of their star half-back jumping fences and hedges. One press photograph showed Ces in mid-air, still on the horse, jumping over a stone wall. The caption was "It's Easy for Cecil".

Warrington

Warrington has a history dating back to Roman times, it also had Tudor and Victorian elements noticeable in the architecture, but is mainly an industrial town which lies on the River Mersey. At one side of the swing bridge over the river was Stockton Heath village and on the other side the village of Appleton, where we lived. It was mainly residential with a golf course and country walks.

Warrington is a typical Lancashire town with a large market and varied industry. In our time it had the Greenall Whitley Brewery, the Crosfields Soap Works and Lockers, a world-wide wire producing industry (in fact the Rugby League team used to be called the 'The Wire'). The Locker family were avid followers of the team and personal friends.

The Wire team colours were primrose and blue. The most famous players in Warrington in the late 1940s and early 1950s were Harry Bath, a second- rower and a mighty kicker of goals - he amassed a points' tally of 1,894 - and Brian Bevan on the wing who scored a record 796 tries.

It was a good time of life, we had wide open spaces, a farm within walking distance, some beautiful walks in Cheshire country lanes and a golf club over the road, also had very friendly neighbours. These were

Owen Bevan, brother of Brian, and Harry Bath, before he returned to the hotel business in Warrington town. We seemed to have 'open house' on Tuesdays and Thursdays when players living in other towns came to Warrington to consult specialists or to have treatment. They would then have a bite to eat at our house before going to Wilderspool for the evening training session. They were our salad days, a happy time.

Our departure from Warrington was more traumatic than when we left Wigan because it meant we were leaving England. This had been a hard decision to make, for Ces was offered a further five-year contract. This would have meant 15 years in all. The decision to leave was partly due to the fact that our children would have been in the middle of serious schooling five years hence making leaving then far more difficult. Also, Ces had a yearning to return to his roots and homeland while I had to contemplate leaving mine.

The farewells were many and very sad. I never hear *Now is the Hour* without that same sad feeling. We were presented with many parting gifts. One of the last farewells was at the Fearnhead Golf Club where Ces was presented with a copper figure of a golfer, suitably inscribed.

The most poignant moment occurred when we were leaving the golf club the entire Warrington team lined the driveway applauding Ces. Many were in tears. As one newspaper scribe wrote: "It was as a father leaving his sons and who wants to leave his sons 12,000 miles away?"

We actually left England from Wigan where my mother and brother lived. After spending two nights with the Owen family, we were about to board the train to Southampton from Wigan when members of the press, who had been alerted, raced up. The train was delayed while photographs were taken on the platform and with our heads out of the train window. It was perhaps fitting that we should leave from Wigan, where it all started.

Forming friendships in Rugby League is quite easy. We were leaving many friends behind us, there are natural ones with team mates and their families, also administrators and their families, but one has to be selective otherwise one becomes the property of the fans. It is all rewarding, but when it comes to close friendships, I can count the numbers on one hand.

Our close friends included Brian Nordgren, 'Noggy' to the Wigan supporters, a countryman of Ces in a foreign land. Brian was a welcome sight at the boat when Ces arrived, along with two Wigan directors. He was able to give Ces a few words of wisdom regarding the signing of a contract, having gone through the experience himself a few months earlier. Maybe this was the first indication of his ultimate career as a lawyer. Yes, there were contract problems, even in those days.

Brian eventually moved to Liverpool to study law and married Marjorie. We then only saw them at intervals when visiting games and functions, but the friendship has continued. When in Auckland we visited them at their home in Hamilton. Old times were discussed with fervour. Our daughters, Anne (theirs) and Carolyn (ours) were born within a week of each other. Our sons, Robert (theirs) and Kim (ours) are much the same age. All met up again in Auckland at Auckland Girls Grammar School and Auckland Boys Grammar School.

Our association with the Bradshaw family also lasts to this day, although Tommy is no longer with us. Tommy was the life and soul of the Wigan team, where he always had a cheeky but funny remark, which dispelled many pre-match tensions. Unfortunately, Tommy was usually physically sick from nerves before a game, but recovered enough to cause mayhem in opposing teams. His partnership with Ces has been well documented, it was like poetry in motion if one can coin such a remark to describe Rugby League - a computer-like understanding to describe it another way, but always a joy to watch. The crowds loved it.

Tommy married Reta and their two sons Rodney and Lindsay were also born about the same time as our children. Rodney was born while Tommy was away touring Australia and New Zealand with the British team. Unfortunately, Tommy suffered a crippling bout of fibrositis and was out of football for a year and unable to work. This was a hard time for his family and painful for Tommy as he had to walk with two sticks for some time. Financially it was a burden as players' pay was a mere pittance in those days. Most players had a full-time job, so a year off work and Rugby League was a real hardship. The closeness between the two men manifested itself in Ces planting Tommy's potatoes while he was away overseas. While he was ill, Ces supplied him with flannelette sheets, a must for sportsmen as far as Ces is concerned. Muscles and tendons should never be placed between cold cotton sheets.

We were shocked to read in the *Auckland Star* that Tommy had died. Minutes later, his son Rodney phoned to tell us. Tommy had been shovelling snow from their garden path on a very cold day when he died. We still visit the family when in England and communicate at Christmas and on each of our children's birthdays.

There was a closeness and caring between all the team and their families at Wigan then. Ces was always a marked man during games, when they could catch him. If they did and there was any dirty work, there was always a price for the opposition to pay. The retribution was usually led by Joe Egan and Ken Gee. When Ces was last in Wigan a reunion for the old players was arranged by Joe Egan, which was very much appreciated by Ces.

Later at Warrington, Australian Harry Bath and Ces were strange team mates. The first time I became aware of Harry was while sitting in the grandstand when Warrington were playing Wigan. Harry's foot slipped while Ces was lying on the ground. The next time I met Harry was when Ces joined Warrington and we were both in the doctor's surgery, so I thought I had better introduce myself. I am sure the slipped foot was on his mind.

Both Ces and Harry were strong-willed people who spoke their minds. The general belief was that they were bitter enemies. Underneath the critical remarks - mostly banter - was a deep respect for each other and our friendship has lasted to this day, even when we lived in different countries. When we made Australia our home we picked up our friendship just where we left off. Harry married Gwen while he was still with Barrow. She travelled from Australia for the ceremony.

Barrow must have been something of a culture shock after Sydney, just as Wigan must have been to Ces. Their daughter Diane was slightly older than Carolyn, their son Harry about the same age as Kim. Diane and Carolyn attended the same nursery school, Marfield in Grappenhall, Warrington. We still have photographs of them at school with the cups Warrington won one season, each holding a handle of the Challenge Cup. Carolyn still speaks of the time Diane hit her with a pink plastic handbag. Diane says it wasn't hard enough – "like father, like daughter", said I. Despite this slight setback they remained friends - in a no-holds barred situation, just like their fathers. Carolyn has lived in Sydney for many years now after graduating from Oxford. The Baths also were living in Sydney at the time she moved there, so Carolyn became part of the Bath family, the help and support given to her by them was as to their own, and will always be remembered and appreciated. We and Kim were also afforded the same help when we arrived on the Gold Coast where the Bath family lived for a while before returning to Sydney.

I have already mentioned the Owen family. It was at their home Elmfield in Wigan Lane where both our children were christened. Betty Owen's father was a retired Minister of the Church. They were for us lovely and moving ceremonies; the house was filled with white flowers and the Owen family were Godparents together with my brother Ron.

The forming of friendships in a new country can be a problem. These days footballers flit between hemispheres like migrating birds. It is indeed a strange fraternity which seems to feed on itself drawing the other half into the same frenetic world. Such is the life of a Rugby League player's wife.

The Mountford family at home at Appleton in the 1950s:
Carloyn, Ces, Edna and Kim

12. My return to New Zealand to keep my promise

Returning to New Zealand after a six-week sea voyage, we spent three weeks with my family on the West Coast and afterwards with my sister May and her family in Christchurch while we decided where to settle.

I renewed acquaintance with many old rugby friends and started initial preparation for setting up the New Zealand arm of the British Trailer Company. I was approached to do this about two weeks before leaving Warrington. Their chairman phoned me – it turned out he lived in the next road to us.

It was a busy time, learning about the product and road rules in New Zealand, which would need changing by the Roads Board if our product could be sold. This meant a parliamentary inquiry which I had to attend in Wellington. There were three days of hearings, but it took a few months for the result to come through.

During this time, I spent so much time in Auckland that we decided that this was the best place to live. We were invited by 'Snow' Telford, the national Rugby League coach at the time, and his wife Alma, to stay with them in Auckland until we found a house.

'Snow' was preparing the New Zealand team to tour Great Britain, so I helped him in any way I could. I did some coaching for the Kiwi team that was preparing to tour Great Britain. The team won the first test at Headingley 29-11, but lost the next two to lose the series 2-1. They were up against a strong Great Britain side, with players such as Billy Boston, Mick Sullivan, Alex Murphy and Neil Fox.

'Snow' is now deceased, but this time was the start of a firm friendship which still exists with his widow Alma. I visited Wellington on a regular basis, and stayed with Ken English and his wife Joan, another enduring friendship.

At the end of the Second World War, Rugby League was a major sport in New Zealand and we had the world at our feet. Yet we lost this opportunity. So the question demands to be asked: what went wrong? Is it that to some extent integrity, ethics and morals are now generally absent? In essence, I feel that Rugby League has lost its soul. I hasten to add this is not confined to New Zealand, but seems to be a world-wide trend. Money payments, what's in it for me and political manoeuvrings take a great deal of time and energy that should be put into improving the game. League is not alone in this; most other sports appear to be afflicted by the same virus. The result is that nothing is done at grass roots and consequently the game suffers. Possibly the commercialisation of sports has brought about the same morality one finds in today's business community. It appears the old values of hard work, honesty and integrity have been replaced by the marketing and public relations gurus of today.

During this time I was also involved with Rugby League as director of coaching. I ran a coaching scheme for the New Zealand Rugby Football League sponsored by the Rothmans Sports Foundation. The Foundation had a dedicated group of individuals covering a wide range of sports. This included Peter Snell of athletics, Don Clarke of Rugby Union, Bert Sutcliffe of cricket, Barry Truman of association football, Marian Smith and Dadir of squash, to name just a few. The directors were John Morris, formerly a headmaster of King's College, Ken Simich, a director of Rothmans and Colonel Frank Rennie of the New Zealand SAS.

These were good years for the New Zealand Rugby League. Wherever Rothmans Sports Foundation went, Rugby League was always there. The national coaching scheme we ran was of a high standard. Often there were sessions attended by the coaches of the various sports bodies throughout the country. We had a very good rapport with the Sports Foundation in all our endeavours. There was none of the back-biting so prevalent in sports bodies today. I think it was the case of the best man for the job, and we all had a sense of fair play, so that we acted for the good of all, not one's particular code.

The importance of my scheme was in instructing coaches how to teach, using the skills of the game and how to train players using the sprint track to improve their speed. 'Keep it simple' was my motto. I always referred to the fundamental skills of the game because I considered that the basics are vital to ensure a winning combination. Many of the senior players thought it was too simple, and didn't take notice of what I required. They thought they knew it all.

If players truly want to be stars they must master the basic skills and in doing so will enjoy the game and give a better display. It is a great pity that some Kiwi teams always looked so fit, yet their skills were so inadequate. This was New Zealand's main failure. The players are there but the dedication, ball skills and positional play are woefully absent. In addition, in my view, most of the New Zealand administration has no real idea of the basic skills so necessary in Rugby League. Talk, we know, is cheap, but action speaks louder than words.

Every month during the time I was with the Foundation I discussed coaching progress with John Morris. We got on very well as we shared many of the same basic beliefs. Coming from the Kings College of Auckland, John had a very good background in understanding human behaviour. He was no snob and set goals and standards for us to achieve. In 1972 he sent a message for me to call and see him, saying that he had received a delegation from the New Zealand Rugby Football League who were very critical of me. This came as a complete surprise because the Rugby League Council had never spoken directly to me on any concerns they may have had. John Morris told me that he didn't understand why the Council were so critical, because the Foundation had always been very satisfied with me and were grateful for the assistance I had rendered to them and the other sporting bodies involved. He advised me that in view of their unwarranted personal criticism I should resign. He said: "They are not worthy of your time. I know them." I accepted his advice and after 10 very satisfying years I left the Foundation. Despite their criticism and the fact that I was virtually ignored by the Council, to my surprise I was made a Life Member of the New Zealand Rugby Football League in 1972. I think that the administration of the game in New Zealand then was damaged by personal feuds between petty officials, many from Auckland. I felt that these were really small time bureaucrats, and totally unsuited for the leadership that New Zealand Rugby League badly needed.

This gave me an opportunity to return to England for a short period with my wife and family during which I helped out the Blackpool Rugby League Club. At this time Carolyn went to Oxford University to complete her education and Kim, who had been ill with glandular fever, was able to recuperate in a new environment. Kim, who was a New Zealand athletics champion and Olympic Games trialist, had caused some controversy at the Auckland Grammar Boys School because he played Rugby League.

Moving to New Zealand by Edna Mountford

So our wonderful and stimulating years in Wigan and Warrington came to an end and we left England in 1961, departing from Southampton on the Southern Cross. I had elected to travel by sea, thinking that we would see more and have a six-week holiday after the rigours of a busy rugby season

- yet I'm the world's worst sailor. We called at the Canary Islands where we had a guided tour, a ride on a camel (much like being on the ocean waves) a shopping trip and a swim at one of the beautiful beaches. This was after we had sailed through an unusually calm Bay of Biscay.

Our next stopover was Cape Town in South Africa, a beautiful city, as was Durban, the following port of call. In Cape Town we were taken around an African market, I felt faintly uneasy that we were intruding on their way of life and that they were being used as an attraction by tour companies. It was unlike any market I had previously seen, none of the bustle and sales talk, just people standing there looking very serious with their wares and maybe a bit reproachful.

There were features other than beauty about these cities, as we noticed on the bus tours. One caught glimpses in the distances of hovels, which contrasted starkly with the luxurious dwellings in the residential areas. However, that was in 1961 - a long time ago.

I'm a poor sailor but I had survived the Bay of Biscay and the Cape rollers into South Africa. Remarks were often made about the Australian Bight – "wait until you get there" which I did with some trepidation, quite unnecessarily because the crossing was incredibly smooth as had been the Indian Ocean during our 10 days there. We witnessed magnificent sunsets on the journey.

Our next ports of call were Melbourne and Sydney. Always on the horizon on this journey was the P & O liner Canberra, on her maiden voyage. There were quite a few teething problems with the Canberra, power failure being one of them. Mingling with the passengers in ports we heard stories of them having to sleep on deck while travelling through the tropics, because the air conditioning had been breaking down. There were other problems too, which is why the Southern Cross kept the Canberra in sight throughout most of the voyage.

Leaving Sydney, I had been lulled into a state of false security about sailing in troubled waters. Out of Sydney, the decks soon cleared as we bobbed about like a toy boat on the huge ocean waves of the Tasman Sea. The storm lasted three days, during which time we all stayed in our cabins listening to the sound of falling crockery and sliding furniture. The stewards and stewardesses also stayed in theirs and I understand that the only people in the dining room were our son Kim, aged seven, and his friend Ian McDonald - we didn't even know where they were half the time. The landfall dinner was cancelled, even the captain was missing, the doctor said he had a stomach upset to which I replied: "He's seasick like the rest of us." One day before arriving in Wellington the storm abated and we rather dishevelled passengers emerged to visit the engine room to get winter clothes from our luggage.

We hadn't been expecting to be met in Wellington, but looking out from the top deck we saw two people waving - it was a while before we realised it was Ces's brother Bill and his wife Isobel, who were on holiday there. I wasn't entirely looking forward to the Cook Strait crossing, but felt that if one could survive the Tasman one could survive any stretch of water. I could go on *ad infinitum* but this isn't a travelogue. Suffice to say we made lots of friends on the voyage and still visit and correspond with the McDonalds in Christchurch.

We spend the first six months in Christchurch staying with Ces's sister May, husband Tom and their two children Earl and Karen. This was after visiting the West Coast for a few weeks including Christmas 1961. Ces at that time spent some time working in New Zealand's largest city, Auckland, located in the North Island. Rugby League also was very strong in Auckland, so we decided that Auckland should be our permanent residence. Since Ces had left New Zealand, there had been a steady drift to the North Island, which meant there would be more opportunities there. So we took up residence in Auckland.

One evening two very apologetic policemen arrived on our doorstep asking for Ces. I told them he was out of town, when even more apologetically they asked where he was on the night of 19 December. Recovering from my surprise, I didn't have any difficulty remembering, because that night we had travelled from Blackball to Greymouth to let the children see Santa Claus arriving with real reindeer - a memorable event for them - and me.

The problem was that a serious offence had been committed against a woman travelling on the ferry between Christchurch and Wellington on that night. The offender had given his name as Ces Mountford, and as the policeman said, they had to investigate. Everything was sorted out eventually, but I did wonder what would have happened had I not been able to remember the happenings of that night. Indeed I did wonder, at that stage, whether we had done the right thing returning to New Zealand at all. I also had to explain the problem to a ten and seven year-old, who were with me listening to the policeman.

My association with teaching English as a foreign language came about because of our good friend Richard Lewis, a former Wiganer, now living in Hampshire. He has language schools throughout the world and as a Wigan supporter has followed Ces's career since his very first day at Central Park. He even remembers the weather on that day. Richard was available whenever Ces was touring and was very helpful in non-English-speaking countries, because he speaks 12 languages.

In 1980 Ces was manager-coach to the Kiwi Rugby League team to tour England and France. I decided to have a break myself and visit our daughter Carolyn in Sydney for about three weeks as a break in the middle of the 12-week tour. It was then suggested by the family that I may as well visit friends I have in the United States and return via Sydney. Then someone pointed out that it wasn't much further to carry on to England. This I resisted for quite some time because I knew what effort would be involved getting one person away, as the weeks before departure are very hectic with all the family somehow being involved with preparation. But for the first time there wasn't anything to stop me travelling at the same time as Ces and eventually I capitulated and began to make plans.

The trip was rather ambitious. First I had to write to relatives and friends inquiring whether it would be convenient to visit on certain dates. In England these visits had to relate to dates the New Zealand team were playing at certain venues. I saw two tests, the first at Wigan, and the second at Bradford, I also watched the Warrington game and the game at Fulham in London. Three weeks were spent in England, two in Sydney and the rest of the eight weeks I was away in various parts of the United States. There were 11 international flights in all.

There was a rule then in Rugby League circles that wives were not allowed to stay with players or managers on tour. In honouring this rule I often wonder whether wives or girlfriends wouldn't be a better proposition than the hangers-on usually associated with touring teams. In honouring this rule it had to be decided who was going to see who off in our situation, my wish was to go a week later than the team enabling me to draw breath after their departure, Ces thought differently and said he would like to farewell to me first so, consequently I made my departure date Wednesday, two days before the team left on Friday. Subsequent departure dates from other centres were also made at the same time. Much to my dismay the team's departure date was brought forward to Wednesday and I was left with the dilemma of whether to change all my flights or leave them as they were. Weak at the thought of all the labour involved, I decided on the latter and I'm sure that no criminal could have felt worse. I hid in a corner of the departure lounge until the team had disappeared from view before running the gauntlet of the farewell party. Once aboard I felt like a lone traveller because I was situated in the business section. I was not allowed to forget my position: the sentence "breaking the rules, eh" was oft heard from people in high places and the situation was caricatured in Tahiti when Ces and I, meeting for the first time since take-off, were walking about during the hour we had to wait looking for a French friend who said he would see us there. Up strode Bill Nesbitt, the tour manager, with a broad grin on his face and a notebook in hand. "Seen at 6am in Tahiti with lady" said he, pretending to write. Our friend eventually arrived, bestowing kisses and garlands of flowers and beads much to the team's amusement.

On the next leg to Los Angeles I had a young man from Nuie Island sitting next to me. It was the following lunchtime before I saw Ces again, when he walked down to say hello and stayed to have lunch with me as there was a vacant seat at the other side of the aisle, and more leg room. After lunch the young man asked Ces to take a photograph of him and me.

My hotel accommodation was also booked in advance. The team stayed near Disneyland, while I stayed near the airport. These arrangements also became a source of embarrassment as the team's hotel was changed at the last minute, to the one I had arranged. It was too late to change, so there I was in Los Angeles committing the unpardonable sin of staying in the same hotel as my husband. The desk clerk must have thought we were dotty, the players thought it incongruous and were vehement that they didn't mind at all where I slept, but in no way did we intend being caught up in the 'politics' of the situation. I crept away to my room, fully prepaid by me. Another rule forbade us females from riding in team buses. For this I cheated a little because I had little choice when the hotel minibuses picked us up from the airport. The touring party left Los Angeles for England the following day while I staying another night before my flight to Washington.

After the first test at Wigan I was forced to change my arrangements slightly and go to Harrogate where there was to be a celebration after the game and a rest day on Sunday. The manager of the Granby Hotel there had arranged for me to stay at a guest house just around the corner from the hotel, number three, I left the function at about 11.30pm with Ces bringing up the rear with my luggage. He insisted that number three on the same road was the place. My instinct was that it was around the corner, however, there was a light in number three and after trying unsuccessfully to unlock the door with the key I had been given we found the door opening. A woman poked her head out at which I said that a reservation had been made for me by the manager of the Granby Hotel, I was asked my name and given a very odd look while being told "this is a home for the elderly". I managed to see the funny side of this, but not Ces who grumbled and heaved my suitcase round the corner to the right number three. I spent two weekends in Harrogate, the second after the second Test, at another guest house on the same road; both were very good.

On the 1982 tour of Australia and Papua New Guinea, I was there for the two tests in Australia. I spent four days with Harry and Gwen Bath at 'Surfers Paradise', reminiscing about our times in Warrington, and the rest of the time in Sydney with our daughter Carolyn. The team, I thought, did very well considering that they sometimes only had four or five days together before each Test, and that during this time players from three countries had to be blended together to play the type of football required. Three to five seasons is the estimated time in England to mould together a team to the coach's requirements, longer in some instances. The tour of England and France certainly put the Kiwis on the map judging by demands from overseas clubs for players.

I didn't travel to Papua New Guinea, but some of the players told me that it was quite an experience and surprisingly still very cold at nights. There were some very nice gifts from the Papua New Guinea officials. One was a large carved shield, just about my height. We could use it to shelter behind and field the flak. There was also a magnificent wooden carving of the Kumul - bird of paradise - the Papua New Guinea national emblem. It is carved from a single piece of wood and the wing span is about three feet with the tail feathers spread about the same height. There is a twin-ended spear attached to the bottom that contains the inscriptions. It is impaled to our lounge wall by half a knitting needle, the wings outstretched ready to swoop on any unsuspecting victims sitting below. At each side is a photograph of our son and daughter and they told me that the spears are pointing directly at their ears.

Our most treasured possession from the tour is a magnificent silver salver, was presented on the last day to the manager/coach and inscribed: "To the Best Coach in the World from the 1982 Kiwis".

13. Interlude in Blackpool

My return to Blackpool in 1972 was not in my schedule when I headed for New Zealand from Warrington in 1961. However, when the request came from Gordon Emery, Chairman of the Blackpool Rugby League Club, for me to try and revitalise the team, which was going through a bad patch, some serious thinking had to be done.

The Blackpool club organised an apartment for us on the Promenade, South Shore. This was very convenient and pleasant, apart from when there was a gale blowing from the Irish Sea and sand was blown up from the beach into the streets and the shopping areas. The Council used a huge vacuum cleaner to suck in the sand and transport it back to the beach.

The Blackpool club was financially impaired. There wasn't an 'A' team and there were no schoolboy teams in the areas to provide footballers of the future and; most importantly; no money to buy players. I did what I normally do to build up a team: start coaching courses for teachers and students.

The club had a short register of players playing in the senior competition. I quickly realised that it wasn't the senior team that was most important, it was organising schoolboy football and finding a way for the young players to become members of the senior team. This then became my long-term plan. My approach to schoolboy football was similar to that of the Rothmans Sports Foundation in New Zealand - organising schools, enabling players to participate in coaching schools and teams and also organising teachers to participate in courses. Such a plan requires time, patience, planning, adequate resources and, above all, finance.

The coaching scheme I taught was originally organised by the late Bill Fallowfield, general secretary of the RFL, who arranged for academics from Oxford and Cambridge to teach coaches how to train and communicate their knowledge and skills. The course was taught initially at Lowther College in Wales and I attended with Trevor Foster and Frank Mugglestone.

The fundamental skills of our code were understood by those attending Lowther College. My plan was proceeding well at Blackpool until I requested finance for schoolboy football, to pay for jerseys, shorts, socks, and such like. There just wasn't any money available. Thus the possibility of Blackpool developing as a Rugby League stronghold was lost. Schoolboy football had to be developed for the club to proceed. I had visited many schools, received much support and had settled on six schools to set up a competition. No one seemed inclined to sponsor them. This was probably due to the fact that Blackpool is a holiday resort with not much industry. So that was the end of that, and eventually there was the demise of the club. They moved from the town, finally ending up at Chorley.

The late Gordon Emery, Blackpool chairman, and his family had put much effort into running a successful club, as had Reg Parker, George Lunn and many others, but like their compatriots in New Zealand, they wanted success immediately. They did not understand that to develop a successful Rugby League club, one has to begin at the bottom and work up. Many clubs around the world have tried to start at the top by buying players. Most have failed. A firm base of local players is necessary to work their way to the top and, when they get there, they need to know that vacancies for their positions will not go to expensive overseas signings; otherwise the situation arises that local players think that it is a waste of time taking up the game.

Mr Emery was in the theatre and cinema business with several venues in Blackpool, where his wife Doreen and children sold ice cream and chocolate in the intervals to raise money for the club. Blackpool was the centre of the entertainment business in the summer so there was always an entertainer at the Rugby League games and at the dog racing circuit, which was around the perimeter of the rugby field. I can remember Danny la Rue, the female impersonator, and many others.

The first team tried hard to reach a position on the Rugby League ladder, but it was always a struggle. We only won a handful of games in my time there, although attendances increased. Economy was the name of the game. Directors' wives did the after-match catering. Without an 'A' team it was a struggle to keep the first team going, especially if there were any injuries.

One charity game played pre-season was at Lancaster Prison. Blackpool was two players short so my son Kim and his brother-in-law were asked to step in, which they did, immediately after lunch. This caused a furore as Kim also played for the Fylde Rugby Union club. He was banned for life by Fylde and the English RFU. Questions were asked in Parliament - this was a topic of conversation for days on television and radio. Letters to and from Rugby Union Headquarters went on for months. By the time he was reinstated we were back in New Zealand.

We decided to return to New Zealand, sold the house and left behind many friends as we also did at Wigan and Warrington.

I have mentioned elsewhere the coaching schools I attended to attain a grade one certificate. The last pre-requisite of this was to personally advertise and conduct a coaching course in a non Rugby League playing town, provide staff and catering and clean out the place afterwards. It was quite a surprise for some people to see Ces Mountford on his knees scrubbing the floor, cleaning up after our courses.

During our time in Blackpool we made several trips overseas in the off-season with our daughter Carolyn and her husband driving through about eight European countries. London was revisited, as also were Wigan and Warrington where we met up with old colleagues and their families. One of our trips was to Winchester and the 15th century home of Richard Lewis and his wife Jane; this is one of their many language schools.

Kim worked for eight weeks in Winchester one summer teaching English as a foreign language and also organising the sports hour at 5pm for students. They were mainly Arabs when we were there so association football was their main interest.

After returning home to Lytham St Annes, near Blackpool, Richard phoned to ask whether he could call on us with a few of the Arab students. After lunch, which required a bit of thought due to their dietary requirements, we showed them around Blackpool, which has a culture far removed from their own. Many photographs were taken and they were quite excited to be going into places unheard of in their own country: Blackpool Tower, the Winter Gardens, Casino, Dixieland and many others. We must be in their photograph albums.

This second stay in England was very enjoyable; our daughter, Carolyn graduated at Oxford University at the time and we revisited Wales, Scotland and France.

While touring France, we met many of our good friends, Raymond Forge, Robert Fassolette, John Chapman, the late Puig-Aubert, Edouard Ponsinet, Felix Berghese, Tas Batieri and their wives and families. What exciting players they were. This was to me a very sentimental trip and well worth the return to England. The great French Rugby League teams of the 1950s, which arose after the Second World War, filled the grounds wherever they played. During the War, the Nazi-collaborationist Vichy government in France singled out Rugby League for termination and banned the code. Not so Rugby Union. Subsequently in France League has fallen on bad times. Competition from Rugby Union was the main cause coupled with the lack of good administration. This allowed the French Rugby Union to assume supremacy. Even when it was officially amateur, Rugby Union in France raided the French League clubs by offering players large signing on fees. It

Blackpool Borough 11 March 1973 versus Swinton.
Back row: From left: Les Greenough, Don Walker, Graham Seddon, Peter Crank, Jim Molyneux, Bob Sinleton, Paul Gamble, Dennis McCann.
Front row: Jimmy Johnson, Joe Aspinall, Joe Egan, Frank Delooze, Dave Gavaghan, Joe Lewis, Doug Robinson. (Photo courtesy Andrew Wheelwright)

was Australia in reverse. In France Rugby Union players have been professional for many years and Rugby League could not compete.

Blackpool: Edna Mountford remembers

Blackpool has seven miles of promenade and three piers, South, Central and North, with a concert pavilion at the end of each, in addition to deck chairs and the usual holiday attractions. The entire length of the promenade has hotels facing the sea, ranging from zero to five or no stars. I always enjoyed walking along, staring in, watching people eating, drinking, dancing and enjoying themselves.

There is just about every kind of entertainment to be enjoyed in Blackpool. One of my first recollections was a ballet in the Tower Ballroom at 4pm daily, given by a children's dance troupe. There was a zoo and aquarium in the Tower and nightly dancing to the strains of Reginald Dixon at the Mighty Würlitzer organ. Recitals were given daily and last, but not least, one could be whisked to the top of the tower to an unforgettable attack of vertigo while looking over the rail.

106

There was also dancing nightly at the Winter Gardens Ballroom and in the same building there would also be a live show. There were many shows nightly in Blackpool with stars of the entertainment world, throughout the summer. After spending the days outdoors, one could attend a different show nightly for quite some time. This was usual fare in most holiday resorts in Britain. That is what I missed most in New Zealand - something to watch at night while on holiday. There is a casino now to which we were taken by Gordon and Doreen Emery and Reg and Shirley Parker. The late Gordon was chairman of Blackpool Borough RLFC at the time and was also in the theatre business. Reg was a member of the Rugby League Council.

We were staying in an apartment on the front and at times sand was blown half-way up the stairs during winter. It was a rough stretch of coastline in winter and a visit to see the lifeboat was a must for us and our children when we were on holiday.

In 1972, it was a kind of a working holiday as we tried to revive the Blackpool club. We originally stayed in an apartment on the waterfront at South Shore while we looked for a house. We decided to live just out of Blackpool at Lytham St Annes. Lytham and St Anne's are two separate resort villages, but lumped together as a postal address. It was to Lytham we went on one of our house hunting expeditions. At the advertised address we found no one at home, but at another house saw two ladies talking over the fence. Ces approached one of them to inquire about the owner of the house we had come to see. She stated that she had been wondering whether to sell her own house and return to the Isle of Man from where she came, because she was homesick. This was on a Thursday. On the following Monday we were installed in the house having brought it lock, stock and barrel and taken the lady to the airport *en route* for the Isle of Man. This was the Mountford method, seeing an opening on the Rugby League field and darting through. He dances like this too, as we weave our way round a dance floor.

While we were in Blackpool our son Kim, who at 16 had grown to the size of a huge second-row forward, took a temporary job as a bouncer at one of the clubs on the promenade. Business in winter was so bad that he said he felt he was hired to bounce customers in, rather than out.

Our happy and invigorating League interlude in Blackpool alas ended all too soon and we headed back to New Zealand - once more crossing the world as ambassadors for Rugby League. The distance between our two countries was more than 12,000 miles, but we always felt strongly the unbreakable bonds that unite League people everywhere.

Great times at Warrington

Warrington 1954-55: Back row: S. Lloyd, H. Bath, F. Wright, R. Ryan, A. Heathwood, G. Lowe, J. Hamblett, E. White, S. Phillips, J. Challinor, T. McKinney, B. Bevan, R. Haywood. Middle: L. Hocknell, S. McCormick, L. Horton, F. Berry, A. Naughton, F. W. Davies, E. Frodsham, R. Price, C.R. Mountford. Front: G. Helme, J. Honey

1959 Lancashire Cup Final: Bevan's try, as Tom van Vollenhoven kicks at the ball (Photo: courtesy Robert Gate)

14. New Zealand again

I returned to New Zealand in 1974 and ran coaching courses at Waitera, Taranaki, Taupo and Turangi. I was interested in coaching and selecting, but was not given the opportunity until 1979 to coach the New Zealand team and in 1980 to select. When the 1979 British tour to New Zealand was planned, I was asked whether I was available as coach for the Kiwi team. I got the job ahead of 17 candidates. I agreed to be coach, but surprisingly I wasn't involved in the team selection, something I thought would be automatic. The trouble was I did not think in the same way as the Auckland members of the New Zealand Council. They all wanted to have a finger in the pie.

The first meeting of selectors was held in Auckland and I was invited to attend even thought I had no say in the selection. The selectors made their choices with the first eight players named coming from Auckland, nominated by the Auckland representative, Bill Sorensen, a former international and an outstanding player. I queried his nominations, saying the selectors were there to select a New Zealand team, not an Auckland one. Bill got to his feet and walked out. He was recalled by the convenor, who asked him to stay, which he did.

The Auckland dominance was still there although I suggested then that the New Zealand Rugby League get its house in order quickly. Professional Rugby Union is now here and we could have a French situation on our hands in New Zealand. Many of the former Rugby Union stars now playing League could go to the Union fold, as could a number of League stars. While Australia would cope, I doubt whether New Zealand could. There are also many Pacific Islanders who have changed codes and could return to Union.

In 1979 we played three games against Great Britain, losing the first test in Auckland and the second in Christchurch. Players badly needed in the team were dropped by the selectors without even consulting me. The selectors just didn't understand forward play and what was required. We then won the third test. With good selection we could and should have won the series. I know that the administration at that time relied on sponsors to keep solvent, but I believe that sponsors should not have a say in the selection. I had my say after winning the third test, which most of the small-time New Zealand administrators didn't appreciate.

In 1980, it was New Zealand's turn to tour England and France. I was left to wait and see who would be the selectors, who was to be business manager and who was to be tour manager / coach. It turned out that I was the last, with Bill Nesbit as business manager. I can say the 1980 Kiwis laid the foundation for the next five years' international Rugby League. Good results were achieved in 1980, with New Zealand sharing the honours with both England and France, but most importantly, the style of football played by the Kiwis encouraged the English clubs to take an interest in our style of play. We played an open game, based on the fundamentals. The British fans liked our methods and we received many appreciative media comments, praising us for the open, fast, innovative and gripping way of play.

In that team there were several players who became legendary: Graeme West, Kevin Tamati, Tony Coll, Mark Broadhurst, Alan Rushton, Howie Tamati, Mark Graham, Bruce Gall, Hugh McGann, John Whittaker, Gary Prohm, Gordon Smith, Fred Ah Kuoi, Dane O'Hara and James Leuluai. Gary Prohm was looked upon as a forward in Auckland but played on the wing and centre for New Zealand, making a success of these positions. One player, who impressed in the second test against England at Bradford, when Mark Graham left the field injured, was Ray Baxendale. Ray made a good impression with the crowd, playing the game of his life. There was always keen competition between Mike O'Donnell and Gary Kemble at fullback, while Kevin Fisher produced good form at centre. Gordon Smith and Shane Varley at half-back were two exceptional players. It was good to be blessed with so much competition for team places.

Our forwards moulded well into an excellent combination. Tony Coll of the West Coast played exceptional rugby. I rate him to be one of the best forwards ever, on a par with the great Charlie McBride. It was with these players that we toured Australia in 1982, unfortunately losing both tests, the first by 11-8 in the last minute of the game in Brisbane. The team played magnificently. Unfortunately, full-back Mike O'Donnell was not available for the tour, so Gary Kemble became full-back. It was a mistake by Gary which lost us the game, though he was consistently a splendid player. Howie Tamati, later a New Zealand coach and New Zealand Universities coach, made the hooking position his own after Alan Rushton was injured.

This tour was the first occasion when New Zealand players based in Australia were called upon to play for New Zealand. There was a noticeable difference, not in loyalty, but in attitude, something rather difficult to define, when using players contracted to Australian clubs. At that time, I believed that when a New Zealand touring team was selected, it should be a New Zealand domiciled team. It was impossible for players to have two loyalties, the club, which is their livelihood, and the touring team, which is really an abstraction. A good manager / coach can build up young players, but I feel that it was almost impossible to get professional players to change their allegiance from their professional clubs. The only time I would have selected players playing in other countries would be for World Cup team competitions, State of Origin games or one-off Tests, but not for touring teams for test series.

It was better to develop and promote players on tour, rather than bring players from overseas to take places in test teams. The selected home-nation based players inevitably get better and they do not have divided loyalties. The reason we had such a fine team in 1980 was that they had come through the ranks from all over New Zealand and been cultivated over the years.

For the 1981 season the New Zealand team more or less picked itself. We had set the foundation the previous year and so we won the test series against France in New Zealand.

Prior to the 1982 season I had written to the New Zealand Rugby Football League informing them that I would be unavailable for the 1982 Australian tour and suggested that it was time to school someone else for the position. We had, at that time, many coaches in New Zealand who had gone through the grades, passed exams and were, in my opinion, capable of following on from me. One I remember was Alan Marshall from Taranaki. Alan's team had beaten Auckland five times, which was an achievement, given the size of Auckland and the relatively minor Taranaki League. I received almost daily calls from New Zealand Rugby League's governing body to remain as the coach and I was finally persuaded to stay. I felt it would be good experience for Alan Marshall to be my assistant coach.

Much has been said in the media about the feud I was supposed to have had with Graham Lowe. The real truth is that I have only met him on two or three occasions. The first time was when Kiwi captain, Mark Graham, brought him to my home in Auckland, because Graham Lowe wished to coach in England and wanted some information about what possibilities there were. I gave him as much information as I could. He went on to England and, as everyone knows, became a successful coach for Wigan. The second time I met him was when I was with the 1982 touring team in Australia. I was told by New Zealand Council members, Ron McGregor and Alan Gore, that Graham Lowe was to speak to the players prior to the Queensland test match. This was done without seeking my views on the matter. To them I was just a coach and had to do what I was told without consultation or discussion. Obviously Graham Lowe thought I had been briefed, but as he himself was to find later, communication was not a forté of the New Zealand administration.

I didn't agree with this as I felt it would interfere with the pattern of our usual preparation. Despite this, Graham duly came along, obviously believing that I had consented to his presence. I can remember a video being shown depicting a blind man running across a desert. I had my doubts about this idea, which came from the gridiron game.

When Graham Lowe was given permission to talk to the players, I did not know that he had already been promised the job of coach until he announced it personally in Brisbane. It would have been polite to wait until the New Zealand Rugby League made the announcement after they had informed me. Lowe understands the media and in true American style used it to perfection. At any rate he proved to be a successful ideas man in tune with the modern game. I know only too well how he felt when Wally Lewis' Australian team defeated New Zealand in the last minute at Carlaw Park. Leading, and with time on the clock, New Zealand kicked down field. The ball was fielded by Wally Lewis, passed to Gary Jack, and on to winger John Ribot to score the winning try. It was ironically the same sort of mistake that caused us to lose the first Test in Brisbane in 1980, when Gary Kemble kicked the ball downfield, when all he had to do was to retain possession.

Lowe's premature revelation was the first I knew of his appointment. My reaction at the time was that my work on the coaching coaches scheme in New Zealand appeared to have been a waste of time. As far as I knew Lowe only had club-coaching experience. He had one advantage. As a relative unknown he had the support of the NZRL Council and the sponsors. I felt that my time travelling the country coaching coaches, instead of being an asset to the game, had been jettisoned overboard by impatient administrators who wanted immediate results and did not recognise or understand the need for building on a stable foundation. Lowe had promised to give them the results they craved. I was also less than pleased when the Lowe announcement was made in such a way as to indicate that I had been given the push. This was not the fault of Graham Lowe, but of the governing body, who over the years had a lot to answer for. In retrospect I felt I was used, bridging the gap until Lowe could take over. I surely deserved better. It was poor reward for years of service.

My real fault was that I loved the game and always acted in furthering its interests. When I was director of coaching, I was also secretary to the New Zealand Rugby Football League, a position for which I received little

112

remuneration. I also represented Taranaki on the Rugby League Council of Management and very much enjoyed my association with Taranaki. I was frequently invited to various functions in the Taranaki province.

At that time, the emphasis by the administration was on saving money. There was no such thing as business class air travel. Many times I paid my own expenses. What a contrast with the present. My mind boggles at the amount of money spent these days on accommodation alone.

Basic requirements

As coach, I laid down certain basic requirements with which all players had to conform. This created problems with some team members who did not like discipline and felt they knew it all. There can only be one coach and he must lead and show the players that he knows the game, and will get the best out of them. I well remember an instance during the 1981 test against Australia. Two of the players appeared to lack the enthusiasm for the hard play that a test always brings forth. I told them both what I thought of them, that I felt they were frauds, that they were only in the team because they were Aucklanders and hadn't the guts to meet Australians head on. I then left the room, though I could hear the uproar my remarks had caused. Both players rose to the occasion and played brilliantly. The end result was that both players received lucrative contracts from Sydney clubs. Their signings were opposed by the New Zealand Rugby League, but the well known criminal lawyer, Kevin Ryan, proved that the New Zealand Rugby League was in restraint of trade and Peter Moore's Canterbury Bankstown were the richer by two players. Interestingly I had used the same legal defence when I transferred from Wigan to Warrington.

Subsequently, the NZRL and the Australian Rugby League agreed to prevent any further signings. In future all New Zealand players going to Australia had to have the written permission of the NZRL.

It was not generally known in New Zealand that although I was the coach, I took no part in the selection of the team. There were many talented players throughout the country who felt they should have been selected and I received much abuse from Auckland and the Waikato clubs' supporters.

It was not until 1980 that I became a selector. Many a time I would receive derisory remarks made to me in the streets when followers of the game thought that my selections didn't conform to theirs. This lack of communication by the New Zealand administration was been another characteristic of the NZRL. Coach Tony Gordon was told about his sacking prior to a team being picked for trials. Lory Blanchard was treated the same way. It is known in New Zealand as the 'tall poppy syndrome'. People like to cut down anyone who is successful - Rugby League is no exception.

Sir Robert Muldoon, a former Prime Minister, used to say nine years at the top was long enough for anyone. Perhaps some of the New Zealand administrators should have taken a good look at themselves and taken Oliver Cromwell's advice, when he said to the Rump Parliament: "Away with you. You have sat here too long".

In New Zealand coaches are in a very tenuous situation. My first experience of this was in France in 1980. Someone said to me: "see you next year", at which Ron McGregor, who was with me at the time, replied: "you won't see him next year, this is his last trip". The same thing happened in Nice, word for word, when former university player John Chapman said goodbye to me. I have heard it said to some coaches at the airport prior to departure. This seems to be the pattern of existing coaches for the last 30 years. Coaching is not a question of taking turns - a share of the goodies, so to speak, or a reward for service. Coaches are in a different situation to council members, many of whom were token figures, wanting a trip as a reward for being on the council. They see anyone with a different approach as a threat, and they act on what is good for them and not for the game.

Confirmation of the problems I faced came in an article by Joseph Romanos in the *New Zealand Listener* in 1994. He wrote: "Mountford was also treated shabbily. On his return to New Zealand, he upset a few crusty officials by suggesting the sport here could benefit from some new blood at the top administrative level. After that he was forever on the back foot. The league recognised his quality, but would not give him the Kiwis. Instead, Mountford instigated the Rothmans coaching scheme - which soon expanded to rugby, athletics, netball and cricket. And, as League's director of coaching, he did tremendous work, touring the country, giving clinics and talks, and setting up coaching programmes. But the league ruled that the national coaching director could not be Kiwis' coach. Why this should be so was never made clear. Mountford, when he was allowed to coach the Kiwis, put together a top-class team. The likes of Mark Graham, Kevin and Howie Tamati, Olsen Filipaina, Gary Prohm and Mark Broadhurst learnt their stuff under him and carried the torch through to the Lowe era."

15. Touring

Touring with a Rugby League party has many facets, the main ones being having to leave one's family for lengthy periods, the pleasure of meeting old friends and making new ones, visiting other countries and getting to know more about one's own.

With a disciplined party there were few problems, a situation I always tried to achieve. There has been the odd player, maybe touring for the first time, enjoying his freedom who thought, mistakenly, that being in another country allowed him to overstep the mark without being noticed. The other players would soon bring such a person to heel. I rarely had to step in.

Although we didn't tour in New Zealand, I did much travelling in my role as national director of coaching for the Rothmans Sports Foundation.

With my fellow coaches, we would attend, in a body, schools, colleges and universities throughout New Zealand, showing teachers how to coach Rugby League and students and senior players how to teach and play. This was the start of university or student Rugby League from which teams were selected to tour overseas.

I also travelled widely during the week in New Zealand at this time. At any venue I was ably assisted by my Maori and Pakeha friends. The amount of work done by these people was amazing, especially the women, who worked long hours cooking and cleaning with no remuneration. We visited country towns and the main cities. The result of those visits was that we were able to put together teams for tours, which, in my opinion, were first rate, in playing ability, behaviour and particularly in public relations. It was a rule that players made the effort to move around and talk to people at functions, not gather together in a group of their own. This was good for the game, the players and the team's public image.

Dressing suitably is an essential discipline. Teams were expected to arrive at their destination looking smart in their uniforms, and should leave their own shores looking the same, changing into tracksuits in the plane for long journeys. They were also expected to attend dinners in their hotels in regulation blazers. Lunch and breakfast were more casual with players in kit ready for training. Players were aware that they had to discipline themselves over sleeping, eating and drinking, knowing that their prime purpose of being there was to play good rugby. There were too many names for me to mention, many of them now out of contact, but I still maintain friendships with some.

I always appreciated a return trip to England, which, after 15 years and a later spell in Blackpool was a second home for me and a first home for my wife and children.

I regularly visited Otago University in Dunedin, South Island New Zealand, for coaching schools and lecturing. It is surprising to find that many students of that time are now in Australia following their respective careers. I sometimes hear from them. During student tours I was ably assisted by Bud Lisle, whose knowledge of the game and general ability was most helpful.

I first visited France with the Wigan team. I was a touring rookie then and didn't know what to expect, but did enjoy the experience. After many tours I began to look upon France as my third home, because I knew so many people there.

I have visited La Cité, Carcassonne, many times to play Rugby League and for holidays. It is walled, very quaint and has winding, hilly streets - I lost my wife there once. It is contained in the larger metropolis of Carcassonne. I am a Freeman of La Cité and on my medal is engraved the name of Simon de Montfort. The history is fascinating. From north to south, France is a fascinating country.

I have mentioned Puig-Aubert - who originated from the Carcassonne area of France and was a prolific goal kicker, but, like me, not orthodox. He hardly ever missed, a true legend of French Rugby League. Another two were Jean Galia, who turned from Rugby Union to start Rugby League in France and Max Rousié, a brilliant back who, at times took off his boots to play. These were but three of many legends of Rugby League in France. Puig-Aubert was not fond of regular training and hardly ever did any, but being a natural, as they say, he played 45 times for France.

During several tours to France and other countries I was assisted by Richard Lewis, the writer of the preface in this book, who is a long time friend and knowledgeable supporter of Wigan and secondly a linguist, whose help was invaluable. I toured France both as manager of the New Zealand team in 1980 and also as manager of the excellent New Zealand Universities team in 1989. On both occasions the French tours followed tough matches in England; the players looked forward to seeing a new country and were able to relax, though of course, they played hard enough once they got on the field.

The French always lived up to their reputation of good hosts and we were treated to wonderful food, not to mention wine, after each encounter. French cuisine is, of course, considerably more exotic than New Zealand food, though their lamb is no better than ours. Whereas a typical New Zealand meal consists of two or three courses, a French dinner may have six or seven courses. Instead of putting several things on one plate as we do - for instance meat, potatoes and salad - they tend to eat things separately and spin out the dinner over several hours. In New Zealand we eat to satisfy our appetite and while the French do that too, a dinner for them is an important social event which can drag on until well after midnight. Very often they don't start eating till around 9.00pm. They are supposed to sit down at 7.30pm or 8.00pm, but usually chat and gossip for at least an hour, sometimes more. Our boys, used to eating much earlier in New Zealand, would be getting hungry by seven and absolutely ravenous by nine. Of course the French would fill in the time drinking wine or *kir royale* - a mixture of champagne and blackcurrant juice. This went down well with our players, too, but I had to keep an eye on them, because they were unused to such an exotic mixture. In general, however, the players disciplined themselves well and did not have too many problems.

When the actual dinners began, we would all be sitting at long dining tables with the French players and officials and very warm socialising would ensue. The French can be tough on the field, but seat them at a dining table and they make the most charming dinner companions that you can imagine. They may win or lose a match, but they are winners every time over dinner. I noticed that French people can drink a great deal of red wine - for hours - without really getting drunk. Of course, they are merry, but always seem to be in control and mindful of their duties as hosts.

On one occasion we had just played the French army in Fontainebleau - a charming city one hour's drive from Paris. The army laid on a splendid dinner for us in a huge dining room at three long tables laid out L-shaped. This meant that we were all looking at each other as we dined - a very sociable and cosy arrangement. I remember the evening went very well. Several French generals attended, looking very impressive in their smart, beautifully-ironed uniforms. They made several speeches saying nice things about New Zealand. Richard Lewis was with us and he translated a lot of what was said, in between a few glasses of red wine. The dinner went on and on, course followed course, speech followed speech. We had to say a few words, too, but of course we were no match for French oratory.

We found that we could better them, though, in one area (apart from the match itself), that was in singing. The French players had started the entertainment off with a vigorous rendition of *Alouette*, but I didn't think they were all that much in tune. Soon our boys responded with some New Zealand songs; we had some good Maori voices in the party and we were clearly in the ascendant. The French did some better numbers later on, but when our players started singing in Maori and doing a *haka*, the French had to admit defeat. Richard remarked to me that when white New Zealanders begin singing in Maori, they actually change their cultural make-up and start behaving like Pacific Islanders. As a native New Zealander, I had never noticed this, but Les Perkins, an Australian friend of Richard's who was touring with us, said the same thing.

Richard's ability to speak French proved useful to our party in an incident which occurred on the same tour when we continued on to the south and played in Limoux. During the game, one of our forwards found himself at the bottom of a pile of bodies and someone accidentally sat on his face. He was in considerable discomfort for the rest of the half and we took him off at the interval. He was examined by a French doctor, who confirmed that he had suffered a rather badly broken jaw. He was taken to hospital to be operated on. Because he was kept in overnight, he missed a splendid Limoux dinner, but he wouldn't have been able to eat anyway.

We were due to leave early next morning, but the doctor told us that John would have to be kept in hospital for a few days. His tour was, of course, over, but there was another problem. He was still under sedation and was not due to be awakened before noon, at which time the doctor would have to give him some important instructions regarding mouth movements while they did some further examination. The difficulty was that nobody in the hospital spoke English (and our forward certainly didn't speak French). An interpreter would be needed and there was no one on hand. Of course, Richard volunteered to stay on, so he waved us off at the railway station. When our player woke up, Richard went through the routines with him and all was well. He was a bit fuzzy to say the least, was wondering where we had all gone and was glad to see Richard's familiar face among half a dozen strange French ones peering down at him. Richard's reward was another splendid dinner that night at the home of the Limoux club's president.

Puig-Aubert

The highlight of that particular tour, for Richard and me, was when we visited Puig-Aubert at his home. He was of course getting on in years, but the old twinkle was there in his eyes (and perhaps in his feet) and he still had a regal presence sitting there proudly on his sofa under a huge photograph of the French team which he had led to victory in the 1951 series in Australia.

He died not long afterwards, but we took away with us an indelible memory of the graceful twilight of one of League's great legends.

Robert Fassolette has long been associated with Rugby League as a player, referee and administrator. He has coached University teams and also French Army teams, from whom I once received a magnificent medal during one of my visits. Robert visited us in New Zealand when he was over there on refereeing duties.

Another colourful French character was Antoine Blain, one-time President of the French Rugby League who usually accompanied the team on overseas trips. Antoine was a great storyteller and usually had an audience around him. His stories always had a twist in the tail.

France was a difference culture altogether. National and University teams visited often and also entertained French teams in New Zealand. Rugby League in France has had a tough time since World War Two. Many individuals have tried to lift the standard of administration which would have ensured success down to the line. French teams are very exciting to watch, flamboyant in fact, and have had some characters during the years.

The war-time ban did great damage. France lost two generations of players, the young ones who were lost to the game when it was banned and the older ones who were playing when the war broke out.

When French teams visited New Zealand they usually played a game in Rotorua, where they were entertained after the game by Maoris who are great entertainers and orators, their speeches being delivered in Maori and English were lengthy. One time the French team rose to leave after the first speech and I had to run to the door to cut them off and turn them back.

Papua New Guinea

Tours to Papua New Guinea are well remembered. They added a unique atmosphere to games, in their colourful dress, huge smiles, not forgetting the music. The players were natural athletes with great enthusiasm for the game of Rugby League, which is a national treasure. At first, they were a big culture shock but the overriding memory is of friendly, smiling people and according to videos seen since, me talking too fast and at great length to players. As I mentioned before we have several outstanding wall hangings from this country and we were well supplied with excellent coffee from their plantations. When PNG teams visited New Zealand they brought a never-ending supply of this product. Teams from these climates really felt the cold in New Zealand. I was also involved with student Rugby League and there was always a team from Papua New Guinea in the World Cup series. While we found it hot in PNG they found it quite cold in New Zealand and wore woolly caps and gloves.

It was the same in Fiji - a very different culture but the same friendly, sincere people who also felt the cold in New Zealand. Both of these nations had very talented athletes and fitness which only needed to be honed into any type of sport they choose.

In PNG spectators would walk for miles and days to watch games and when they arrived their grandstand would be branches of trees. They didn't have to travel so far in Fiji but the enthusiasm shown by spectators helped greatly in the progress of their athletes.

At home

Of course, I was also often involved in meeting teams touring New Zealand, both at professional and student levels. Tour parties to New Zealand found Rotorua amazing but usually declined an invitation by the Maoris to swim nude in the hot pools in bath houses. These were the equivalent of health spas and very beneficial, especially for injured footballers.

In 1954, the New Zealand Rugby League wrote to Ces to congratulate him on Warrington's success in the 1953-54 season.

16. No problem mate, no worries

My involvement in the game saw me receive some honours. In 1987 I was awarded the MBE in the Queen's Birthday Honours list. This was quite a surprise. I received a letter a few weeks before the announcement, but was not allowed to disclose it to anyone. Early in the morning of the announcement Edna and I were driving to Taranaki, listening to all the announcements on the car radio. We were going to a function or Howie Tamati's wedding, our memory isn't what it used to be. Brian Nordgren phoned us at 7.00am thinking he would be the first to offer congratulations, but we missed his call and many others. We think it was Rugby League followers who organised support for me to be given the honour.

We travelled to Wellington for the ceremony, which was held at Government House. The presentation made by the Governor General, the Rt Rev. Paul Reeves, we had previously met the former Archbishop. When I was receiving my medal from the Governor General there was a rather longer than usual conversation. When I returned to my seat Edna asked me: "What was all that about?" I replied that the Governor General said that he was the "Ring in" who married our daughter some 12 years before. This was correct. Carolyn was married at the University chapel, Auckland, the then Rev. Paul Reeves was called upon to stand in for the University Chaplain who couldn't be present on that day. He is also the uncle of Howie Tamati, a friend and Rugby League player in my teams of the time. There was a reception afterwards at Government House where we were able to recall those past moments with the Governor General.

The Hall of Fame

The Hall of Fame ceremony had a different procedure to the MBE. In December 1990, I received a letter saying that I had been nominated for the award together with an invitation for us both to visit Wellington for three days. This we did and met up with other nominees at the hotel. As this was the inaugural ceremony there were 75 sportsmen and sportswomen and seven teams. The time range was over 150 years, as New Zealand was celebrating its 150th anniversary, to a cut off point of 1979. Some of the awards were posthumous, but most of those elected were there. It was great to renew acquaintances. They came from near and far, A few names I can remember include Sir Edmund Hillary, Peter Snell, the late Jack Lovelock,

Jean Batten, Des White, Bert Sutcliffe, Bob Charles, Barry Briggs and Dame Naomi James. We all assembled in the auditorium of the hotel to be told that all nominees had been selected; then each was presented on stage. It was a live television programme, then there was entertainment and dinner together with breakfast the following morning when the recipients were questioned for live radio and answered with their mouths full of bacon, egg, toast, etc.

It was a very impressive, well-organised function. The Hall of Fame is now housed in the magnificent railway building in Dunedin.

Legend of League

We flew from the Gold Coast to Auckland for the ceremony. The citation is very long in a large frame, to be honoured by Rugby League was very special.

Local politics

While living in Auckland (Mount Albert) I was nominated for the Mount Albert Council and duly elected being involved for several years which was a change from Rugby League. In Wigan I had a deputation to our home asking me to stand for Parliament, this I declined.

Moving to Australia

My life took a new turning when we moved to Australia's famed Gold Coast, 'Surfers Paradise'. I still follow Rugby League.

It would be wrong of me to say that I am completely happy and contented, because I miss the hurly-burly that is associated with Rugby League. It is part of my life, to which I have dedicated my whole energies, sometimes to the detriment of my family and most importantly, my wife and ever loyal supporter, Edna. Professional footballers' wives do make many sacrifices, often unseen and unheard. My immediate family have suffered the barbs of officialdom.

Like the English language, Rugby League is a living game. It changes to suit modern conditions. It must do so or it will perish.

The game was born in adversity and over the last 100 years there has always been a division between the affluent, public school types in the south of England and the working class people in the north. The concept of true blue amateurism was trumpeted to the full by the snobbish Union administrators, who were vocal in their criticisms of Rugby League.

In my own country, the first Rugby League touring team was sneeringly called the 'All Golds' because it was assumed they were only playing for money. That team had the last laugh as they had a very successful tour, both financially and on the pitch. In Australia especially in New South Wales and Queensland, Rugby League quickly became the number one winter sport. There it has always met the challenge of Rugby Union. Like the Coasters, the Australians have always been advocates of a fair go. This to some extent was due to the quality and brilliance of the initial Australian players, many of whom transferred from the 15-a-side game.

Edna Mountford: Moving to Australia

I enjoyed our involvement with University Rugby League. I never thought that at the age of 70 I would be selling raffle tickets in downtown Auckland and other shopping centres to raise funds for University Rugby League. The first time accosting a pedestrian was the most difficult. After that it was a piece of cake. The worst part was a cold wind blowing from the harbour.

Neither did I expect to be cooking sausages, etc. fund raising for University teams after games or selling t-shirts to French players, helping them to try on for the right fit. Janet Lubbock and I enjoyed these times.

Australia

Just when I thought we settled into retirement in New Zealand, we arrived in Australia. It was a difficult decision to make in some ways, but not in others because our children had been here for some time, Carolyn in Sydney and Kim in Surfers. Moving countries isn't ever easy, although we had become almost experts having moved from England to New Zealand, New Zealand to England, England to New Zealand and now New Zealand to Australia. This last time was somewhat more difficult, because prior to moving, Ces spent five weeks touring England and France with the New Zealand University Rugby League team while I attempted to sell the house.

We had already visited Australia many times for holidays, family visits and rugby tours and always found people to be most helpful. Help is required when one arrives as a settler but "no problem mate, no worries" was the standard reply to any request we made. Australia must be the only country we have lived in with so few problems and worries. It is truly the 'lucky country'. The help we received from all concerned was phenomenal and even though moving was a big hassle, we settled without too much trauma and a resolve that this was definitely the last move.

Without the worries of Rugby League, life here seems like a constant holiday. We watch Rugby League on television and compare then and now. There is no comparison really, either in the pattern of play or remuneration. Players are well paid these days, but they have different worries: more money means more responsibility and more pressure with cheque books ever at the ready and more criticism if one's play doesn't perform to expectations.

We weren't entirely out of the League scene, because Ces spends many hours reminiscing with Harry Bath and Bob McMaster when our families meet regularly. We were also invited to functions along with Gold Coast players. Ces was also able to play golf, which he didn't have much time for before, except when teams were preparing for tests as a means of relaxation.

There isn't as much change in the lifestyle from New Zealand to Australia as there is from Great Britain to New Zealand though there is a much warmer climate in Queensland. For the first time Rugby League hasn't played a major role in our lives.

I believed that the Wembley Challenge Cup Final was the Zenith in Rugby League but since residing in Queensland now I'm not so sure. The State of Origin games in Australia are something quite unlike anything I have ever experienced before. I have watched them on television and attended a game in Brisbane.

The atmosphere in England centres on the two towns involved in the weeks preceding the Challenge Cup Final. The rivalry was usually friendly. In Sydney and Brisbane it's much more, the atmosphere is there in large measure and colours the whole time between games. There isn't much work done after noon on State of Origin day and woe betide anyone who has the temerity to telephone between the hours of 7.30 and 10.00pm.

When all is over, the victors race to all parts of the field where the followers bend low in admiration and adulation. There is much hugging and kissing between players and management and partying goes on until all hours. The vanquished slink off, with my sympathy, and no hugs or kisses, maybe a consoling pat on the back. There is no victory round for them, and if there is partying it is more to drown the sorrows than a celebration. After the three games it is all over until the following year.

Now we are in Australia, in our twilight years, living in Robina. I think this must be the area where retired players are put out to grass. Tommy Bishop who played for St Helens, Ken Kearny who played for Leeds and more recently Kurt Sorenson, all live here, to mention a few.

It wasn't really a difficult decision to make this, hopefully, last move. Our son, daughter and grandchildren were already living here. One has to be ruthless with possessions, but not the box loads of rugby memorabilia, which travel with us everywhere. It wasn't easy for Ces to cut his links with Rugby League. However, we do appreciate the almost eternal sunshine and warmth that is kind to old rugby injuries. I know now that apart from family and friends in New Zealand we should have been here years ago.

The very relaxed lifestyle is a far cry from the frenzy of rugby life and the cold in England and sometimes New Zealand. A gentle breeze here is considered cold.

Our time is spent between Sydney and the Gold Coast. Our daughter and her family visit us at Christmas and Easter, while we visit Sydney between times and sometimes when Carolyn goes overseas in a 'child-sitting' capacity. Our son Kim lives with us, retired from a very active sporting life in New Zealand. He is a businessman, and is recovering from a car accident.

What better homecoming (and perhaps resting place) for a hardened magnanimous West Coast veteran and hero, with his wife than the welcoming golden sunlight of Australia - that generous amicable English-speaking southern ocean heaven and a Rugby League stronghold to boot.

1961: Leaving Warrington for New Zealand

1961 Championship Final: Ally Naughton (Warrington) tackles Eddie Ratcliffe as Brian Bevan watches. (Photo: courtesy Robert Gate)

Leaving Wigan station for New Zealand.
From left: Carolyn, Edna, Ces, Kim, Mrs Webster
(Ces's former landlady), Edna's brother Ron.

Part 2: Memories of Ces Mountford

Harry Bath, Ces Mountford and Johnny Raper

The 1982 Kiwis: Back: P. O. Mellars, M. E. Broadhurst, A.J. Leuluai, G.E. Kemble, O. G. Wright, H. J. McGahan, W.P. Dwyer, G.J. Stokes, G.J. Prohm, H. K. Tamati. Middle: O. O. Filipiana, J. C. Griffin, K. L. Fisher, D. B. O'Hara, K. R. Tamati, L. E. Hudson, B. P. Gall, A. P. Coll, D.C. Field, Front: C. R. Mountford, S. Varley, M.J. Gillespie, M.K. Graham, G.L. West, J. A. Whittaker, F. Ah Kuoi, G. J. Smith, C. Friend, J. J. Campbell.

Where it all began: At The George, Huddersfield.

1989 Student World Cup Kiwis in England.

17. The Mountford family

Edna Mountford

Fifty-five years of marriage plus two previous years, where does one start? At the beginning I suppose.

As mentioned elsewhere, Ces arrived in Wigan on a wet Sunday night in June 1946. The following day we met when Brian Nordgren brought him into the radio station where I worked. They both lived in 'lodgings', across the road from me and were very visible, especially Ces in his maroon West Coast blazer.

My first impression of Ces was of a friendly, approachable person with a generosity of spirit. Also, being from a large family and a small community he would smile and speak to everyone he passed in the street.

It has been an amazing career, a mixture of Rugby League and academic pursuit for both Ces and Brian, probably the first full-time students in Wigan Rugby League history. Brian is now the oldest full-time criminal lawyer in New Zealand. He works in Hamilton and still has an amazing memory.

The rugby history has been well recorded, but his five full years of academic study were interesting. There were students from all over the world at the Wigan Mining College and some firm friendships formed. One in particular was Angelo from India who, with others, often came to our house with Ces for a taste of home, which would have been very different from their usual abode. We were often invited to visit Angelo in India. We received invitations from all over the world but unable to take advantage due to the tight Rugby League and study schedules. We were often invited to the home of Mr Chalmers, head of department, who was very helpful to Ces as he was to all overseas students in a strange country.

As a change from the football field Ces would often go with his fellow students to visit mines in Wigan, Newcastle and other places. He found these very different to mines in New Zealand, where he had been a deputy manager. All this meant a very busy week with college, home study, training on Tuesday and Thursday nights, a game on Saturday and sometimes a midweek game. Thankfully, Sunday was a rest day.

The birth of our two children didn't conform to rugby's needs. Carolyn was born in Wigan in the early hours of a match day, which didn't deter Ces scoring three tries to celebrate. Kim was born in Grappenhall, while we lived in the Cheshire side of Warrington. This was an early Friday morning arrival. The President of the Warrington club, Dr McClelland, assisted me; he came at 2.00am before catching a train to London at 9.00am to attend a Rugby Union dinner.

With all these activities, it was a very full life. We did have a holiday in the off-season each year and a trip to New Zealand at the end of the three-year contract with Wigan. Before our 1961 journey to New Zealand, Warrington had asked Ces to stay for another five years, which would have made 15 years at Warrington altogether, but the promise to return to New Zealand to "put something back into the game" was uppermost in his mind.

There was also an offer to join Parramatta as manager-coach, which was made by Jack Argent, their president, and manager of the Australian Rugby League team that toured Britain in the 1959-60 season and was based in Stockton Heath near where we lived. Jack later married a nursing sister from Warrington hospital where some of his players spent much time. They both said farewell to us from Warrington and met us on arrival in Sydney six weeks later we stayed two nights with them before the boat left for New Zealand. Ces was taken to the Parramatta club, but didn't change his mind.

We could have stayed another 10 years in England, as it took all of this time for Ces to be reluctantly accepted back into the fold of Rugby League in New Zealand. The original attitude of some was that we "don't want any of your Pommy ideas here." Ces would never accept a position where he wasn't in complete control as manager / coach. It was a very outspoken Ces who gradually persuaded the Rugby League organisations outside Auckland to join him in his efforts to have players throughout New Zealand recognized for international teams, not just Auckland players.

At Wigan and Warrington, wives and girlfriends were close knit because we lived a life slightly different to normal. We had to watch our conversation as our comments regarding players, teams and the clubs were often attributed to being the thoughts of our partners, which was not always the case. There are some friendships which carry on long after the last kick. In Wigan, it was the late Tommy Bradshaw, his wife Reta and two sons, Rodney and Lindsay, with whom we still communicate; and also Brian Nordgren and his late wife, Marjorie, their son and daughter, Bob and Anne, who are the same ages as our two. In Warrington, it was the Bath family, Harry, Gwen, the late Diane and young Harry. This friendship is still ongoing though not much rugby is discussed; more the ongoing problems of old age. In New Zealand, it was Bud Lisle, Janet Lubbock and many team members from both the national and university teams.

Carolyn Mountford

Even to his grandchildren, Ces is known as 'CR'. What many people don't realise about 'CR' is that he was an outstanding all round sportsman. He was chosen to play for the New Zealand association football team when he was only 16 years old. Fortunately for Rugby League it was decided by the football pundits that he was too young to be sent overseas and he switched to League. On his occasional trips to the golf course he embarrassed those playing with him

130

with his seeming effortless ability to sink balls. He also fielded a cricket bat looking like he was a professional, and he was a good horseman. That, combined with his enduring fitness, from taking food and supplies to the miners up the mountains behind Blackball from a very early age, formed the basis for his outstanding career.

Being the daughter of a famous person in Great Britain had its ups and downs. Sport is one of the few areas that allows one to move between the classes in Britain and indeed around the world. That provided me with a very good opportunity to learn how to handle people from all walks of life at a very early age. The down side affected Kim more than me, because he was always "Ces Mountford's son". A fact not lost on Peter Snell, the Olympic middle-distance runner, who took great glee in announcing 'CR' as "Kim Mountford's father" when Kim was the New Zealand 100 metres men's sprint record holder.

'CR' spent a lot of his time helping young Rugby League players learn how to make the best of themselves and their opportunities. White collars, manners and the ability to talk to people were a must. We lost count of the number of white shirts he gave away.

'CR' also thought outside the square and that made him even more 'different'. Change and New Zealand were not synonymous in the 1960s, but he battled hard to bring New Zealand Rugby League up to world standards. Finally it worked but it did take a long time for people to recognise it. He very much deserved the MBE he was awarded in 1987.

For me, he insisted I become well qualified 'just in case' I was ever in a position where I was left to raise my children alone. It was not usual for fathers to insist on education and careers for their daughters in those days. His wisdom has meant that after the death of my husband from cancer our two teenagers Andrew and Sarah don't want for much. As a grandfather he is just adored.

Last, but not least, the partnership that he and my mother Edna have cannot go unmentioned. They have been a remarkable team by anyone's standards. They get on better than just about any couple I have ever met. She endured long absences while he coached weekend after weekend, provided him with support and never complained. For those of you who thought all my father's weekly newspaper articles were brilliantly written, well it wasn't the editor it was his ghost-writer Edna. The 'CR' and 'AE' team wrote many an article; his concepts, her literary ability.

Nowadays he is not quite as fast on his feet as he used to be. The knee injury that finally stopped his Rugby League career gives him quite some pain. But just when you think he is not listening the quick comment with a twinkle in the eye keeps the teenagers smiling and on their toes.

Kim Mountford

I was born in 1954, and thus did not see my father play Rugby League in England. The only time I did see Dad play was in a 'Golden Oldies' game in Auckland. Harry Bath was visiting as coach of the Balmain team, in 1965, from Sydney. Somehow Harry and Dad talked each other into playing.

There were flashes of genius from both in the first half, however, as Harry would remember years later, my father pulled his hamstring and Harry Mackwood had a stroke. The other factor in the game was the 'banter' between Dad and Harry and the humour that was ever-present in their company. To this day the Bath and Mountford families have been very close.

I do know that when my father arrived in New Zealand in 1961 to the end of the Rothmans Sports Foundation in 1972 he worked unceasingly to develop the game in country areas and create the New Zealand Rugby League Coaching Scheme.

My father was away from home a great deal trying to 'help' the game in New Zealand as he had promised to do after refusing a further five-year contract at Warrington. Life was always interesting in New Zealand with Dad having a core of people against what he was doing and conversely some good support. 'CR' as we called him, was certainly not afraid of speaking his mind, and often did so.

While I was at school there was a pro-Rugby Union, anti-Rugby League sentiment present. I was in the athletics team with Bob Nordgren, son of Brian who played at Wigan with Dad. We created the first Rugby League team to represent Auckland Grammar School. Bob and I played, Brian Nordgren was the coach, and Dad was the manager. We weren't allowed to use the school name so we were called 'Epsom Grammar'. We were then asked to play in the Schools' final as a curtain raiser to the Auckland Champion of Champions game.

The school board of governors would not allow it, consequently the Nordgren and Mountford families complained hard with petitions and letters for the game to be allowed, but to no avail.

My father was asked to coach the New Zealand international team in 1979 and did so until 1982, developing a 'new look' team. Many of these Kiwis went on to play professional Rugby League in England and Australia. Dad took much interest in the progress of Kevin and Howie Tamati, Mark Broadhurst, Gordon Smith and Graeme West. Of the players he developed Graeme West went on to captain Wigan to the 1985 Wembley Challenge Cup Final – Graeme was the first New Zealander since Dad to hold the Cup aloft. In 1992 Graeme coached Wigan to beat the Brisbane Broncos in Brisbane for the World Club Championship.

The main thing I have learned from the good times and bad is that Mum and Dad - Ces and Edna - created a very strong feeling of family which with my sister Carolyn has endured to this day.

18. Playing colleagues

Bob Aynsley
Ces was as astute on Rugby League as observers claim he was. For me, his forté was using his brilliant acceleration to make breaks from second-phase play. A quick play-the-ball and Ces would be away to exploit any gaps in a slow defence. Some of the local derbies involving Blackball were torrid affairs yet Ces always stood out on attack and was totally uncompromising on defence.

Bob Aynsley was a member of Ces's Blackball team in the 1940s. Kiwi hooker 1946-49, six international matches. President West Coast Rugby League, 1976-82. Life Member West Coast and New Zealand Rugby Leagues.

Harry Bath
My 10 years of playing in English Rugby League from 1947 to 1957 gave me the opportunity to play with and against many of the greatest players of all time. It is in this vein that I speak of Ces Mountford both as a player, coach and friend. We had many battles while playing against each other, and certainly disagreements when he coached me but over the years we have maintained a close personal relationship. I am sure fans of yesteryear would be surprised to know that our families have remained friends over the years.

Harry Bath came to England to join Barrow, but in March 1948 signed for Warrington. He became the club's greatest try-scoring forward, and scored 90 tries, 812 goals and 1,894 points in 346 appearances. He returned to Australia in 1957, played for St George, and coached St George and Australia.

Charlie McBride
Ces was the complete five-eighth. His acceleration was remarkable and he was very quick over 50 yards. He was a great tackler with tremendous courage. Ces was absolutely dedicated to training and in his will to succeed. I have no doubt that had New Zealand not lost Ces to Wigan in 1946 he would have gone on to be the star of the 1947-48 Kiwis in Great Britain with his all round brilliance.

Charlie McBride was in Ces's Blackball team in the 1940s; played 21 internationals for New Zealand, 1946 to 1952. New Zealand 'Legend of League'.

Bob McMaster
How do you comment on the career of Ces Mountford? It is a long story from a humble beginning in New Zealand to the enormous accolades and success as a

most talented player, first with the Wigan Rugby League team, then at Warrington, followed by a lengthy period in coaching and administration at the Warrington Rugby League club.

I played five seasons for a fine Rugby League club, Leeds, and my friendship with Ces began the latter months of 1948 with an instant rapport, which exists more strongly than even after all these years. When I think back on those playing years, I realise how privileged we were to be part of the very finest Rugby League in the world. I now realise the toughness of the competition, the hard work we had to indulge in and the overall discipline insisted on by the finest of coaches.

I also appreciate how fortunate the Rugby League world is to be represented by people like Ces Mountford. Quietly spoken, deep thinking, always controlled, super fit, and a credit to a game he loved and graced.

As a Leeds player in a fine side I always found Ces a redoubtable opponent and I have never ceased to be amazed at his skill and courage in a Wigan Rugby League team I considered to be finest Rugby League team I had ever seen.

In 1948 the British Rugby League formed 'Other Nationalities' to join its international competition with England, Wales and France. The 'Other Nationalities' proving a huge success with the help of Australians, New Zealanders, South Africans, etc producing brilliant sides.

Playing with Ces in such top company just reinforced my admiration and respect, and I thank him for his leadership, advice and help. I count it my privilege to have known Ces. I could not speak more firmly than that. To get back to my opening question: it's easy, his record speaks for itself. It is just impeccable and amazing.

'Wallaby Bob' McMaster played 179 games for Leeds between 1948 and 1953. He also played for Other Nationalities

Brian Nordgren

Although Ces Mountford and I were both born in or near Greymouth we did not meet until 1945 when his West Coast team lost 8-7 against Auckland at Carlaw Park. We met there again a few weeks later in New Zealand's big game of the year: North Island 18 South Island 8. If there had been a Kiwi team that year it would have been captained by North's captain Arthur Kay or South's captain Ces Mountford.

When I arrived at Wigan in February 1946 I was asked if there was a good first five-eighth in New Zealand. I nominated those two captains. Arthur Kay was then 32 and Ces was in his mid-20s. Wigan went for Ces and he arrived at Wigan in August 1946.

Over the next five seasons Ces showed that he was probably the finest five-

134

eighth in the world. The position was called 'stand-off half' in those days. It was a period of great stand-offs in England. Dickie Williams of Leeds, Jack Fleming of Warrington, Barrow's Willie Horne and Willie Davies of Bradford spring to mind.

Ces was of stocky build – a pocket battleship. He had all the expected qualities in attack and defence. He had real pace over 30 yards or so. At times from a scrum, his pace enabled him to run diagonally across the field towards the opposing inside centre and outside centre, creating uncertainty between them. Should one centre tackle Ces and thus leave his opposite number unmarked? A well-timed pass from Ces could then put a Wigan centre into a gap or create an overlap for the winger.

Ces was a great favourite with those Wigan crowds of up to 40,000. His combination with test scrum-half Tommy Bradshaw was a talking point. It was often a turning point in Wigan's wins.

Although Ces scored memorable tries, I remember him best for one day in 1950, which was probably the highlight of his career. A few weeks earlier, Wigan had been thrashed 24-5 by Huddersfield – it proved to be our biggest defeat in my 10 seasons with Wigan. Immediately after that loss, the British team to tour Australia was chosen. A record eight Wigan players were chosen. Only one player was chosen from the Huddersfield team, whose overseas players were not eligible for Great Britain. Wigan had finished top of the table, but now had to tackle the top-four play-offs for the Championship without those eight tourists – Egan, Gee, Bradshaw, Ashcroft, Hilton, Cunliffe, Ryan and Ratcliffe. Ces Mountford took over as Wigan's captain. We were not expected to win the semi-final at home against fourth-placed Halifax. We managed a 5-all draw and seemed to have little chance of winning the replay at Halifax. However, we won 18-2, but the odds were heavily against us beating Huddersfield in the final. After all, our full team had been beaten 24-5 only a few weeks earlier by what was virtually a team of internationals capable of beating Australia and the Kiwis.

About 65,000 turned up at Maine Road to watch the Championship Final. After five minutes or so, from a scrum near the touchline, Mountford made a diagonal run and managed to get between Huddersfield's inside centre and their outside centre Pat Devery. At the right moment, Mountford flung out a long overhead pass towards young Nat Silcock, a forward who was Wigan's right winger that day. Silcock caught the pass at full gallop and kept ahead of Huddersfield's winger Lionel Cooper for about 25 yards to score. The quality of that try may best be judged by the fact that Devery had been Australia's test captain and 14 stone Cooper his test winger. Both were in their prime and a much feared centre-wing pair. Behind them was New South Wales' full-back Johnny Hunter. Wigan's stand-in full-back that day was veteran centre Ted Ward, a Welshman who had captained Great Britain. He converted Silcock's try

135

from out near touch and Wigan led 5-0. About five minutes later, at halfway I intercepted a pass to Devery, rounded Hunter and scored by the goalposts. The conversion made it 10-0. Soon it was 10-2, but there was no further scoring until we added two converted tries in the final minutes, and won 20-2.

"The greatest ever upset in a major final," claimed Wigan's coach Jim Sullivan. Mountford's early brilliance and his subsequent play and captaincy decisions made this day a highlight for himself and Wigan's supporters, players and coach. That same depleted Wigan team grew in stature and remained undefeated for about 10 games into the new season before Wigan's eight touring players returned. Their return created selection problems.

Although Wigan went on to win the Challenge Cup Final at Wembley in 1951, then the Championship Final in 1952, there were signs that Wigan's great run over around seven seasons was coming to an end. Joe Egan had gone to Leigh, Mountford to Warrington and others had retired. By 1953, only Ernie Ashcroft, Jack Cunliffe, Billy Blan, Frank Barton and I remained of that 1946 team. That team had started the great run of six successive Lancashire Cup Final wins, four Championship Final wins, two Wembley Challenge Cup Final wins – and an additional 13-12 Challenge Cup loss at Wembley when four of our best players were absent on the 1946 Great Britain tour to Australia. Ces was a leading light in most of these 13 finals.

By 1954, English Rugby League clubs had been striving for almost 60 years to win the coveted double – the Championship and the Challenge Cup in the same season. Only Hunslet in 1908, Huddersfield in 1915 and Swinton in 1928 had succeeded. I could have done it for Wigan in 1946 if only I had landed a 53-yard penalty attempt in the last minute at Wembley.

In 1954, under Mountford as manager, Warrington won that rare double, although the team had to survive a 4-4 draw at Wembley, an 8-4 win in the replay 12 days later at Odsal and three days later an 8-7 win in the Championship Final.

With his background, there was no better man than Ces to coach the Kiwis. His 1980 Kiwis drew the test series in England.

By huge coincidence, his son Kim and my son Bob were both at Auckland Grammar School in the 1960s. Kim was a big strapping lad who shaded Bob in the 100-metre sprints. With two other fast youngsters they became the fastest-ever sprint relay team to represent any secondary school in New Zealand. Kim ran 100 metres in 10.7 seconds to become the holder of the official New Zealand under-19 sprint record which I had once held.

Brian Nordgren played 294 games for Wigan between 1946 and 1955. He scored 312 tries for the club. In 1949-50 he was the top try scorer in British Rugby League with 57 tries. He also represented the Other Nationalities team.

19. Wigan, Warrington, Blackpool and France

Alastair Brindle

Ces Mountford, in my opinion, was Warrington's most successful manager. In the period he was in charge, Warrington won every available trophy. His last trophy was the Lancashire Cup in 1959, beating St Helens in a very hard fought game. Warrington had last won the cup 22 years earlier. Later, in 1961, he must have been very disappointed when in his last game as manager we were beaten by Leeds in the Championship Final.

Ces signed me on in 1956 as a 17-year-old, and after a season in the second team, promoted me to the first team. His approach was to take you to one side and have a quiet word. His assistants did the coaching on the field.

Ces was one of Wigan's all-time greats from the late 1940s and early 1950s. He was the first overseas player to life the Challenge Cup at Wembley and also to win the Lance Todd Trophy for man-of-the-match in the Final. He was a great player, a great coach and a very nice person.

I had the pleasure of meeting Ces and his wife Edna in 1998 at their home in Robina in Queensland. Joe Whittaker (another former Warrington player) and I spent a very enjoyable day there, reminiscing about the old days. He looked a very fit and suntanned 80-year-old. I feel very privileged to have been signed by him, played for him and to have known him.

Alastair Brindle played for Warrington from 1956 to April 1969, making 277+3 appearances, scoring 7 tries and 1 drop goal.

Robert Fassolette

When I was a young French Rugby League player, in the late 1960s, I had never heard of Ces. In fact, we, French, were not much aware at all of what happened in Rugby League in other countries as it was even difficult to know anything about the game itself in France. It was only when I became a regional development officer for the game, 10 years after, that I could get access to some exotic knowledge about Rugby League, thanks to my English.

One of my first great missions was to be in charge of the visit of the 1980 Kiwis to my country as the French leg of their European tour started in my home town of Roanne, one of the 10 pioneer clubs of the French venture of the game, back in 1934. And one of the most titled French clubs. So, as Roanne was the French Champions in 1947 and 1948, they had a sort of a challenge against their British counterparts, Wigan, where a certain Ces Mountford, from New Zealand, was already starring. And it was the same Ces that I first met as coach of the current Kiwis. He was very pleased to be in Roanne and immediately asked me if it could be possible for him to meet his opposition player of the time, the famous test scrum-half Pierre Taillantou. As I knew Pierre very well, the meeting was arranged in a minute and I obviously acted as an interpreter for that new meeting, one-third of a century later. Straight away, pictures and papers came out of Taillantou's drawers and heaps of comments went on. I was only 27 by the time and those two, both of whom could well have been my father, really impressed me as you could believe the game was played the night before, so precise were the memories they kept of all sorts of action and moves.

As usual, mid-week games during a tour are a good opportunity for the home side to have a good go against high standard opposition. Before a packed house of 3,500, Ces's Kiwis had a hard time that November night against Roanne, to finish 16-11 ahead after a game that pleased everyone there.

Another stop on the tour route was prestigious Rugby League stronghold of Carcassonne, also home of the legendary and greatest among the French greats: the now late Puig-Aubert, but by the time a real living myth. As I was still with the Kiwis, I also arranged for Ces to meet "Pipette". He warmly welcomed us in his modest house and he was obviously smoking one of those dark tobacco French cigarettes, a Gauloise or a Gitane. It was another big moment for me, being the young and privileged witness of the meeting of those two great names in the whole history of the game. Puig-Aubert's health was already not very good and I could see, afterwards, how that affected Ces...

When you ask someone not coming from Rugby League circles to describe a typical player of our game, he will certainly mention a tall, big, a bit rough and solid guy. When I remember those three above-mentioned players, they all are – despite great names – small in size, and Ces certainly the smallest of the lot. But ask their opponents about their passing, swerving and side-stepping techniques...

As a former first-class player, it was natural for Ces to involve himself in coaching because he also develops a high quality in human relationships, with on top of that a great sense of humour. I noticed how respected he was by his players, themselves great names in the game: it was indeed the time of the Tamatis, Kemble, Graham, Leuluai, Ah Kuoi, Prohm, West, Broadhurst and the likes. I am pretty sure that they all owe something to Ces that was part of their success in their playing time and, for some of them, coaching career.

In the very early 1980s, video was still something, if not odd, at least futuristic, and people of Ces's generation were absolutely not used to it. To one of my questions about him eventually using it to help him as a coach, he promptly answered that the best video system was his own eye. Certainly, nowadays that appears to be a bygone attitude, given the sophistication of the actual computerised machinery a contemporary coach is provided with. But Ces was brought up in Rugby League in a time where all that did not exist at all and it was only a really experienced view that could record details to be said to players and then worked on at training. When I talked with the above mentioned players, they all were very admiring in Ces's ability to pick up every relevant detail of a player's performance.

Then a few years later, in 1983, I was to meet again Ces in France. This time he was the coach of the Students Kiwis on their European tour and I was very much involved in the University Rugby League as students are a key for the future of the sport. A game was arranged in the winter Olympic city of Grenoble against the local PE training centre, as they were the current French university Rugby League Champions. A game quite delicate to organise as some of the trainees were first class Rugby Union players and the president of the French Rugby Union in person, Mr Ferrasse, threatened the players to be banned from Union if they took part in a game of Rugby League. He even put a hard pressure on the Head of the training centre to stop the game. Finally, the game could be played, only without the two local first division players from Grenoble RU who was told by the Rugby Union authorities not to play the forbidden game before their own public. And this despite the fact that a University sport registration allows every student to practise any sport. This situation in which Ces was involuntarily involved just helped him to even more understand the hard conditions faced by Rugby League in France. The game also was played in hard conditions: rain and mud gave the game a Carlaw Park atmosphere that probably helped the Kiwis in their 18-14 win.

It was in 1989 when Ces came again to Europe as Kiwis national coach, this time for a Student World Cup in Britain. On their way they had a couple of friendly games in France, including one in Fontainebleau, near Paris, against the famous French Armed Forces Sport Unit, the Battalion of Joinville which I was the coach of. For the first time Ces and I were directly opposed as coaches of national sides and it was a really great occasion. Firstly, our common friend Richard Lewis, the languages and cross-cultural training maestro and one of Ces's earliest fans in Wigan, made it especially from England to attend the game. Then, when both national anthems were played I experienced a strange feeling because in 1985 – the year of the Rainbow Warrior affair – a game was originally planned in Paris between the French Army side and the Kiwis as opening game of the French leg of their European tour. But in November of that year two French officers of the Secret Services were still in jail in New Zealand and the Brigadier in charge of sport in the French Forces radically opposed such an official game against an "hostile country": he probably considered that France was at war with New Zealand. And the Army side was replaced for the occasion with a President XIII. So, four years later, that game in Fontainebleau, played on a military sport ground, was the very first official contact between the French

Forces and New Zealand in sport. Once again sport was of a beneficial use to restore official relations. I was extremely pleased that Ces and I were taking part in completing the rapprochement of our two nations. And that Rugby League was used for it was also remarkable as our sport was somehow making history in those circumstances.

As one can see, quite a few memories with Ces; all good memories. In fact, how could it be different with such an enjoyable person who will remain forever as a great character in the world of Rugby League.

Robert Fassolette is a PE teacher by education, then qualified in Rugby League for the French Ministry of Sports. Had to stop his playing career at 19, due to serious shoulder injury. Became a young referee and, at the age of 26, as he was regional Rugby League development officer in Lyons, was also appointed by the French Rugby League Council as national technical director of referees for four years, in order to restore confidence in the French whistle holders. Initiated the first international (Franco-British) referees seminar in 1980. Then turned to coaching and was appointed (1985) national coach of the Army side, in the time of conscription (now abandoned in France) when sport governing bodies were allowed to give their young elite players a real professional training for one year in the sport battalion, instead of normal military activities that could have hampered their career.

He is also an historian, specialised in the political conflict between the two codes of Rugby; graduated of both French Sport Institute and Political Sciences Institute. Now president of "XIII Actif", an association arguing for compensation for the harm done to French Rugby League by and after the ban of the game during the Vichy Government years of the Second World War.

He has lived in Vichy since 1999, with Bernadette and three children (Eric, Hugo and Lisa) where he works as a general trainer for coaches in the Auvergne regional sports centre and has contributed to the formation, in 2002, of the first Rugby League club in that highly symbolic town for the game.

Paul Gamble: Signing for Blackpool Borough

As a young teenager, I had played for the Blackpool Borough youth team. Then, just before Ces Mountford became Blackpool manager in 1972, I moved up to play for a local amateur side. That team became the ICI amateur team, and that was where Ces saw me play. Most of the other players were older than me.

He asked if I would sign for Blackpool Borough. He said I had the skills and ability to play professionally. He was an icon for me, I knew about his coaching. It was a great experience for me to be coached by him; of course I was far too young to have seen him play. He signed me in September, when I was 16. I turned 17 the following February.

As I coach, I remember him as being very strict, but quietly spoken. But he always could put his point over. He asked me to sign for the club in a friendly way, asked if I wanted to bring my father along to discuss terms. He said what he had to offer – and the club didn't have much money – and told me to go and think about it.

As there wasn't an 'A' team, Ces introduced me into the first team gradually. He put me on the bench and would give me a game. I played in the second row.

In conclusion, I would say he was an old-style gentleman of the game. He made his presence felt, and got his point over. He picked me out as a youngster, and that was special for me. And then he signed me for the club. I went on to play for Blackpool Borough for 17 years, and hold the club appearance record.

Paul Gamble played for Blackpool Borough until the 1986-7 season, and then a final season with Springfield Borough, as the club moved to Wigan. During that time he played for the club in the 1976-77 John Player Trophy Final, which was lost 25-15 to Castleford. He was also in the Blackpool team that achieved promotion in the 1978-79 season.

Harold Genders

I remember the great Wigan team after the war. They were brilliant, big and fast players, and it was very hard to beat them. Ces Mountford and Tommy Bradshaw at half-back were a wonderful combination, and they were the key to that team. Ces was regarded as the best stand-off in the world at that time. There were a lot of good stand-offs, but Ces Mountford was the best.

I was raised in Warrington, but signed for Rochdale Hornets in 1949, and then played for Blackpool and Widnes. I joined Blackpool when they were managed by Chris Brockbank, who had left Warrington in 1951. I played against Ces Mountford once when I was playing for Blackpool, and he was at Warrington. I couldn't get near him. I couldn't catch him to tackle him.

Harold Genders played for Rochdale Hornets, Blackpool Borough and Widnes before retiring to develop his career in the building industry. In the 1970s he was a director at Warrington before resigning in 1980 to set up Fulham RLFC.

Parry Gordon

In 1961, I was playing for the Warrington Colts side as a fifteen year old, although I was born in Wigan. Ces spotted me and asked me to turn professional. With two directors, he 'wined and dined' me, and I signed for the club at midnight on my sixteenth birthday: 17 February 1961, at Wilderspool. I think the club did this to make you feel important, but it was special, and it is something I've never forgotten.

Ces left Warrington at the end of that season, so as a 16-year-old I didn't play for any of his teams. I continued to play for the under-17 side. The club had quite a lot of half-backs when I signed, and Ces asked if I was happy. "Any more money?" I cheekily asked. Ces replied that he could change the contract – you got a few hundred pounds to sign and a further £150 when you had played 10 first team games. He suggested an extra £10 every time I played for the first team. I settled for the £150, but his offer gave me some confidence. And to think I went on to play over 500 first team games…

I was raised on Rugby League in Wigan, but I didn't see Ces play. However, my Dad had photos of him. I knew his history with Wigan, and he was well respected.

The first thing he said to me after I signed was: "Have you got any spikes? You need speed." So I turned up with my spikes, and at training we were always on the track first. I was just a colts' player, and he was with the first team. But I do remember this diminutive figure – he could really explain how he wanted things done – with his own inimitable style. He was a disciplinarian, always on the ball; you couldn't slip anything by him.

A few years after he returned to New Zealand, Warrington was playing New Zealand, and he sent me a 'good luck' telegram before the game.

After about 15 years I got to international level, and I played for England in the 1975 World Cup in Australia and New Zealand. Ces came to see me when we were training in New Zealand. He took me out for the day in Auckland and I met his family. He must have followed my career – it was a nice thing to do.

When I finished playing, I was on the coaching staff at Wilderspool, and also helped set up an amateur club in Shevington, where I lived. Two school teachers had set up the team. Warrington was playing at Blackpool, and Shevington had organised a concert to raise funds. I had to leave Blackpool straight after the game to get there, and when I arrived there seemed to be a lot of people I knew. As a 'thank you' for the work I had done for them, the two teachers had organised a 'This is Your Life' for me, with a red book and everything. I was so surprised and delighted. But the highlight was a tape that Ces had sent for the occasion. I still have it, and still remember him saying when he signed me: "You'll make it son."

I hold Ces Mountford in high esteem, and I always proudly say that Ces Mountford signed me for Warrington.

Parry Gordon was Ces Mountford's last important signing for Warrington. He played 528+15 games for the club, scoring 167 tries. Only Brian Bevan played more games for the club. He played for England in the 1975 World Cup, and on retirement joined the coaching staff at Wilderspool. His loyalty to the club was recognised by him being given two testimonial seasons.

Reg Hughes

I signed for Warrington, from local amateur Rugby League, in the autumn of 1950, as a centre. The secretary-manager was Chris Brockbank, a winger in the famous pre-war Swinton team. Chris had decided to retire at the end of the season, and this set up a storm between old rivals Warrington and Wigan for the services of Ces Mountford. Wigan insisted on retaining the contract of Ces as a player, while the Wire offered the great Kiwi half-back the chance to become the first full-time player-manager in Rugby League. The RFL eventually accepted Warrington's case and so Ces became a man of primrose and blue instead of the cherry and white. After his illustrious career at Wigan he became a true 'hands on' coach at Wilderspool.

As a youth I watched Ces form a wonderful partnership with Tommy Bradshaw. Although like quicksilver over 10 to 20 yards, I couldn't understand why he didn't appear to glide past lots of opponents or score more individual tries. It was only when I appreciated his skill at first hand that I realised one of his many ploys was merely to 'commit' two opposition players, say the stand-off and first centre, before sending his own centre through the gap he'd created with a perfectly timed pass. He maintained it was often unnecessary to beat his direct opponent when a clever piece of wrong footing could prove more profitable. In one particular reserve match his coaching vision from the sideline showed that he had a true rugby brain. I was first centre in a standard passing movement heading towards the right wing, when I heard the cry "straighten up" – without looking up I changed direction 45 degrees to my left and sailed amazingly unopposed between two startled defenders to the try line. Ces had the gift to think two moves ahead of the opposition. He soon settled into his dual role at Warrington and could readily switch hats from a players' man to his role with the directors. You just hoped that you picked the right time in your personal dealings with him.

Ces became quite ruthless in his search for major honours. The previous season we had won the 'A' team league title quite comfortably with a lot of former first team, senior players in the side. He decided to release many older players like Harold 'Moggie' Palin, Jimmy Featherstone and Jack Atherton in the pack, and bring in the likes of Austin Heathwood, Gerry Lowe, Ted White and Sid Phillips. I suddenly became reserve team captain at the age of 22. Future stars like Laurie Gilfedder, Jimmy Challinor and Eric Fraser made their debuts in the back division with me. The average age of the squad dropped dramatically.

One match saw us beat Liverpool City 'A' 64-2 at Wilderspool. I played centre alongside the 17-year-old giant Gilfedder, scoring six tries between us out of the 10 tries the threequarter line scored. Laurie and I walked off proudly, only to be met by Mr Mountford who stated that the wingers should have scored five tries each, not the centres. No bigheads allowed with this hard taskmaster.

Ces gave me enough chances of first team rugby and I played centre, wing and loose-forward on several occasions. In the reserves I played every position except prop forward and scrum-half. This versatility might have fitted into the modern squad rotation system, whereas in the 1950s specialisation seemed to be the preferred option to secure a regular place.

First team

During one heart-to-heart conversation with Ces he stated that I fell between two stools for a regular first-team place: "You are not quite fast enough for the backs and a bit light for the pack," even though I tended to play above my weight with hard tackling. He even suggested that as a hooker I might walk into the team. At 6ft 1in this seemed highly unlikely, although Ces was forever the innovator, prepared to try something different.

On 11 October 1952, I was selected to play alongside the great Brian Bevan, with Ces at stand-off against the mighty Australian tourists. Within the first 15 minutes I broke a bone in the back of my hand in a stamping incident. Although I felt it crack, Ces and the trainer told me to swap places with Ray Lambert on the left wing and they would examine me fully at half-time. During the interval my left hand had swollen threefold and when strapped up the flesh broke through like a bacon joint with string. I winced through the second half marking test winger Noel Pidding, who fortunately didn't manage to get much ball. We ended up being soundly beaten. The doctor later verified my broken hand.

When I recovered I found myself only 'A' team reserve. I took some time to re-establish myself as a potential first teamer and it somewhat spoiled my relationship with Ces, although the board probably had the major say in team selection. This showed me why players can be dissatisfied with an unfair decision, especially when they feel they are giving 100 per cent at all times. Substitutions in Rugby League didn't happen until 1964, so I had to play on against the Australians. Now they even leave the field with a bloody nose. Alan Prescott once played half a test match against Australia with a broken arm – did he get dropped for his gutsy performance when he recovered?

The low point in Ces's playing career came almost a year later, in October 1953. Playing Hull KR, and cruising to victory with 42 points on the board, Rovers had a breakaway on the left. The ever-keen player-manager attempted a last-ditch tackle that on the winger diving in for a consolation try. Ces's flying tackle took him over the Hull player at the Railway End at Wilderspool, and he flew across the cinder track, beneath the trestle seats and into the concrete boundary wall with a sickening crash. I watched from the home bench as he was stretchered off with the worst knee injury I have ever seen. His kneecap was displaced, and there was ligament and cartilage damage that needed major

144

rebuilding. It was soon obvious that his illustrious playing career was over.

A few months later I was sitting next to Ces in the club's treatment room, when he opened his heart to me about his injury. His left leg was now shapeless compared to the strong thigh and calf muscles on his right leg. His knee was encircled with a U shaped scar from his thigh and round his repositioned kneecap. He said: "Reg, I know I will never play again, but without this job as full-time coach I would end up disabled. The availability of first-class electronic equipment and the chance to have the correct treatment four or five times every day at least gives me the chance of a fully mobile future." He added that every time he thought of the accident and the sight of his shattered knee he broke out into a cold sweat.

The retirement of Ces Mountford as a player heralded his progress as an excellent manager. Warrington had welcomed the 1953-54 season with confidence. Ces had moulded a strong squad of youth an experience into a match for any side in Rugby League. Despite my own lack of first team chances I was always ready to support the team in any capacity.

The club took all the players to witness the cup and league double, including the titanic Odsal replay against Halifax. Mountford's tactics, Eric Frodsham's captaincy in the absence of Ally Naughton and the mercurial Gerry Helme, helped to overcome the luckless Halifax side.

Ces continued his magic during the 1954-55 season, which culminated in a further championship win against Oldham at Maine Road.

I left the Warrington area during the following season to get married, although I remained on the club's retained players list for a further two seasons.

I am proud to have been involved with the only club I ever wanted to play for, and with managers Ces Mountford and Chris Brockbank, who together with some of the club's greatest players provided one of the club's finest eras and greatest achievements in its history.

Enoka Macdonald

When I came across from New Zealand to play for Halifax in 1948, Ces Mountford was just starting to make a name for himself as one of the best stand-offs to ever play for Wigan.

Although we are both South Islanders, we had never played against each other prior to being in Great Britain at the same time. I was from Marlborough at the top of the South Island, and a Rugby Union background, before shifting down further south to represent Otago and New Zealand Maoris in Union in 1947. Ces, on the other hand, came from the West Coasty, which was a Rugby League stronghold.

I played against him on three occasions, and knew how highly regarded he was by the Wigan people. As a result, he was always looked upon by us at

Halifax and other teams as a key player, which sued to make him an obvious target to try and knock back. Although the game has changes considerably over the past 50 years and it is difficult to compare players of different eras, he nevertheless had similar qualities as Stacey Jones today. He was not big, but extremely quick off the mark.

The first time I played against him, Wigan showed no mercy in comprehensively beating us, but the second time it was a much closer affair as the general play by both teams was similar.

My final memory of him is playing a couple of charity matches together at the end of the season. These games were always fun and were an opportunity to meet your previous rivals as a now adopted team mate. Ces took it somewhat easy for the first three quarters of the game, before playing an explosive final 20 minutes, which was enough to see us through to win.

It was a pity that New Zealanders back home never saw him as a player than had him regarded in Great Britain as one of the best that ever stepped onto a Rugby League field.

Enoka MacDonald played in Great Britain for Halifax. His nephew played for the club at the same time. On his return to New Zealand, he played for Otago and then South Island against the Kangaroos.

Geoffrey Moorhouse

Ces Mountford was, quite simply, the greatest stand-off / fly-half / second five-eighth (call the position what you will) that I ever saw; and I'm including some outstanding players in both codes of rugby over the past 50 years, from Willie Horne and W. T. H. Davies, through Phil Bennett and David Watkins, to Brett Kenny and Wally Lewis. He had every skill to perfection - handling, passing, sidestepping, acceleration, tackling - and on top of this he had all the other virtues coaches hope for in their rugby footballers. He was quite the most durable person who handled the oval ball during his years with Wigan, a stubby little man who bounced back from constant battering (when his opponents could get their hands on him, that is) like a piece of India rubber, and hardly ever missed a match through injury during the whole of his time at Central Park. He had quite remarkable stamina that saw him going hell-for-leather from start to finish of every match; his work rate, in the fashionable football jargon of today, was phenomenal. And he had a terrific brain, that intangible asset which separates the really great players from the merely good and enables them to see potential moves and the openings to them, that split-second before anybody else - or, in some cases, whole seconds earlier. It made his fabulous half-back partnership with Tommy Bradshaw one of the most successful ever seen on a rugby pitch (at least as good as Morgan and Edwards or Kenny and Sterling) and

146

the source of many Wigan triumphs in the years they were together.

I remember the sensational winning try Ces scored against Leeds in 1950. I was there and it remains in my memory as one of the two greatest tries I've ever seen; the other, of course, being Brian Bevan's unique diagonal, when he shimmied and shot past 13 Wigan players in the Wardonia Cup.

One other indelible memory I have of Ces concerns a tackle he made at about the same time against Bradford Northern's Frank Whitcombe, a very solid, around 18-stone, piece of prop forward with a Billy Bunter face. Ces found himself the only Wigan player between Whitcombe and a winning score at the clubhouse end of the ground, with not many yards left before the Welshman would charge over the line. And charge he did, straight at this half-pint Kiwi who was clearly going to be flattened en route by the impact (It wasn't worth the effort of going round Mountford, so certain was Whitcombe that he couldn't be stopped if he just ran straight). But the prop made the mistake of sticking out his arm to flatten Ces with a classic hand-off. So fast that I didn't see it (though I was only yards away in the boys' pen), Ces had him by the wrist and dug his own right heel into the turf as a pivot, all in a flash. Then he swung Whitcombe off his feet with exactly the same twirl used by the hammer throwers in Highland Games - and only let go when the number 10 was briefly airborne, before coming to earth with a crash against an advertising board. It was seconds before a dazed Frank picked himself up, too, and he couldn't have had much push left for the subsequent scrum. Talk about mind over matter! Talk about hyper-dexterity!

Geoffrey Moorhouse is a Fellow of the Royal Society of Literature, and supported Wigan as a youngster after the Second World War. His work on Rugby League includes the collection of essays *At The George* and *A People's Game – The Official History of Rugby League 1895 to 1995*.

John Owen

The first time I saw Ces Mountford play rugby was in the late summer of 1946. He had just arrived from New Zealand and turned out in a pre-season practice match at Central Park. There was a large turnout for the game to run the ruler over the new half-back. Wigan fans were still smarting over their 13-12 Challenge Cup Final defeat at the hands of Wakefield Trinity in May. A late disputed penalty had cost them the game.

It is hard to recall how war weary Britain was after 1945. People had been starved of sport and in the immediate post war period Rugby League in the north of England drew huge crowds. During this golden era which equated approximately with Ces's stay in Wigan, the gates were regularly closed for home matches. It was wise to be in one's seat or favourite vantage place at least an hour before the kick-off.

My father and Ces became friends as a result of their mutual interest in rugby and horses. Ces used to ride on Sunday mornings to get rid of his aches and pains picked up the previous day. He had steady blue eyes, a firm handshake and those admirable qualities of the old dominions - steadfastness, modesty and frankness.

For a young sports-mad boy these were heady days. The Wigan coach, the legendary Welshman, Jim Sullivan, was a hard-driving, even ruthless operator. He assembled a gifted side which was led on the field by Joe Egan, but the team's real dynamo was Ces Mountford. For six years he hardly missed a game. I never saw him have a disastrous match, his consistency was without peer. He had no technical weakness apparent to a young fan, and was, as the locals said "a big little 'un", fast, fearless, a superb passer of the ball and a pre-eminent team player. His side-step was poetry.

One highlight: I recall his 1949 exceptional individual try against Leeds [described elsewhere in this book]. The crowd rose to a man and thousands refused to leave the ground at the end of the game. It was a magic moment.

Perhaps the outstanding result of those years was Wigan's victory in the Championship final in 1950 against Huddersfield. Wigan had lost eight players needed for the Australian tour. Ces, captaining the side, drew out a performance from a mix of veterans and apprentices which saw Huddersfield destroyed 20-2.

Throughout this period Wigan's main rivals were Warrington, Leeds and Bradford Northern. It was a competitive league. Ces was a huge favourite with the Central Park crowd, and thus survived his controversial decision in 1951 to become player-manager at Warrington. There his playing career was halted by a knee injury, but he became a brilliant coach particularly of young players.

In more than 50 years of listening to experts on rugby I never met a man more succinct or interesting on the game. He believed in speed and logic, not passion, and never rubbished his opponents. He was gregarious and straight forward and perhaps as only a New Zealander or Welshman can, truly loved the game.

Though the Mountfords now live in Australia, our two families have been in close contact for over 50 years, and through four generations.

On a trip to New Zealand in 1996 my wife, Sue, and I made a visit to Blackball. This is a pretty remote place and the main hostelry was named, obviously tongue in cheek, the Blackball Hilton. Inside were two very interesting photographs, one dated 1918 was of Ibrox Stadium in Glasgow and pictured King George V presenting a Sergeant of the New Zealand Regiment with the Victoria Cross. 70,000 spectators were present. The other showed a smiling Ces Mountford shaking the hand of King George VI at the 1948 Wembley Cup Final. Here were two favourite sons of Blackball.

Eric Silcock

I, along with countless thousands of supporters watched Ces Mountford play for Wigan. Although he was a small man, he was such a brave player. He was superb in every aspect of the game. To see him come away from the scrum, running at full flight, at an angle of 45 degrees, it seemed to me, was marvellous. I also remember the way he would kick the odd goal: he would address the ball, swing one leg back with no run-up and bang it over. I saw him play many fine games for Wigan. He will always be remembered with great esteem here in Wigan by all who saw him play. He was also a gentleman, as I was to learn a little later on.

By the time I had completed my national service, Ces had joined the Warrington club as player-manager. I got to know him personally because I had a few games in the 'A' team there. This was in the days of Brian Bevan, Ally Naughton and company. Ces moulded a great team – his regime was very strict, but he was very fair and treated everyone the same.

The ritual at the end of a hard training session was that everyone started in the corner of the pitch at Wilderspool, Ces would blow the whistle, and we would all go hell for leather round the outside of the pitch. Woe betide anyone who didn't try his best – in this case Ces would send everyone round again. Needless to say that didn't happen many times.

My first introduction to Ces, and Warrington, was when I attended a summer school – a pre-season sprint and training session. I went there through the auspices of Billy Cunliffe who was the chief scout. Incidentally, he was instrumental in signing Jackie Edwards, who turned out to be a great player for the Wire. After one training session, Ces, Billy, Jackie and I walked across Warrington to the bus stop for the Wigan bus. As there was a little time before the bus came, we slaked our thirst in a pub.

We chatted about this and that, and I remember Ces mentioning that he used to go to the pit back home in Blackball on a pony and trap – he was a miner of course. As well as playing rugby in Wigan he studied at the Wigan Mining Technical College.

Ces married Edna, a Wigan girl, and was a family man. He would set the washing machine running and take the kids to school before going to Wilderspool for the day.

That was Ces – a great player, well remembered by the public of Wigan. He was a renowned coach who accomplished many great triumphs at Warrington, and is well remembered by players and supporters there.

I will be 71 in July 2003, and have seen and met many great players, and witnessed their feats on the field. Ces Mountford is up there with the very best of them. I am proud to have known him.

Colin Thomson

I have supported Bradford Northern since 1944, and I recall Ces as one of the greats. He was always outstanding against Northern, probably the open spaces at Odsal gave him more room for his artistry. The main thing I recall about him was the way he held the ball, as if it was an egg, hard to describe, but as if his hands were the egg cup with the ball stuck up. Most unusual.

I include him in my all time top six players. He had to be great to catch my eyes as they have always been coloured red, white and amber. Pity he always was outstanding against Northern.

Chris Wilson

In 1994, I was fortunate enough to be present in Brisbane to watch the World Club Championship match between the Brisbane Broncos and Wigan. My seat just happened to be right next to Ces and his wife Edna. We got talking and, after the game, Ces introduced me to Graeme West and Shaun Edwards who graciously stayed to talk and to sign my programme.

Ces was modest about his achievements with Wigan, Warrington and New Zealand and the esteem that he is held in on this side of the world. That June night, he was enormously proud of his protégé Graeme West and his achievement in winning the world title in Brisbane.

Since then, we have remained in contact and the Mountfords' is the first Christmas card I receive each year. In it Ces reveals that he still follows the fortunes of Wigan and often has a perceptive comment to make about the English game.

Chris Wilson is a southerner who moved to Wigan in January 1985 and began his Rugby League education. He has been writing on the game since 1987 and has regularly contributed to Wigan RLFC's programme between 1987 and 2000. He has also contributed to *The Greatest Game, London Calling!* and books *When Push Comes To Shove 2* and *From Fulham to Wembley*. In April 2001, he moved to Gloucester and became the Gloucestershire Warriors RLFC's media manager the following year. In 2003, he was elected chairman.

20. New Zealand international players

Lory Blanchard

I first met Ces in 1951 in England. He came to meet the Kiwi touring team. He was not very impressed and so he took over training for an hour. I learnt more that morning about Rugby League than any other time.

I met Ces again on the 1955 tour. I was injured so he took me to Warrington, where he was the manager, for treatment, but I did not run into him again until he came back to New Zealand. He was appointed coach for the Rothmans New Zealand coaching scheme. I was also privileged to tour with Ces twice. He was a very good manager – nothing was a problem as far as the players were concerned. If ever I wanted advice on League matters I only had to ask. My only regret was that I never saw Ces play. From reports he must have been one of the best in Rugby League in England.

Lory Blanchard MNZM, DSA played 16 internationals for New Zealand from 1951 to 1956, including the 1954 World Cup. He also coached the Kiwis.

Tony Coll

I was extremely fortunate to be playing for the New Zealand Kiwis under the coaching regime of Ces Mountford between 1979 and 1982, during which time we played two test series against England, two against France, one series against Australia and a single test against Papua New Guinea.

This period was the most satisfying and enjoyable during my 11 year time in the Kiwis. Prior to this era, results at international level were mediocre and there had been an extremely high player turnover. Ces bought the Kiwis stability and established a high level of professionalism, on and off the field, which previously had not been implemented at this level. He instilled a hunger and passion to achieve a very high standard of Rugby League in every game regardless of the quality of the opposition. This was one of Ces Mountford's great attributes and there was a level of pride to wear the Kiwi jersey not previously seen. Ces was an absolute gentleman, a masterful coach and a pleasure to work under. I can honestly say that during the Mountford era, I played some of my best rugby and enjoyed the greatest team camaraderie, which is still there today whenever we happen to cross paths.

Tony Coll made 30 international appearances for the Kiwis between 1972 and 1982, including the 1972, 1975 and 1977 World Cups.

Ken English JP

I first met Ces Mountford in England with the New Zealand Rugby League team in 1951. Ces was with Wigan and it was a brief encounter.

We met properly in the 1960s, when I was chairman of the Wellington Rugby League. Ces had returned to New Zealand and been appointed by the NZRL with the sponsorship of Rothmans to establish coaching schools throughout the country.

When visiting Wellington, Ces would always stay at my place, and we talked well into the night about Rugby League. Ces was a tremendous enthusiast and extremely passionate about the sport.

His coaching ability and technique was refreshingly new and one could not help but become a devotee. His visits to Wellington were timely, because Wellington was reviewing its coaching and selection policies and had already established procedures to bring in younger players to receive coaching at representative level. Ces put the icing on the cake and players and coaches alike all were enthused by his passion. From then on Wellington Rugby League developed well-trained and well-coached teams at club and junior levels. The success of his coaching of coaches schedules was reflected in the better performances at representative levels as well as at club levels.

Ces's involvement with Rugby League moved into other areas including administration, where he became Wellington's representative on the NZ Rugby League Council, until Wellington, along with other Leagues, opted for direct representation.

Ces Mountford's return to New Zealand was great for Rugby League in this country. Not only was he a tremendous enthusiast, he was also a great ambassador for Rugby League in the days when one was definitely needed. New Zealand was the loser when he drifted away to retire in Australia.

Ken English JP played two internationals for the Kiwis and is a former chairman of the Wellington Rugby League.

Graeme Farrar: Ces Mountford "Simply the Best"

There are two decades between Ces and myself so naturally, I never saw him play, but everywhere we went on the 1961 British tour there was praise for the little guy from the West Coast. When people knew that we were visitors from New Zealand, they would say: "Ee lad, that bloke Mountford of yours, he was a great player." He must have been something special for the Poms to rave about him 10 years after he finished playing and, of course, he was. As a player he was a legend, but it was as a coach that I knew him best. Not many great players become great coaches but Ces achieved just that.

152

His style of coaching was considered controversial at the time when he returned to New Zealand in 1961 from a successful playing and coaching career at Wigan and Warrington. He later became New Zealand Coaching Director, where he had a hand in bringing many young players through the grades from outside the main Rugby League centres to play for their country.

When he arrived he taught us that to win in Rugby League you must first stop the opposition from scoring. His patterns of defence were flawless, he was the instigator of the front-row forwards taking control of the game, looking after the middle of the field on defence and running onto the ball at pace and offloading, giving your backs some space to work. He brought a new dimension to our game. After starting and running coaching schools all over the country in which he spent hours and hours talking to people about Rugby League, he then took on the job of coaching the Kiwis and brought through a lot of his former pupils to the test arena. He introduced some of our most exciting talent in the time he spent as national coach. For years after his term as national coach, a lot of those playing test Rugby League can thank him for his time and methods in helping them get to the top.

As a former pupil of his I can say that I have never met a man more knowledgeable and as passionate towards the game. He was probably the very first person to bring the science and thinking side of Rugby League onto the blackboard, of which he was a master. Like many of his kind, he was, as they say, "before his time". We have had other good coaches in our great game, but probably none more likeable and who knew more about the game, or how it should be played. On and off the paddock he was one of the all time Kiwi greats. He was, and still is "Simply the Best".

Graeme Farrar is a former New Zealand captain, and made four international appearances between 1961 and 1966.

Jim Fisher: Ces Mountford - Man of Vision

Ces Mountford was a Rugby League man of great vision. As a coach he was also very particular to emphasise the need to master the basics of the game.

He is still a legend on the West Coast, where he was born and honed his own skills, and in Wigan, where he was renowned at the Blackball Bullet during a sparkling career as an inside back and captain.

They were still talking in glowing terms about Ces when I was fortunate enough to tour Britain with the 1971 Kiwis, and no doubt they still are as stories about him are handed down from fathers to sons.

Ces Mountford came back to New Zealand in 1961, when Rugby League could often degenerate into barging football with teams separated by only a couple of yards and unlimited tackles enabling one side to dominate possession for long periods.

He was contracted by the New Zealand Rugby League to develop national coaching schools, and I was fortunate to attend two of them. The second, in 1963, culminated with the School XII playing the Kiwis in deep mud at Carlaw Park before the tour of Australia.

By then Ces's influence was taking effect. His vision enabled him to improve and develop the game throughout the country, and his emphasis on correctly playing the ball, passing the ball, and turning in the tackle brought out the best in a lot of young players.

Every outstanding Kiwi of that era graduated through Ces's coaching courses. He had the foresight to make Rugby League a more attractive game and the ability to sport talent, strengths and weaknesses in individual players.

To me Ces saw the game into another era. So many of us owe him a debt of gratitude that we were given the opportunity to realise our potential and gain even greater enjoyment from our sport.

Jim Fisher played nine test matches for New Zealand between 1963 and 1972.

Michael O'Donnell

As a child growing up in Blackball on the West Coast, the Mountford family, and Ces in particular, were a highly respected family in the district. Ces, mainly due to his deeds in England, had a cult like status with people of my father's generation.

When Ces first selected me for the Kiwis in 1980, I hardly knew him personally, but over the next few years my admiration for him as a coach and person grew considerably.

His technical knowledge of Rugby League was astute and so were his people-handling skills - always ensuring that if you could not say something positive about someone you should say nothing.

It has been an honour and privilege to have known and been coached by Ces Mountford and I regard it as a highlight of my Rugby League career.

Michael O'Donnell played 11 international matches for New Zealand between 1977 and 1981.

Colin O'Neil

I am very honoured to be asked to pen a few sentences about Ces Mountford whom I regard as one of the great men of Rugby League in New Zealand.

Many people influenced my Rugby League career, none more so than Ces Mountford. As a teenager I had read, of course, of his marvellous exploits as a player and coach for Wigan in England, which are chronicled elsewhere in this book. However, I first came in personal contact with Ces when he was director of coaching for New Zealand and he came to Wellington.

Ces was the most passionate and knowledgeable Rugby League person I have ever known and during the 1960s and 1970s his impact on the game at the national level was legendary. You were either a 'Mountford man' or not, and fortunately the former outweighed the latter by a huge number, especially outside Auckland. A little-known fact is that the international Rugby League numbering system used only by Britain at that time but used by all countries today, was brought about by Ces's insistence of numbering the correct Rugby League way. From team numbering, to the correct way to pass, to the correct way to play the ball, to positional play on defence and attack, Ces had foolproof teaching methods that he has been able to pass on and these methods have stood the test of time. He also backed his views by cold hard logic.

As a director of coaching, Ces introduced certification courses for coaches into New Zealand. The game in New Zealand was suffering from dominance by Auckland where it experienced great popularity, but it was not progressing elsewhere and there was no recognized provincial competition. Ces concentrated on bringing the rest of New Zealand up to a competitive standard with Auckland and ensuring that the basics of the game were taught at all levels. Ces had his knockers during those days especially in Auckland where it was said that if we all played the same way, the game would be boring and predictable.

However, coaches throughout New Zealand took on board what he was coaching and good coaches used those basics as a springboard to success. It is often said today that players should get back to basics; I firmly believe that the basics must come first and, without them, the razzle-dazzle we like to see as spectators could not happen. The proof of the pudding is in the eating and the Mountford influence could be seen in the marked improvement in the standard of performance of provinces outside Auckland (and even in Auckland itself). Mountford adherents in Wellington, such as Jim Campbell and the late Ossie Butt, ensured that Wellington became a force on the national scene.

Ces was immensely proud of his sport and impressed on us all the necessity to ensure that at all times we dressed and behaved in a manner that did not bring the sport into disrepute. These standards too have enhance Rugby League's reputation with the wider public.

I knew that, like myself, many players from outside Auckland (and also from within) owe a great debt to Ces for giving them, through his coaching system and his coaching schools, the opportunity to reach their potential as Rugby League players. Indeed, New Zealand owes Ces a great debt for making the game competitive on a national basis.

I had the privilege of touring with Ces twice, once with him as coach and the other as manager. I recall a team mate, the late Bill Burgoyne – a very good

155

imitator of Ces's Lancashire accent – having the team in fits at the back of the bus by giving a very good rendition of Ces giving a team talk, a measure of the esteem in which he was held. I can still hear the words 'turn in the tackle' in a Lancashire accent resounding in my ears.

Colin O'Neil captained the New Zealand international team, and won 21 caps between 1965 and 1971. He played in the 1968 and 1970 World Cups.

Gordon Smith
Ces was a man of very high morals and was particularly strong on discipline. He was a gentleman and expected the same behaviour from the team. He had team walks and runs before breakfast each day, and expected a blazer and tie to be worn to dinner each night. He also had a sense of humour. He was very good with one-liners. Some of these are still etched in my memory, such as:

"If you can't say good, say naught."

"One man marking, one in behind and one either side."

He encouraged players to improve their speed by running with the correct arm and leg movement. Most players under his coaching improved their sprint times over 40 metres. He was responsible for turning a bunch of amateurs into professional players on and off the field.

Gordon Smith won 14 caps for New Zealand between 1979 and 1983.

Howie Tamati MBE
I reflect on my time spent with Ces Mountford. It started in January 1979 when word that Ces was coming to Taranaki, set the Rugby League officials in a buzz.

In my youth, I had heard of him and talk of the Rothmans coaching scheme and Ces's system of coaching had been implemented by Taranaki coaches since that time, with the box attacking system 8 and 11, 10 and 12, the number 9 at acting half. Coaching by numbers; positional play around the dummy half and outside backs marking their opposites. It was instilled in me by people who were following Ces's system.

Why was it so good? It was the basics - the skills of the game. It taught everyone their roles and it empowered the coaches who in the main were working class men.

Ces's system enabled you to learn by heart, the way to teach the basics of Rugby League. The words spoken were the same in Kaitaia as they were in Otago. Brilliant in its simplicity, the system provided the springboard for aspiring coaches to go on and develop their own teams and their own personality, keeping in mind the basic structures and roles required by the game at all levels.

I remember his visit well, listening intently and trying my best to impress this

156

man, who in less than six months would introduce me to international Rugby League. Ces took over the Kiwi coaching job following the 1978 team's disappointing performances in Australia. He came back after being sent into the wilderness in 1970. Political infighting saw him removed from the game's highest levels. Yet in 1971, the Kiwi team coached by Mountford devotee Lory Blanchard, and using Ces's system, beat Australia, Great Britain and France.

By 1978, the Kiwi team had lost its way. It had no other credible coaching option and turned back to Ces. He started again with a new group of young men, few of the original 1978 team survived. He spent the next four years coaching and training new players, to understand their roles at the international level. He also made them into men that New Zealand could be proud of, both on and off the field.

He made them tough enough to play 80 minutes non-stop. He demanded we play at our best and, more often than not, he got it. All without yelling, swearing or abusing.

We set standards of behaviour and discipline that showed on the Rugby League field. It was his players that became household names in the 1980s.

The coaches that followed did not have to teach those men how to play test Rugby League. All they had to do was make them want to play. When other selections began to dominate the New Zealand test teams, they ceased to be as successful.

Every moment of time spent with Ces was valued. He was a special New Zealander who enhanced the game of Rugby League and our country. Ces Mountford had a huge influence over me and the men that coached me. I am what I am today because of him. I am honoured to have known him.

Howie Tamati played for New Zealand between 1979 and 1985, winning 24 caps, and played for Wigan. He was the Kiwis' coach between 1992 and 1993.

Kevin Tamati: A tribute to Ces Mountford

No amount of praise that could be bestowed upon this man would be enough to acknowledge the high respect and admiration I have for Ces and his family. His professionalism and mannerisms had a great influence on me, so much so, that I tried to emulate him when my managerial (coaching) career began. He was always the professional: "Treat people the way you expect to be treated" was one of his favourite sayings.

The news in 1979 that Ces Mountford was going to be the new Kiwi coach was, the best news for a lot of players like myself who came from south of the Bombay Hill. After gruelling trials, at last, I was selected to play for my country. What a great memorable moment, one which I will never forget. It was Sunday evening; the radio was turned up loud so that I could hear it anywhere I was in the house. I knew the team was being announced that night and I knew I had a better chance of selection this time. When the team was announced, I could not believe it. A Kiwi at last. Shortly after, our then club coach called to congratulate me and I knew I was on my way.

Ces was a British coach, a former professional player for Wigan and manager for Warrington and Blackpool, so it was obvious that we would learn the British style of playing Rugby League.

Your role as prop forward, he would say, was to take the ball up hard, hit the tackler and at the same time pivot, thrusting the hips and buttocks into the tackler, twisting the upper body away from the tackler, clearing the ball, looking to unload to the supporting back-rower. "Turn in the tackle, look to make the ball available", Ces would always say. It was a skill I feel I mastered and it became part of my game forever more.

In defence, it was one man marking, one in behind, two forwards either side, loose forward open side, stand off blindside, centres left and right with wingers and full back covering. A very simple and very successful pattern when performed correctly.

Another of Ces's favourite sayings was: "You are ambassadors to your families, your club, your province, your country and the game of Rugby League. Dress and act accordingly. Sell yourself."

It was a pleasure, honour and privilege playing for Ces. I have no doubt at all that his influence instilled pride into our players, the game and the country and what a great feeling it was. Oh, if only I could turn back the clock!

Arohanui Ces and Whanau.

Thanks for the faith

Kia Kaha

Kevin Tamati played in 22 test matches for New Zealand between 1979 and 1985. In Great Britain he played 105+11 games for Warrington, and then coached Salford for four years. He was Salford's first overseas coach since Lance Todd, and under his direction the club won the Second Division and the Divisional Premiership. He also coached Chorley and Whitehaven.

Graeme West

I first became involved with Ces in about 1978-79, when he was New Zealand development director and New Zealand national team coach. He travelled around the country to each of the provinces educating players and coaches on his very simple but also very effective method of approaching the game.

I learned more from his first two-day session than I had learned in the previous six years. That is no criticism of the previous coaches because they worked very hard, but Ces had it all. He gained instant attention by his no nonsense approach and knowledge and the way he could put it across. In his system everyone had a job and if you did it well the team would benefit.

If you had flair, by knowing your role, it enhanced your individual performance. His loyalty to each player was second to none. If he thought you were doing things wrong he would tell you, if he had seen improvement he would say so, an attribute that not many coaches of that time had.

At that time Auckland had a strong hold on the game in New Zealand, they would win most of their provincial games and by doing that would provide most of the New Zealand squad. Ces changed this by providing top class coaching to the 'country boys' - everyone outside Auckland. In turn Central Districts and South Island defeated them in the District series in 1979, 1980 and 1981. By being successful, a number of the players outside Auckland then gained New Zealand selection. He was also very successful in his New Zealand coaching role, beating France and Papua New Guinea, drawing with Great Britain and pushing Australia to the limit.

Over a three year period the team got stronger and worked better together and was expected to get even better. In 1982 the New Zealand League decided to sack Ces as coach and development officer. In my opinion, they were wrong in doing that. They had made some ordinary decisions over the years so it did not surprise me. To sack him as development director was especially sad because his input for periods of time in two decades had seen New Zealand produce some fine players and a system of developing them that worked.

By learning his system it enabled me to play and coach successfully at the highest level and I thank him for the interest he showed in me.

In closing I would like personally to acknowledge the finest coach I ever played under. He was honest, loyal, and knowledgeable and was a statesman of the game of Rugby League. I wish Ces, Edna and the family all the best for the future, and like so many of my era thought he was 'simply the best'.

Graeme West played 18 test matches for New Zealand between 1975 and 1985. He also had a very successful career in British Rugby League, winning every honour in the game, including captaining Wigan to the 1985 Challenge Cup Final victory over Hull, and coaching Wigan to the 1994 World Club Challenge victory over the Brisbane Broncos.

Gary Woollard

It was during 1964, while attending a Wellington Rugby League squad training session supervised by manager-coaches Ossie Butt and Jim Campbell at the Wellington Show Grounds, that the players were introduced to the New Zealand Rugby League director of coaching Ces Mountford. My first impression of Ces was his enthusiasm and the personal interest he took in the players. He was also the most analytical coach I had during my playing career. The breakdown into the stages taken to successfully complete the disciplines of Rugby League: how to carry the ball, how to play the ball, how to pass the ball, how to kick the ball, how to tackle front on and side on were instilled into the players with ball security as the main priority. The importance of 40-metre sprint training with track shoes was instilled into us.

Ces was a coach who encouraged positive Rugby League and it was a pleasure to play in his sides because he was a "keep the ball alive when able" coach, and this does make the game more enjoyable to play. He was a coach who preached many statements such as: "Speed doesn't make a good player, but it does help", and "If you can't say anything nice about a player, don't say anything".

I was fortunate to have played in a number of Rugby League teams that Ces coached and he was very approachable and professional. One of the happiest experiences was being a member of the 1970 Kiwi World Cup team touring Great Britain and France, with Ces as manager and Lory Blanchard as coach. I also realised the very high regard that people in Europe held for Ces when he was a star player there in his playing days. More importantly, Ces was a gentleman and I would rate him as one of my top coaches.

Gary Woollard played 12 international matches for New Zealand between 1963 and 1971, including the 1970 World Cup.

21. New Zealand Rugby League

Smiley Burnette

In the late 1960s, while playing under one of the great post-war backs, Morrie Robertson, who by this time was entrenched as a coach of equal ability, I was invited to attend one of Ces Mountford's training schools. My attendance was without much blessing from Morrie, as he had many conflicts with Ces's philosophy of how the game should be played.

After just a few hours of very basic drills, more suitable I thought for under-sevens, I was leaning towards Morrie's point of view. Ces kept reiterating: "get the basic right and the rest will follow." How right he was. Even today, with Rugby League an entirely different game, many a result may have been reversed if the ball had only been played correctly on the first tackle, or the tackler had gone low etc. – just basics.

I have been able to continue the friendship with Ces, Edna and family; when they moved to the Gold Coast I was able to assist a little in their relocation. Ces was able to introduce my son Kurt to play in England, where he met and married his wife from Wigan, Samantha Fox (not that Samantha!). So I also have to thank Ces for that. He truly is a Kiwi who has been a great ambassador for New Zealand, not just as a sportsman, but as a citizen of New Zealand.

Paul and Phil Bergman

It was a great honour to be selected as teenagers to tour Australia, England and France by a man who had played and coached at the highest levels. It was an exciting time for us, as Ces had the ability to pick players and turn them into legends.

Initially, we struggled and were frustrated with his unique coaching style in comparison to the New Zealand and Australian coaching methods that we were conditioned to. However, what we learnt through his discipline, manners, straight talking, honesty and integrity set us up in life as well as Rugby League.

We owe Ces tremendously for a wonderful start and tuition for becoming men. He is a super coach, a champion bloke and our game is blessed with having him in it.

Paul and Phil Bergman played for the New Zealand Universities against Australia in a curtain raiser prior to the State of Origin in Brisbane. This was the only time a New Zealand University team played in front of such a huge crowd.

Ray Cody

When I first heard of Ces Mountford I read in a short newspaper review that the New Zealand Rugby League was having some doubt as to whether they could use him in any capacity. At that time I was president of the Otago Rugby League and my first thought was how strange it would be to overlook a person like Mountford who had great experience in England - he was the best man I could think of to help us with Rugby League in Dunedin. Fortunately, after a couple of months went by he became a kind of director of Rugby League during which course I met him and I do not think there was anyone else who had such a sublime knowledge of the game.

I was planning to move to Auckland when I realised that Mountford was having difficulty gaining acceptance. He would have made an ideal coach of the national team but others were being considered ahead of him. Eventually he became the Rothmans coaching director which is when most of us began to take notice of him.

I had read a lot about Ces Mountford and I recall forever him being nicknamed the "Dazzling Bullet". All of the Mountford family had reached representative standard in one code or another.

To talk to Ces Mountford was an education which I had never experienced before. His knowledge of Rugby League was outstanding. He eventually became a member of the New Zealand Rugby League Council. Later, he moved to Australia and has remained there. Many Kiwis value the aid they received from Ces – he was a great 'little' man - but his horizon was twice as high as anyone I knew in the game. In England the admiration that was his was beyond any recognition he received in New Zealand.

Ray Cody MNZM is a Life Member of the NZRL, and a former president of Otago Rugby League.

Peter De Goldi: Ces Mountford – The consummate gentleman

We were privileged to have Ces Mountford as our coach for the 1989 Universities World Cup Rugby League tournament held in York, England. For most of us, this tour was the sporting experience of a lifetime, but more so because Ces was the coach with his reputation and experience to guide and lead us.

Ces was a stickler for time management, very rarely raised his voice in anger, which was a major strength when motivating a group of young, over enthusiastic university students who generally perceived that they knew it all. This I took as a genuine sign of respect for the man.

Ces's legendary style of rugby was encapsulated in the coaching regime he preferred – attack with quick plays and get the ball to the wings to score.

To Ces the game wasn't finished just because we had come off the paddock. We had to not only learn from our mistakes, but also continue to act professionally and dress accordingly o meet our public and New Zealand representative obligations as Rugby League players.

Finally, although our team may not have been as successful as perhaps it could have been, a number of players have moved onto higher levels in both sport and business. This tour, under Ces's guidance, no doubt helped to provide some useful life-skills experiences.

Peter De Goldi was captain of the 1989 New Zealand Universities World Cup Rugby League team, and has played for the Canterbury representative side.

Hon Brian Donnelly MP

For a kid like myself growing up in a Rugby League family and community, Ces Mountford was something of a legend. Not only had his skills taken him to the pinnacle of the game in New Zealand, but also to the loftiest heights in the tough professional circuit of England.

I came to know the man better during age grade rep competitions and later playing at senior level. To Ces Mountford the notion that Rugby League was the greatest game in the world was indisputable fact. His aim (and I'm sure he imposed the same standards on himself as a player) was to motivate and train all involved to play the game perfectly. Not just well. That wasn't good enough for Ces. If you were fortunate enough to have the chance to play the game, you had to play it perfectly.

To that extent Ces was a techniques man. Woe betide the player who made a sloppy 'play the ball'. I well remember his demonstrations on passing the ball. I also remember clearly his insistence on the use of the offensive box which multiplied the options available to the attacking team.

His desire was to have very player entering senior ranks with these techniques already honed to perfection. To this end he worked tirelessly over the years that I knew him during my playing days. One fact is indisputable. Ces Mountford's contribution to Rugby League in New Zealand was monumental

Hon Brian Donnelly MP played for the first New Zealand Universities team to tour Australia in 1969. He also played for Auckland and was a Kiwi trialist.

John Hales: Over the Paparoas

Being born in Dunollie a small suburb of Runanga in 1946, on the West Coast of the South Island, of New Zealand was indeed a great privilege. This coal mining town on the western side of the Paparoa Ranges (which was rich with coal seams), harboured some of the roughest, toughest Rugby League players this country has seen. Some even possessed brilliant rugby minds. I was brought up in my grandparents' household, Jack Curragh and Norah (née Kelly), the sister of William, (Bill) Kelly one of the early pioneers of Rugby League in New Zealand and Australia.

Next door by just the separation of a number eight wire fence, lived the great rugged Kiwi of the late forties, early fifties, Jack (Chang) Newton and his family. Others who visited or came to get their haircut numbered among them, legendary Kiwis such as Norm Griffiths, Bill Glynn, Jock Masters, Arnold Green, Geordie (the little master) Menzies, and the great bullocking World Cup centre Reecey Griffiths. Others whom I played with as contemporaries, were Gary (Moose) Smith, W.K. (Billy) Johnson, and Spencer Dunn.

Over the other side of the Paparoa Ranges almost nestled out of sight in a deep bush clad valley was the coal mining town of Blackball which also boasted a good percentage of tough, brutal, brilliant Kiwi Rugby League players. The rivalry in those early days between Blackball and Runanga could be likened to the modern version of Australia's State of Origin. Both towns often battled it out for premiership honours, and to mention the word Blackball in our town bought frowns and gruff retorts.

With League being played on a Sunday on the West Coast, even Sunday church often took a backseat to Blackball Domain, Wingham Park, or O'Brien Park when these two teams came together.

Blackball produced the likes of J. Dodds, R (Bob) Aynsley, Bill (Ginger) Mclennan, Ray Nuttral, Robin Schofield, and not to mention the numerous members of the Mountford family, of which a number stood out, and generally small in stature were feared by other teams for their tenacity and guile.

Two who became Kiwis were Bill Mountford 1946, and Ken who represented New Zealand 1947 and 1948. While the Mountford boys were great stalwarts of Blackball, they continued to represent their province the playing field and later in administration, management and coaching on the West Coast, however early in 1946 it was another brother Ces who after playing for his beloved Blackball, West Coast and South Island, was encouraged to leave his job as a mining engineer in Blackball and leave his homeland for England where he was a player, and captain for Wigan, where he became a Rugby League legend captaining Wigan to the Wembley Cup Final in 1951, and also the recipient of the Lance Todd Trophy for player of the match. Ces continued both playing and coaching with Warrington before returning home to New Zealand where he became national coach fashioning a proud record and laying the foundation for other coaches such as Graham Lowe and a playing contemporary of my own, Frank Endacott, to build on into the modern era of professional Rugby League in New Zealand.

My first recognition of Ces, apart from stories I heard around the coal range

164

as a young lad, was a programme front cover with him being held shoulder high by his Wigan players after their win in 1951. As fate would have it this was the programme for the only test match that I can recall being played at Greymouth's Wingham Park. This was in 1954, the Kiwis winning 20-14 indeed with once again a good spattering of tough West Coasters including the miners from both Runanga and Blackball. As a seven year old I played in a curtain raiser that day with boys from Blackball and Ngahere in a game for Country against Town.

After moving to Christchurch in 1964 and while playing for Linwood and Canterbury in 1968 and 1969 I was to come across Ces Mountford while he toured New Zealand conducting coaching schools as national coach. During this period I was coached by D. L. (Lory) Blanchard who was a member of the 1954 Kiwi test team and later to follow in Ces Mountford's footsteps as New Zealand coach. My recollection of Ces Mountford at that time was that of a small, balding, almost English speaking gentleman, who spoke with wisdom and positiveness in his words, never losing his temper at failure, but raising his chipper voice to suggest "try that again boys". Those that have known Ces will know what I mean. His voice and phrasing was one of his distinctive features.

From one so young and many games of Rugby League apart, it was an honour to have heard stories about Ces Mountford, remembered and learned from him later in life and yet again, had the opportunity to meet up with him again in 1997, at New Zealand Rugby League headquarters. Even then he hadn't changed a bit from that first photograph I had seen way back except he was older. He was balding in 1946 – it would seem from wearing his hard coal mining hat while working deep down in the Blackball mine over the Paparoas.

John Haynes: Student Rugby League

The starting point for Ces's role in Student Rugby League was when he very graciously accepted the coaching position offered to him in 1984. I was at that time President of the New Zealand Universities Rugby League Council. I asked him if he would be the coach following his terrific success and personal popularity with the Kiwis in Britain and France in 1981.

The NZ Universities tour in 1984, the first to the northern hemisphere tour by any southern hemisphere Universities team in any code, broke new ground. Ces was 64 years old, but the longer the tour went on the younger he seemed to become. He immediately imbued the team with his personal credibility, a terrific public platform to work from. He demanded high standards from players about dress, conduct and how they played. The players responded very well and the tour was a great success.

His 7am morning team walks (in the snow in Leeds in January 1985) were a great time for people to get along side him and talk. It was during these that he told me that his rugby started at Blackball Primary school where he learnt the basics. He also said that Johnny Dodds, an American, who played for the West Coast and New Zealand was a star and guided the young Blackball players.

On tour in England Ces made a point of introducing the team to players such as Herb Cooke and Arthur Clues from past great eras. He had the happy knack through his personal fame of being able to get people of any age to talk about Rugby League. Quite simply he crossed the generation gap with ease. Ces also still had access to the highest officials in the Rugby League and when the tour was such a success those countries responded enthusiastically when asked by our Universities Council if they wanted to come to New Zealand for an inaugural Universities World Cup in 1986.

Trevor Patrick (former Kiwi) had by 1986 succeeded Ces as coach building on Ces's success. New Zealand won this World Cup, with Howie Tamati as captain having just returned from playing for Wigan, being influential in that outcome. The concept of holding a Students Rugby League World Cup had had its genesis when the 1984 team was due to return from England and France. Both Martyn Sadler and Robert Fassolette, independently had asked me if I would consider hosting a tour by their countries to reciprocate our tour. The cost of two tours in short order seemed prohibitive. I then decided to invite Australia and Papua New Guinea having in mind that a triennial World Cup would form a for future international competition. Ces's role had been pivotal in establishing New Zealand's credentials to host a tournament. The rest is now history with the Student World Cup a much anticipated and enduring international fixture.

John Haynes represented New Zealand Universities Rugby League in the first test matches played against Australian Universities. He later organised the inaugural tour of England and France in 1984-85 and the 1986 Student World Cup. He has received New Zealand's prestigious Montana Book award and taught history before joining the Office of the Parliamentary Ombudsmen.

Les Huston

I first met Ces Mountford a few days before he arrived in Christchurch at the end of a very successful career in Rugby League in England. I was impressed with his keenness to share his accumulated knowledge of playing, coaching and managing Rugby League. It was well known that this advice started a new train of thought and action in Rugby League circles in New Zealand. Ces became a very good friend of mine and I enjoyed his many tales of experiences in England that he sometimes used to reinforce and to embellish a point he was making. I admired his high standard of dress code and his dictum: "If you don't have something good to say about a person – don't say anything."

Les Huston is a life member of the NZRL.

Peter Kerridge

The West Coast of New Zealand's South Island has produced many fine Rugby League players, some exceptional, and even a few deserving of the tag 'great'. Perhaps the greatest of them all was Ces Mountford of the Blackball club who found wider fame with Wigan and Warrington. Ces's move to England before he wore the Kiwi jersey has not diminished his standing in New Zealand.

Down under, New Zealanders in general and West Coasters in particular, thrilled to hear about and read of Ces's Rugby League exploits before huge crowds in that halcyon post-war decade. He is a benchmark against which the completeness of a Rugby League player is measured. Seldom is Ces described in sporting circles as other than "the great Ces Mountford." With his personal qualities and physical attributes he would have been a champion in any sport, lucky for us he chose Rugby League.

Peter Kerridge has been the president of the West Coast Rugby League since 1997 and is the West Coast Rugby League's historian.

Gordon Nuttall

My first recollection of Ces Mountford goes back more than 70 years. We attended the same primary school, although there was an age difference of several years. In his last year at the Blackball school he won the senior sports championship which was the start of an illustrious sporting career. As well as playing schoolboy Rugby League he was also very adept at association football, but his great forte was League. He became a member of the Blackball senior team at a very young age. From then on his rise to greater heights was meteoric and his selection in West Coast and South Island teams was a matter of course.

Probably his greatest moments playing in New Zealand was taking part in the final trials for the selection of the Kiwi team to tour England and France. It was a great surprise to almost every Coaster that his name was not in the touring side. It was later suggested that it was probably that the selectors were aware of his youth and did not want to risk him in the hurly burly of a very hard tour playing seasoned English professionals. This was in 1939, but in 1946, he proved this was no great handicap when he was signed by Wigan and went on to become one of the really great players in the British competition.

Gordon Nuttall played for the Canterbury representative team.

Hon Damien O'Connor MP

As MP for the West Coast of New Zealand's South Island I am proud and privileged to represent a unique area with special people. West Coasters have distinguished themselves in many ways and particularly in sport. I am mindful of the special regard in which Rugby League is held in my electorate and I value highly my position as patron of the West Coast Rugby League Inc.

When the all time stars of the game are discussed it is inevitable that Ces Mountford's name is to the fore. My Rugby League education is deemed to be proceeding satisfactorily when I refer to the 'Blackball Bullet' who found fame on the Rugby League fields of northern England some 50 years ago.

Ces Mountford is also recalled with pride for honouring the promise he made in 1946 on the eve of his departure from the West Coast, to return to New Zealand eventually and put something back into his sport.

From all I've read and heard about Ces Mountford he was the original role model we would wish to see in sport: a brilliant player, a fine sportsman and a credit to himself on and off the field. I join in saluting a champion.

Hon Damien O'Connor is MP for West Coast / Tasman and is the Patron of the West Coast Rugby League

Roy O'Courtney: Dedicated to Ces Mountford

A fine sport and gentleman

Life holds no gift of finer worth
Than friendship, loyal, selfless, pure
Friendship, which can, unscathed, endure
The myriad numbing shock of earth.

Thrice-blest are they to whom is given
This flawless jewel from above
Whose facets do reflect the love
Which permeates the hosts of heaven.

Impervious to the flight of Time
Steadfast as stars that know no wane
It stands on an exalted plane
Because it is a thing sublime.

Therefore, should Destiny's secret plan
Divide our separate paths for aye
I shall remember you always
As a good friend and kindliest man.

Kia Ora

Roy O'Courtney was from Christchurch, but spent most of his time in Australia, working as a wool chaser. He met the New Zealand team during their 1930 tour of Australia, and donated the magnificent O'Courtney Trophy, which was competed for by Australia and New Zealand. During a visit to New Zealand, he called to see Johnny Dodds, and all the players met him. His friendship with Ces and Edna continued. He wrote to them in New Zealand, sent food parcels, and met them in Sydney on the way home in 1961. They heard on the radio that he had died, and two days later received a letter from him, which must have been the last one he wrote. He said he had been busy, but was very tired. Ces and Edna found it disconcerting and sad, almost like a voice from the dead. It is believed that he died alone in Victoria, in farming country working as a wool chaser. The text is on an illuminated address that Ces and Edna treasure to this day. The O'Courtney trophy is on display at a Leagues Club in Sydney.

Mark Pfeifer

The first time I heard the name Ces Mountford was from my father, who was born and bred in Greymouth, and played League for Marist. He referred to him as the 'Blackball Bullet'; and said he was a great player. When Ces was appointed as Kiwi coach, Dad said that he wouldn't take any nonsense.

When I was selected to tour with the New Zealand University League team to England and France, I had an idea as to what to expect from Ces as a coach and my expectations were met.

He trained us hard, but the thing that impressed me the most was that he focussed heavily on developing basic rugby skills, which a lot of coaches just assume we as players have. These basic skills included how to beat a man, off-loading the ball, turning in the tackle and how to side step.

I found Ces to be a very quiet man who commanded a huge amount of respect, especially from League supporters in England. The whole tour was a fantastic experience. I learned just so much and for that I truly thank Ces.

Judge Anand Satyanand

Rugby League is now an establishment sport in New Zealand with fans and players from all walks of life and parts of the country. It wasn't always that way and 50 years ago miners and wharfies and other blue collar workers were the main lifeblood of the game for playing, financing and support in other ways. The glamour and high finance associated with much of the game today simply wasn't present. But there were some people who, by their ability were able to point to a new future. Ces Mountford was a pioneer who after playing the game on the West Coast and for his country went over to play in the English competition successfully. Not only that, but when his playing days ended he turned to coaching and came to put back what he could impart back in New Zealand.

169

Under his encouragement a new generation of New Zealanders went on to wear the Kiwi jersey and to play in Australia and Great Britain. In any write-up of Rugby League and its development in New Zealand, Ces Mountford is a hero.

Judge Anand Satyanand is one of the three Parliamentary Ombudsmen in New Zealand. He was on the New Zealand Rugby League Council in the late 1970s and early 1980s.

Bill Whithead

I first met Ces Mountford when I was a boy during the Second World War, on the West Coast. He was a star in the West Coast teams that savoured many wins over talented opposition, including victory over Great Britain in 1946 when Ces had already left to join Wigan. However, Ces's brothers Bill and Ken did play in that team.

Ces played for West Coast in the Northern Union Cup. I saw him play three times against Inangahua. He played at full-back in 1938, when the Coast won 11-8, at centre in September 1940 when the Coast won again 7-5, and finally in August 1941, with the Coast winning 17-4. Ken Mountford played in that game as a 16 year old.

Ces was a very deceptive runner with the ball, had a great sidestep, and his career at Wigan is legendary. It was a pity he never got to play for New Zealand, but there was no doubt he could have, had he not decided to take up a professional career in Great Britain.

Ces introduced the Rothmans coaching courses into New Zealand Rugby League, and was a member of the NZRL Board, as well as secretary / manager for a while. He was always readily available to pass on his various skills, and came out to my club, Marist, training sessions on many occasions. He was the type of administrator the game lacks today, too many seem to have their own agendas and have trips in mind all the time, instead of getting down to basics, and supporting the game at the grassroots, where it counts. Even Rugby Union is saying this these days.

When I was a board member with the Canterbury Rugby League I met Ces on many occasions. One of my duties in Canterbury included liaison officer to many visiting teams. One of these was the 1980 Kiwis, which Ces agreed to bring to play in a benefit match against a Brereton invitation team in 1980. Mocky Brereton, a member of the famous 1971 Kiwis, had suffered a motorcycle accident in 1979 and the match was for him. He recovered from his injuries to become Marist's assistant manager.

Many Kiwi players would have had some connection with Ces, 'the little master', and all would vouch for his ability to pass on his skills to others. Ces was also a great supporter of schoolboy Rugby League and acted as the representative on the senior council for the schoolboys' council. I was also involved with this for more than 20 years. Ces ensured that grants were made available to the junior body to conduct national tournaments and arranged tours to Australia for our young talented players.

I also remember Ken Mountford, who first played for West Coast as a teenager, and was killed in the Strongman mine disaster in the 1960s. Bill Mountford died in Blackball some years ago. He was a strong supporter of the schoolboy game as well, and was the West Coast coach for schoolboy grades and a selector for higher sides, as well as a referee. Both played for the Kiwis. Jimmy Mountford was a schoolboy Kiwi in 1951, having led the South Island against the North. Bill and Ken were both capped by the Kiwis.

To have known Ces Mountford was a privilege. To have seen him play the great game of Rugby League was a delight to behold, especially his brilliant footwork. There was also his uncanny ability to pass on what he had learned at Wigan and Warrington. To pay a full tribute to Ces's work is not easy, because he had so much input into the improvements of the organisation of Rugby League in New Zealand. The Mountford coaching schools would be the most lasting impression of his work. His name will live on for yonks...

Bill Whithead is a Life Member of the NZRL and has a lifetime's involvement in the game in New Zealand, particularly with the Marist club, and schoolboy Rugby League. He was manager of three schoolboy Kiwi teams in the 1980s, including the 1986 tour to Australia.

Appendix 1: Ces Mountford's British playing record

Compiled by Robert Gate

Wigan

Debut: 31 August 1946 versus Belle Vue Rangers (away)
Last game: 5 May 1951 versus Barrow (Wembley), Challenge Cup final

	A	T	G	P
1946-47	48	17	27	105
1947-48	45	8	-	24
1948-49	42	13	4	47
1949-50	38	19	-	57
1950-51	37	13	24	87
Totals	**210**	**70**	**55**	**320**

Warrington

Debut: 4 October 1952 versus Bradford Northern (home)
Last game: 3 October 1953 versus Hull Kingston Rovers (home)

	A	T	G	P
1952-53	26	5	2	19
1953-54	11	1	-	3
Totals	**37**	**6**	**2**	**22**

Career Record

	A	T	G	P
Wigan	210	70	55	320
Warrington	37	6	2	22
Internationals	5	-	-	-
Representative	1	-	-	-
Overall Totals	**253**	**76**	**57**	**342**

International matches

22 October 1949	Other Nationalities 6 Wales 5 at Abertillery
15 January 1950	Other Nationalities 3 France 8 at Marseille
10 December 1950	Other Nationalities 3 France 16 at Bordeaux (captain)
11 April 1951	Other Nationalities 35 England 10at Wigan (captain)
15 April 1953	Other Nationalities 16 Wales 18 at Warrington

Representative match

| 4 October 1950 | The Rest 16 1950 Great Britain Tourists 23 at Wigan (captain) |

Major Finals

Challenge Cup

| 1948 | Wigan 8 Bradford Northern 3 at Wembley | |
| 1951 | Wigan 10 Barrow 0 at Wembley (captain) | 1 goal |

Championship

1947   Wigan 13 Dewsbury 4 at Maine Road, Manchester
1950   Wigan 20 Huddersfield 2 at Maine Road, Manchester (captain)

Note: Mountford gained a Championship winners' medal in 1953-54 with Warrington but did not play in the final. His eight games in league fixtures entitled him to a medal.

Lancashire Cup

1946   Wigan 9 Belle Vue Rangers 3 at Swinton
1948   Wigan 14 Warrington 8 at Swinton
1949   Wigan 20 Leigh 7 at Warrington
1950   Wigan 28 Warrington 5 at Swinton (captain)

Note: Mountford was injured and missed the 1947 final when Belle Vue Rangers were beaten 10-7 at Warrington. He had played in all the previous rounds and so earned a winners' medal.

Mountford gained Lancashire League Championship winners' medals in 1946-47 and 1949-50 with Wigan.

Appendix 2: Ces Mountford's record as manager of Warrington and Blackpool

Compiled by Robert Gate and Peter Lush

1953-54
Championship winners
Challenge Cup winners
Lancashire League winners

1954-55
Championship winners
Lancashire League winners

1955-56
Lancashire League winners
ITV Trophy winners

1959-60
Lancashire Cup winners

1960-61
Championship runners up

Season by season

	P	W	D	L	Pts	Place	Ch Cup	Lancs Cup
1951-2:	36	24	1	11	49	6	Round 3	Round 1
1952-3	36	20	1	15	41	9	Semi-final	Semi-final
1953-4	36	30	1	5	61	2	Won	Semi-final
1954-5	36	29	2	5	60	1*	Round 1	Round 1
1955-6	34	27	1	6	55	1**	Round 1	Semi-final
1956-7	38	21	1	16	43	10	Round 2	Semi-final
1957-8	38	19	1	18	39	13	Round 3	Round 2
1958-9	38	22	0	16	44	9	Round 2	Round 1
1959-0	38	22	2	14	46	7	Round 1	Won
1960-1	36	27	1	8	55	2	Round 2	Round 2
Totals:	**366**	**241**	**11**	**114**	**493**	**5.9 (average)**		

Over 10 seasons, the team won 67.34% of the points available.

*On points difference from Oldham.
** Belle Vue withdrew, table decided on points %.

Blackpool

1972-3	34	4	0	30	8	29	Round 1	Round 1

Blackpool also lost in the first round of the John Player Trophy. This was the last season of one single division in Rugby League, so Blackpool had a tough fixture list. Ces's old club, Warrington, finished top of the league. Blackpool's victories were against Doncaster, Barrow, Hunslet and Huyton.

Appendix 3: Ces Mountford's record as New Zealand national team coach 1979-1982

1979:
New Zealand 8 Great Britain 16 Auckland
New Zealand 7 Great Britain 22 Christchurch
Lost series 2-0

1980:
New Zealand 6 Australia 27 Auckland
New Zealand 6 Australia 15 Auckland
Lost series 2-0
Great Britain 14 New Zealand 14 Wigan
Great Britain 8 New Zealand 12 Bradford
Great Britain 10 New Zealand 2 Leeds (Headingley)
Drew series 1-1 with 1 draw
France 6 New Zealand 5 Perpignan
France 3 New Zealand 11 Toulouse
Drew series 1-1

1981:
New Zealand 26 France 3 Auckland
New Zealand 25 France 2 Auckland
Won series 2-0

1982:
Australia 11 New Zealand 8 Brisbane
Australia 20 New Zealand 2 Sydney
Lost series 2-0
Papua NG 5 New Zealand 56 Port Moresby
Won series 1-0

Overall record	P	W	D	L	Percentage
	14	5	1	8	39%

Versus:					
Australia	4	0	0	4	0%
France	4	3	0	1	75%
Great Britain	5	1	1	3	30%
Papua New Guinea	1	1	0	0	100%

Appendix 4: The Mountford family name

When I first arrived in England I spent some time at Somerset House trying to find my origins, which I managed to a certain extent. Our son Kim went further with the investigation so here is a potted version of the Mountford family history.

Certain members of the de Montfort family arrived in England with William Duke of Normandy, shortly before the Battle of Hastings took place in 1066. It is on record that four Knights Templar broke through the English lines in that battle and killed King Harold of England. It is recorded and shown in the Bayeux Tapestry that one of these Knights was named de Montfort.

Historians still maintain that the name de Montfort was the original French name of the English version of Mountford. Admittedly there were other English variations of Montfort.

In France Simon de Montfort was given the task, by the Roman Catholic Church, of wiping out the Cathar religion in the South of France. The task of the French Albigensian Inquisition was successful in that it wiped out most of the Cathar sympathisers in the South. France. Simon himself died in one of the major battles while trying to enter the walled Cité of Carcassonne. This particular Simon de Montfort is still hailed as one of the saviours of Carcassonne; his son, Simon de Montfort, was given the title Earl of Leicester by King John of England in 1206. He married a sister of Henry II and was one of the instigators of the Baronial Civil War against King John that resulted in King John signing the Magna Carta. Simon Junior, although working hard towards Royal Concessions, did not witness the signing of the Magna Carta, as he was killed at the Battle of Evesham in 1265.

The Norman state was conquered by Rollo, a Viking Chieftain. The King of France at the time gave Normandy to the Vikings and used the Viking Norman assimilation as one of his main fighting forces. One of the results of this is that Normans to this day have blue eyes and blond hair. William the Conqueror was a third generation Viking.

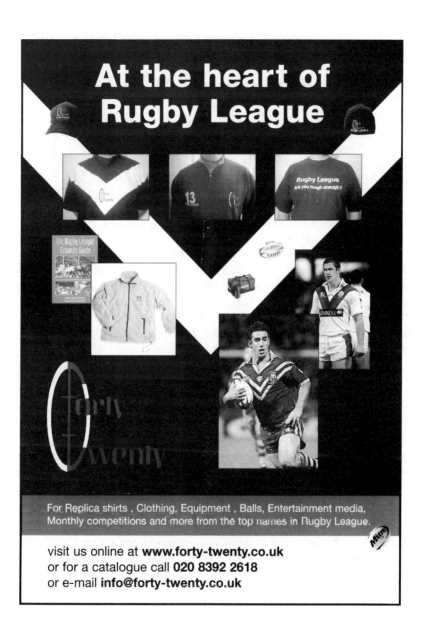

Rugby books from London League Publications Ltd

The Great Bev
The rugby league career of Brian Bevan
By Robert Gate

Brian Bevan is one of the few rugby league players to rightfully be called a Legend. He scored 796 tries in British rugby league, a record that will never be surpassed. This is the first book on Brian Bevan.

Published in August 2002 at £14.95. ISBN: 1903659-06-X
Special offer by post: £14.00 post free in UK.

I, George Nepia
The Autobiography of a Rugby Legend
By George Nepia and Terry McLean
Foreword by Oma Nepia - New edition with new material

George Nepia is arguably New Zealand's greatest ever Rugby Union player. First published in 1963, his autobiography covered his early years, the 1924-25 All Black tour; and his Rugby career. This edition has new material on his life and times in Union and League, including at Streatham & Mitcham and Halifax.

Published in September 2002 at £13.95. ISBN: 1903659-07-8
Special offer by post: £10.00 post free in UK.

A Westminster XIII
Parliamentarians and Rugby League
Edited by David Hinchliffe M.P.

MPs and Lords write about their favourite Rugby League team.

Published in November 2002:
Hardback: £12.95. ISBN: 1903659-08-6. Paperback: £9.95. ISBN: 1903659-09-4
Special offers by post: Hardback £10.00, paperback £9.00 post free in UK.

Rugby League Bravehearts
The history of Scottish Rugby League
By Gavin Willacy

Despite never having a professional club, Scotland has a rich Rugby League history. This book covers that history and the game today in Scotland.

Published in June 2002 at £9.95. ISBN: 1903659-05-1
Special offer by post: £8.00 post free in UK.

Order from: London League Publications Ltd, PO Box 10441, London E14 0SB. Sterling cheques payable to London League Publications Ltd, no credit cards. Add £1 per book for overseas orders. All books can be ordered from bookshops. For free catalogue, email: peter@plush.worldonline.co.uk or write to the above address.